Dafydd ap Gwilym Poems

Series Editor   Lynn Hughes

DAFYDD AP GWILYM
A SELECTION OF POEMS

RACHEL BROMWICH

GOMER PRESS

First Impression—September 1982
Second Impression—February 1987
Third Impression with revisions—September 1993

British Library Cataloguing in Publication Data

Dafydd, *ap Gwilym*
   Dafydd ap Gwilym.—(The Welsh Classics)
   I. Title   II. Bromwich, Rachel
   III. Series
   891.6'611   B2273.D3

ISBN 0 85088 815 8

Text composed in Trump Medieval and printed
on Basingwerk Parchment from Abbey Mills, Treffynnon, Clwyd.

Printed in Wales
at the Gomer Press, Llandysul, Dyfed

Cyflwynir y gwaith hwn
i'm hen fyfyrwyr

ACKNOWLEDGEMENTS

These translations are based on the text of Dafydd ap Gwilym's poems as edited by Sir Thomas Parry in his monumental *Gwaith Dafydd ap Gwilym* (U.W.P., Cardiff, 1952), and I gratefully acknowledge the courtesy of the University of Wales Press in permitting me to reproduce the original Welsh texts from this work. My primary debt of gratitude therefore goes to Sir Thomas Parry, whose fundamental scholarship has alone made it possible for a translator to follow in his footsteps. In addition, Sir Thomas has been kind enough to read my English translations, to propose certain corrections, and to save me from a number of errors. I am further indebted to Sir Idris Foster, who read my work in typescript and again in proof, gave essential help for my interpretation of the final poem and made a number of helpful suggestions. Such errors as remain are of course my sole responsibility. I wish to thank Gareth Bevan, editor of *Geiriadur Prifysgol Cymru* for allowing me to make use of as yet unpublished lexicographical *data*, and Robert Jones for his kind assistance in sending me references from the Dictionary's slips. Finally, I am deeply grateful to Lynn Hughes for the unfailing assistance, encouragement, and friendship which he has extended to me throughout the years in which this work has been in progress. Not only has he scrutinized my text with the greatest care and made helpful suggestions with regard to phrasing, but I have benefited greatly from his expert ornithological knowledge, which has cast valuable light on Dafydd's birds and bird-lore. Without Lynn Hughes's invitation to contribute this inaugural volume to *The Welsh Classics* series I should not have embarked upon the precarious task of attempting to render into English this selection from the poems of Dafydd ap Gwilym. My thanks go to the Gomer Press for the care with which they have produced this book, to the Welsh Arts Council for their financial assistance and to the cartographer, Anne Mainman, for her map of Dafydd's neighbourhood.

RACHEL BROMWICH

CONTENTS

Contents

Contents

FOREWORD

Far more has been written about Dafydd ap Gwilym than about any other Welsh poet, and the nature and the merits of his poetry have been discussed extensively by scholars of various nationalities. As far back as 1878 the noted Orientalist, E. B. Cowell, included within the wide range of his intellectual interests a study of Dafydd ap Gwilym, in which he started the vogue of comparing the themes of Dafydd with those of Continental poets of his own and previous generations. In 1908 a German scholar, L. C. Stern, published an extended study. A Welshman, in the person of Ifor Williams, entered the same field of inquiry in 1914 with a lengthy article, and in 1927 the Dutch scholar, Th. M. Chotzen, published a comprehensive study. Fifty of Dafydd's poems were rendered in English verse by Idris and David Bell in 1942.

Nothing is more gratifying to a scholar than to find that some publication of his has inspired others to pursue the same line of inquiry, but with an expanding awareness and the capability of deeper penetration. Such has been my experience during the years that have elapsed since the appearace in 1952 of the book, *Gwaith Dafydd ap Gwilym*, in which an attempt was made to establish the canon of the poet's work, as far as that was possible after six centuries of erroneous attribution and uncritical evaluation.

In recent years there has been a great revival of interest in Dafydd, not only in Wales and among Celticists, but in other countries and among mediaevalists generally. This interest has resulted in suggested textual emendations, critical assessments of individual poems, a reappraisal of aspects of the poet's art, a new interpretation of possible biographical references, further exploration of Dafydd's debt both to the native tradition and to foreign models, together with studies of the historical background in fourteenth century Wales.

Among students of Dafydd ap Gwilym Dr Rachel Bromwich has an honoured place. In her book in 'The Writers of Wales' series, her monograph *Tradition and Innovation in the Poetry of Dafydd ap Gwilym*, and in a number of articles, she has, by her deep knowledge of the poet's literary background in Wales and elsewhere, and by her imagination tempered with a balanced judgement, contributed substantially to our understanding of this important figure in our literature.

Dr Bromwich's critical and scholarly approach to the poetry developed, as with some other scholars, into an appreciation of its merits. She could not fail to recognize Dafydd ap Gwilym's pre-eminence as a poet, and it was this that inspired her translations. She says candidly in her introductory remarks that the translator of poetry can only partially succeed in conveying the impact of the original, and this is particularly true of Welsh strict-metre poetry, because its complex alliterative pattern is entirely lost in translation. It is one of Dafydd's prime achievements that he is able to embody his poetic sensibility in a medium which is governed by extremely intricate rules of prosody.

However, certain important attributes of the poet's temperament and art are retained. The themes of his poems, many of them international, his love of women and of the birds of the woods, his enjoyment of life, his exuberant fancy, the structure of his poems, are all features which the attentive and sympathetic reader can discern in translations. It is to be hoped that this will be a sufficient incentive for the reader to fulfil the translator's desire that he should come to understand and appreciate the originals.

THOMAS PARRY

Bro Dafydd ap Gwilym

INTRODUCTION

The poet

Little is known of Dafydd ap Gwilym apart from what he himself has chosen to reveal in his polished and sophisticated verse, and this slender information is ambiguous in the extreme. It can be supplemented only by a few allusions made to Dafydd by contemporary and near-contemporary poets: there is also a well-authenticated genealogy which gives the name of the poet's father as Gwilym Gam ap Gwilym, and traces his descent ultimately to a certain Gwynfardd Dyfed, who was the semi-legendary progenitor of a number of families in south-west Wales. Such a descent accords well with the description of Dafydd by his fellow-poet Madog Benfras as *eos Dyfed*, 'the nightingale of Dyfed'. His family originated from the *cantref* of Cemais in Pembrokeshire, and it had in earlier generations included several officials who had held positions of high authority in the same area under the English crown. The few datable allusions which Dafydd makes to contemporary events all point to the middle years of the 14th century as his period of maximum poetic output: he may thus have been born about 1320—a slightly older contemporary of Geoffrey Chaucer.

Tradition places Dafydd's birth at Brogynin in the parish of Llanbadarn Fawr, a few miles north-east of Aberystwyth, in a substantial mansion or *plasty* which lay adjacent to a farm-house still retaining this name. It is believed that he lies buried not far away, near Pontrhydfendigaid, within the precincts of the monastery of Strata Florida. Several poems indicate that the neighbourhood of Aberystwyth and north Ceredigion was more familiar to Dafydd than any other part of Wales, yet he appears to have travelled widely throughout the length and breadth of the country, and to have been well-acquainted with places in Anglesey such as the borough of Rhosyr or Newborough, and with Bangor and Caernarfon in Gwynedd. He may also have visited Chester, whose famous Cross is the subject of a poem which has latterly come to be accepted as belonging to the canon of his work; but there is no indication other than this that Dafydd ever travelled beyond the borders of Wales. He describes himself, no doubt fancifully, as a member of the *clêr*: these were the Welsh equivalents of the *clerici vagantes* or 'wandering scholars' of other countries, and Dafydd may indeed have qualified at an early period of his life for minor religious orders—a not uncommon practice. But the indications are that he was a man of birth and breeding, and of no fixed occupation, who had sufficient means to travel at will through town and country, visiting the taverns in the Norman boroughs, and the homes of his cultivated friends over a wide area of Wales. And in both tavern and *plasty* there were no doubt to be found audiences fully capable of appreciating the *cywyddau* which, in their different kinds, he composed for their entertainment.

Dafydd's range of personal contacts included his fellow-poets Gruffudd ab Adda, Madog Benfras and Gruffudd Gryg—the last being an Anglesey poet with whom Dafydd exchanged a sequence of *cywyddau* in the form of a debate concerning the proper subjects to be treated of in the newly-introduced *cywydd* verse-form. Among his friends and acquaintances were also *uchelwyr* or men of hereditary station in Ceredigion and further to the south—men such as Rhydderch ab Ieuan Llwyd of Glyn Aeron and his family, and his uncle Llywelyn ap Gwilym, the constable of Newcastle Emlyn, who appears to have been a powerful educational influence upon the poet's early life. Dafydd's uncle may, perhaps, have been the first to have introduced Dafydd to the 'two cultures'—that is to the native bardic tradition as well as to the language and poetry and romances of the Anglo-Norman world. There was in addition Dafydd's friend and patron Ifor ap Llywelyn or 'Ifor Hael' of Basaleg in present-day Gwent. To all of these men he addressed praise-poems which by the very fact of their existence provide an authentic framework, however exiguous and inadequate, for the bare facts of the poet's life. For in all his other compositions but these few poems, fantasy intermingles with fact to such an extent that it is impossible to distinguish the one from the other, or to estimate the degree of reality which lies behind what Dafydd ruefully presents as his perpetually thwarted love-affairs. Love and Nature are the prime subjects of his poetry, and the two are very frequently blended, for he presents his love-theme most characteristically in an idealized woodland setting, in which he imagines himself as building a *deildy* or house of leaves and branches in which to shelter with his chosen sweetheart—'Morfudd' or 'Dyddgu' or some other un-named girl, making his retreat with her in the wilderness, as an escape from the hampering restrictions of conventional society. But as often as not it is the forest setting itself which is the poet's real subject, together with its natural inhabitants, the animals and the birds. The device of the *llatai* or 'love-messenger' poem may seem at the outset an artificial convention, yet for Dafydd it provided an ideal combinaton of fantasy and realism; the fantasy of sending some bird or animal as a messenger to his sweetheart serving as his means of introducing what were for him the most serious of realities, his most profound responses to the miracles of the world of Nature. In one of his most famous poems, indeed, it is the Wind itself which is imaginatively dispatched on such an errand. Such themes as these were entirely new in Welsh poetry, and on occasion they inspired Dafydd to flights of imagination which far transcended anything that might be expected in a framework suggestive of the light poetry of love's intrigue.

During the century of political upheaval and social turmoil which followed the loss of national independence in 1282,

Dafydd ap Gwilym introduced innovations into the subject-matter and metrical techniques and language of poetry which effectively gave a new dimension to the poetic art in Wales. He accomplished a daring and original synthesis by integrating into the established bardic tradition elements emanating from the contemporary European cult of 'courtly love', thus drawing Welsh poetry, if briefly, into the mainstream of European literature. He is without doubt one of the great poets of the Middle Ages. But the difficulty of conveying in another language even an approximate idea of his poetic artistry has served as a permanent obstacle to the recognition of this fact.

Metrics, Language, and Poetic Artistry

The primary appeal of Welsh poetry has always been to the ear rather than to the eye. Mediaeval poetry was accompanied on the harp, and Dafydd ap Gwilym shows considerable technical knowledge of harp-playing, and makes it plain that he could accompany his recitals of his own poems on this instrument. His chosen metre for by far the greater number of his poems was the *cywydd deuair hirion* ('song' or 'poem of two long lines'—to distinguish it from the *cywydd deuair fyrion*, whose lines had only four syllables). In general usage this became abbreviated to *cywydd*, as the *cywydd deuair hirion* progressively increased in popularity over the succeeding centuries. The *cywydd* is a couplet of seven-syllabled lines which rhyme unrhythmically; i.e. an accented final syllable rhymes with an unaccented final syllable, either of which may precede the other in the first line of the couplet. *Cywydd* also denotes a poem composed in this metre. Dafydd's *cywyddau* are normally between 30 and 60 lines in length—only rarely do they exceed this length or fail to come up to it. The musical appeal of the *cywydd* was enhanced by bestowing on each line full *cynghanedd* or 'harmony'. *Cynghanedd* is a technical term used to denote the regularized pattern of alliteration combined with internal rhyme which developed during the twelfth and thirteenth centuries in the *awdlau* or praise-poems composed by the professional poets attached to the courts of the Welsh princes. There are four types of *cynghanedd*, any one of which may be employed in a line, and all four may appear in the individual lines in any given *cywydd*. The simplest type is:

Cynghanedd Lusg ('dragging *cynghanedd*'), in which an accented penultimate syllable rhymes with some earlier syllable in the line, which may be either accented, as in

Cydblannu *bedw*, gwaith *dedw*ydd   (Poem no.11, l.29)

or unaccented, as in

Paun asgel*las* din*as*tai   (no.2, l.37)

Cynghanedd Groes ('cross *cynghanedd'*). Here the line is divided into two halves. The consonants are repeated in the same order before the main stress at the end of each half, and between the two halves is a *caesura* or pause:

Breuddwyd ýw, ebrwydded óes   (no.17, l.36)

Ar las báncr eurlais býnciau   (no.25, l.10)

Cynghanedd Draws ('across *cynghanedd'*) differs from the last only by the fact that there are one or more unrepeated consonants at the beginning of the second half of the line:

Cwcyllwyd edn cu callais   (no.25, l.12)

Lle briwddail fal llwybr Adda   (no.35, l.50)

Cynghanedd Sain ('sound *cynghanedd'*) has both alliteration and internal rhyme. The line is divided into three parts. The first and second parts rhyme, and the final word in the line alliterates with a word in the second part, whether this be a monosyllable or a di-syllable. (This is the oldest type of *cynghanedd*, and was the kind most frequently used by Dafydd and other 14th century poets):

Yng nghor Deinioel Bangor doe   (no.9, l.6)

Hawddamor, glwysgor glasgoed   (no.1, l.1)

Each of these four types of *cynghanedd* is further subdivided according to the differing balance maintained between the stressed and unstressed syllables in each of the two, or three, parts of the line. (For full discussion and analysis see J. Morris-Jones, *Cerdd Dafod* (Oxford, 1925, reprinted Cardiff, 1980); in English, Eurys Rowlands, *Poems of the Cywyddwyr* (Dublin, 1976), and Gwyn Williams, appendix to *An Introduction to Welsh Poetry* (Faber, 1953)).

Dafydd not infrequently leaves individual lines without *cynghanedd*, usually the first line in a couplet (exx: poems nos.38, 41 and 52). This is the more understandable when it is recognised that the *cywydd* developed during the first half of the 14th century out of the older, popular metre (as distinct from an official bardic metre) known as the *traethodl*. This was a seven-syllabled couplet like the *cywydd*, except that it lacked *cynghanedd* other than occasionally, and that the unrhythmical type of final rhyme was not obligatory—though this too occurs sporadically. The language is simple and almost entirely devoid of the types of metaphor and inversion favoured by Dafydd and his contemporaries, which are discussed below. An example is Dafydd's dialogue with the Grey Friar, poem no.43 (see n.).

Cynghanedd was an organic growth which, like the *cywydd* itself, became permanently stabilized in its lasting form during the 14th century. It had evolved slowly over the previous two centuries in the long lines of nine or ten or twelve syllables in the *awdlau* composed by the court poets who were Dafydd's predecessors. Their *awdlau* were long panegyric poems, originally bearing a single end-rhyme throughout (*awdl* is the same word as *odl* 'rhyme'), and composed in one or more than one of a recognised number of *awdl* metres. The unit was the single line—its length allowing fuller scope for experimentation and variety in *cynghanedd* than did the short line of the *cywydd*—but frequently the lines were bound together by the device known as *cymeriad*, which means the beginning of a series of lines with a single initial letter. The *awdl* retained its status as the most honourable and distinguished of metrical forms for centuries after Dafydd ap Gwilym's day, and Dafydd himself composed *awdlau* on occasion. Only a handful of these have come down (and they are not represented in this book): one is a poem to Christ and the others are praise-poems and elegies to certain of his friends and patrons. They are of mature technical accomplishment and are highly traditional in their employment of compound words, of conventional epithets, and in their frequent references to the legendary Welsh heroes and heroines for purposes of illustration. Certain of the metrical and other features of the traditional *awdl* Dafydd transferred into his *cywyddau*; sometimes employing a monorhyme throughout a whole poem (as in nos.2 and 3), sometimes employing *cymeriad* throughout a whole poem (as in no.54) or more frequently for inset passages (exx. no.5, 1s.17-22; no.8, 1s.1-14; no.11, 1s.25-42; no.29, 1s.9-24), and employing with imaginative creativity the freedom assumed by the court poets who preceded him to make new compound words at will.

Dafydd also employs the verse-form of the *englyn* in his panegyric poems; sometimes by itself, sometimes prefacing an *awdl* with a few introductory *englynion*, as had become a common practice by the early 14th century. The Prayer, which is the final poem in this book, is composed in the form of an *englynion* sequence, and the structure of the *englyn* therefore requires a brief description in this place. The *englyn* is the oldest of Welsh metres to be recorded in writing, and the *englynion* composed even at the present day retain the essential features of their ninth-century prototype—an unbroken metrical tradition which has lasted over a thousand years. There are several varieties, but the *englyn unodl union* ('straight monorhyme *englyn*') is the form most commonly employed from the 12th century onwards, and is the one employed by Dafydd. It approaches more nearly to a stanza form than any other in mediaeval Welsh, being composed of four lines. The first two form the *paladr* or 'shaft', the second the *esgyll* or 'wings'. The *paladr* is normally printed as two lines of ten and six syllables respectively, in which the one, two, or three syllables at the end of the first long line (the *gair cyrch* or 'link phrase') stand in parenthesis, while the main rhyme is carried by the syllable immediately preceding this 'link phrase'. The *esgyll* which follows is a seven-syllabled couplet with unrhythmical rhyme: in fact, it corresponds exactly to the *cywydd* couplet. Both *paladr* and *esgyll* have full *cynghanedd*. The *englyn* is the most tight and compact of Welsh metres and is peculiarly well adapted to concise, emphatic, and epigrammatic statements.

Certain stylistic features in Dafydd's practice of the *cywydd* need brief comment and explanation here. Since the couplet of seven-syllabled lines was the natural unit of the *cywydd*, sentences of any length or complexity—particularly such as described a series of consecutive actions—could not easily be confined within its limits, subjected as were these to the discipline of *cynghanedd*. Frequent use of the *sangiad*, or parenthetical phrase, was the device developed by Dafydd and his contemporaries to overcome this difficulty. In their simplest form such phrases occupy part of a line only (most frequently the second half), but in Dafydd's *cywyddau* they are sometimes carried over one or more lines and run parallel to the poet's main statement, underlining or giving emphasis to it, but always subordinated. *Sangiadau* are usually of an exclamatory or descriptive nature, their linguistic constituents being conditioned by the requirements of the *cynghanedd*, yet only on very rare occasions do Dafydd's *sangiadau* fail to contribute in this way to his total meaning. *Sangiadau* are used effectively in no.40 'Trouble at an Inn' where the rapid and excited movement of the passage (ls. 21-46), describing the poet's successive misadventures, is richly enhanced by the *sangiadau* which alone make possible its abrupt and jerky progression. Another example is the story of Peredur, narrated in no.13 (ls.35-52). Dr Parry has emphasized that the practice of a difficult and involved style which was 'sentence-structured' rather than 'couplet-structured' with lavish employment of *sangiad* and *torymadrodd* (i.e. tmesis, or inverted constructions) was an embellishment of their poetic artistry which was deliberately cultivated by Dafydd and his contemporaries.

An embellishment no less cultivated by the *cywydd* poets, but one which could be accommodated easily and naturally within the confines of the couplet, was the device known as *dyfalu* ('comparing' or 'describing'), by which a creature, object, or natural force is described by means of a string of imaginative comparisons and hyperbolical similes which draw upon the whole range of the poet's resources in vocabularly and ingenious imagery. It is noticeable that Dafydd employs *dyfalu* 'pejoratively' for the purposes of satire and abuse far more frequently than he employs it 'positively' for that of praise. Most frequently of all he uses it to abuse some creature or object which has acted as an obstruction to his love-making. Examples of the latter are his abuse of the Magpie (no.25), of the Owl (no.26), of the Clock (no. 32), of the Mist (no.36), and his diatribe against his Shadow (no.52). Some superb examples of the 'positive' employment of the device are 'The Wind' (no.29) and 'The Star' (no.30). It has been suggested that *dyfalu* had its origin in the art of riddle-making, as exemplified in both Latin and in Anglo-Saxon poetry. There is indeed a Welsh analogy for such a riddle in the poem on the Wind in the Book of Taliesin, perhaps of the tenth century, and perhaps known to Dafydd. But the much greater frequency of pejorative *dyfalu*, employed for the purposes of abuse and vituperation, over the positive kind, suggests an even closer alignment with the richly figurative and elaborately-compounded language of bardic satire than it does with riddles. In 'The Wind' and 'The Star' Dafydd expressed through this device his deepest responses to the wonders of the universe. And in 'The Wave on the River Dyfi' (no.33) he gave a clear indication that for him *dyfalu* constituted the very essence of the poetic art. Both *dyfalu* and *sangiad* can be paralleled in the work of the Gogynfeirdd as well as in the earliest Irish poetry: it is evident that the origins of both devices lie very far back in the poetic tradition which was shared in common by both branches of the Celtic peoples.

The amazing richness of Dafydd's vocabulary arises from the fact that he had at his command not only an extensive knowledge of the language of Welsh poetry of the preceding centuries, but could also draw upon words of French origin—borrowed words such as had been rapidly infiltrating the Welsh language during the previous two centuries, and which he constantly employed in a metaphorical or figurative manner. These borrowed words consist almost invariably of nouns denoting concrete things: buildings and furnishings of all kinds (in terms of which he describes his woodland *deildy* or house of leaves and branches); weapons of various sorts (as when Morfudd is compared to the bent stick which discharged a *mangonel*, a very up-to-date siege weapon, no.17, 1.45); different kinds of currency—*coron* 'crown', *fflwring* 'florin', *copr* 'copper coin', *mwnai* 'money'; and—less concretely—words dealing with the law and the official administration, *ustus* 'justice', *sieler* 'jailer', *fforffed* 'forfeit', *corodyn* 'pensioner'. And when these borrowed words are used, they are employed almost without exception in a figurative sense, and right out of their normal prosaic context, in order to give the shock and surprise of the unexpected. The leaves of May are florins on the tops of the branches, they are *iawn fwnai* 'true currency'; the stars are golden pieces of wrought metal—*goldyn o aur melyn mâl*; everyone is only a copper coin compared with Dafydd's friend the poet Madog Benfras, *copr pawb wrthaw*. In addition to his employment of metaphor in his use of *dyfalu*, there are poems in which Dafydd elaborates a metaphor throughout a number of lines or even throughout a whole poem, as in

'Morfudd Like the Sun' (no.8) or in the passage in which he compares the growth of his love and his final loss of Morfudd to the action of a farmer who sows his grain and watches it grow, only to find it destroyed at last by a storm when it is ready to be harvested (no.6). Dafydd displays a superb artistry in playing on the rich nuances of his vocabulary, and makes a constant use of innuendo and double meanings. His ability to encompass lively, idiomatic conversation within his exacting verse-medium was another novelty in Welsh poetry (nos.18, 25, 42, 52), so also was his evidently wide-ranging familiarity with the details of a number of crafts and professions: clock mechanism (no.32), agriculture (no.6), the law—both the native 'law of Hywel' (nos.23, 54) and more recent administrative terms (no.21), carpentry and building (no.5; no.48, ls.25-8), up-to-date weaponry and armour (no.17, 1.45; no.36, ls.28, 46), especially of the cross-bow and its adjuncts (no.23, 1.62; no.47, 1.12), music and harp playing (no.10, 1.22; no.20, 1.17; cf.GDG nos.142,148).

The Poems

This selection gives the texts, with translations and notes, of just over a third of the cywyddau accepted by Dr Parry as belonging to the authentic canon of the poet's work, and edited by him in his Gwaith Dafydd ap Gwilym. I have arranged the poems in sections according to their subject matter, and in order to bring out certain comparisons and resemblances; but inevitably there is frequent overlapping between the sections. This re-arrangement has involved re-numbering the poems, though for convenience I have retained the original numbering of GDG alongside the Welsh text in parentheses. Since the titles of the poems in GDG, appropriately bestowed on them by Dr Parry, do not actually appear in the original manuscripts, I have felt at liberty occasionally to make slight variations in the English titles. But here again, Dr Parry's original titles appear above the Welsh text.

A number of themes, attitudes, and devices characteristic of the poet will be seen to recur continually throughout the selection. Prominent among these is the device of Personification, by which Dafydd attributes the capacity for human feelings and emotions not only to all sentient creatures, but also—in the case of the Ruin and the Haycock—to man-made artefacts, and even to the Wind, the Star, and the seasons of the year. In his fabliaux, and other poems of incident, Dafydd's pose of ironic self-depreciation, alleging continual failure and misadventure in his pursuit of love, is equally characteristic. Though this pose was something quite new in Welsh, it was also affected, interestingly enough, by Dafydd's contemporary Geoffrey Chaucer.

When Dafydd alludes to those for whom he intended his cywyddau it is an audience of girls of whom he speaks ('the girls of Gwynedd', no.43, ls.83-4; an un-named girl, probably Morfudd, no.12, ls.1-4), and he recalls the 'seven score and seven *cywyddau*' which he has addressed to Morfudd (no.10, 51-2). Yet where are these poems, which Dafydd actually composed for girls, and in which he claims to have 'sown' the praise of one or other girl throughout Gwynedd, or carried it through the whole of Wales? Barely one of the *cywyddau* which have come down can be called a love-poem in any usual sense: it is exceptional for him to address a girl directly (as in nos.12, 37, 41, all of which poems—and others—are expostulatory). The lyrical passage in no.11 'Love Kept Secret' and in the poem 'To Invite Dyddgu' (GDG no.119) are the nearest of all Dafydd's extant compositions to genuine love-poems. The interest never really centres on Morfudd or on any other girl: even when a comparison between Morfudd and the Sun is elaborated throughout a whole poem (no.8) one feels that it is the image and the comparison, rather than the girl herself, which is what really most interests the poet. Dafydd's prime concern is with himself, and frequently with the fanciful elaboration of the effects which his passion for Morfudd have had upon him. Of the genuine nature of his passion there need be little doubt. But in detailing his experiences he makes a bid for the sympathy and appreciation of the listening audience of familiar friends whom he addresses (cf. no.13, l.56; no.18, l.2), and whom he could please and amuse by the recital of his real or fictional escapades and awkward misadventures. Other than himself and his passionate love he had a single absorbing interest, and that was his interest in the entire world of Nature. Hence the extended descriptions, often lovingly phrased, which he gives to his *llateion* or love-messengers, and his heart-felt greetings to the seasons of spring and summer, which brought freedom to wander abroad, to find privacy for his love-making, and to indulge in minute observation of the ways of the forest creatures, in particular of the birds. Ideas of freedom and 'escape' recur in other forms, and in a manner which is potentially significant. The poet observes that both Sun and Star are far above and beyond the reach of predatory human hands (nos.8 and 30); the Skylark climbs to heights which liberate it from the fear of any chance arrow (no.23); while the two hunted animals, the Roebuck and the Fox, elude pursuing hounds (nos.27 and 28), and the Wind itself is essentially a symbol of freedom (no.29). With all major poets the ephemeral and transitory nature of life and of beauty is a perennial theme: it is one which is implicit, and sometimes poignantly expressed, wherever Dafydd is at his most serious.

Section I, 'Love at all Seasons', brings together the poems of joyful greeting to May and to the summer months which gave freedom to go about outside and to build 'houses' for love out of leaves and branches in woodland solitudes. The obvious comparison is made with Winter's inclemency which enforced long incarceration indoors: Winter is however the season preferred by

Yr Eiddig, the 'Jealous Husband', who had already become a conventional figure in European poetry. The evergreen Holly, 'lad with a green tabard' is praised as offering a shelter for illicit love, even in the depth of winter. Personification is rarely more prominent than here: May is 'a strong horseman' and 'a free and generous nobleman' who causes lavish and abundant growth; Summer is 'a fair woodward' (forester) who departs when August comes. In one poem Dafydd watches his love grow throughout the changing phases of the agricultural year, only to find that all his care has been in vain when an unseasonable storm causes him to lose the confidently expected harvest, in some unexplained but catastrophic disappointment.

Section II, 'Morfudd, Dyddgu, and Others', places in the foreground the two girls whom Dafydd aspired to love but was unable to win. Morfudd, his most cherished sweetheart, who continually eluded him and rarely granted her favours, had for him an enchantment as of magic, but her vacillating and exasperating behaviour drove him to distraction. In spite of her marriage to that enigmatic character *Y Bwa Bach*, 'the little hunchback', the *liaison* continued, and Morfudd's husband figures several times in the conventional role of *Yr Eiddig*. In contrast, the aristocratic, virginal, but for ever unattainable Dyddgu is celebrated in some eight *cywyddau*, of which two are given here. In other poems, certain more ephemeral loves are glimpsed, but only infreqently, and they are nearly always unnamed. There is strong evidence that Morfudd was a woman who really existed, and the same is probably true of Dyddgu: but this is a very different thing from accepting at its face value all that Dafydd tells us about either girl. Apart from Elen, the English merchant's wife who repaid his praise-poems with good woollen stockings, Dafydd's constantly repeated complaint is that he never receives from any of his sweethearts the payment in the form of favours which he regards as his due for 'sowing' their praise abroad widely in his *cywyddau*—a payment evidently felt to correspond with that which the bards had always expected from their patrons in a more material form. Continental influences blend with this traditional bardic viewpoint in Dafydd's portrayal of love's sudden onslaught upon him with pangs which are as sharp as those of any spear, followed by sickness and lack of sleep. The literary conventions of *amour courtois* come into open collision with bardic custom, however, when the necessity of preserving secrecy in love's affairs is stressed (nos. 11 and 15), since such a taboo is manifestly inconsistent with 'sowing' a girl's praise abroad, and winning from her a reward for doing so.

Section III 'Birds and Animals' gives Dafydd's finest bird-poems, together with two of his three poems about hunted animals. The Song Thrush, the Nightingale and the Skylark are envisaged by Dafydd as Nature's own poets, in whose activities he discerns the implicit counterpart of his own. The Nightingale and the Thrush celebrate Mass in the forest as though they were ordained priests, and the birds sing together a paean of praise to their Creator for the great and small miracles of His creation. Birds have figured in many literatures as *exempla* from whose activities man may profitably learn, but the distinctive feature of Dafydd's bird-poetry is that personification is always counterbalanced by close observation of each bird's true and individual characteristics—its colours, its behaviour and appearance, and its distinctive notes. Dafydd's references to the nightingale (*eos*) raise interesting questions: not only to do with ornithology but to do with literary convention and his own observation and experience. Distribution of the nightingale does not, according to modern records, extend much further west than the Welsh border—except in isolated instances. Such is the precision of Dafydd's observation of the natural world (see all poems and notes in this section) that we must ask whether climatic or other conditions favoured a wider distribution of the nightingale in the 14th century, whether Dafydd's observation took place outside Wales or whether he could have merely been paying lipservice to a popular convention dating back to Biblical and Classical sources. Confusion of the nightingale with the black cap was frequent, and persists, due to the rich variety of its singing by day. The singing of both woodlark and sedge-warbler which frequently sing loudly on summer nights has often been taken for that of the nightingale. Dafydd, though, would seem too keen an observer to have made such a mistake. Exact and accurate observation, and in the case of the Skylark and the Seagull, an almost mystical reverence, pass into the world of fantasy when these birds are dispatched as *llateion* or love-messengers to Morfudd or to some other girl. Bird-messengers abound in other literatures, but for the *llatai* convention as developed by Dafydd ap Gwilym no foreign parallels appear to exist, and there are only very slight indications of this *genre* in antecedent Welsh literature. These poems all follow a similar pattern, though with slight variations. They begin with an address to the messenger, followed by a descriptive passage in its praise, generally in elaborate *dyfalu*; a request to carry a message to the poet's sweetheart, in which details may be given of the destination, of the dangers of the journey, or of the girl herself; and ending with a prayer for the messenger's safe return, perhaps with a message or—in the case of the Roebuck—with a kiss for an answer; in conclusion there may be the invocation of a saint's protection upon the messenger. In contrast to the *llatai* poems, the Owl and the Magpie incur the poet's displeasure in a torrent of vituperative *dyfalu*, the one for disturbing his sleep by its raucous hooting, the other for its gratuitous and interfering advice. The Fox (like the Hare, GDG no.46) threatens the success of Dafydd's tryst by appearing suddenly and unexpectedly before the girl arrives: the *dyfalu* seems here to express the poet's somewhat reluctant admiration for the vivid flash of colour which the animal presents.

The device of the *llatai* is imaginatively extended in the following Section IV 'Other Messengers of Love'. Here the Wind itself is deputized as Dafydd's message-bearer to Morfudd, and in lines of superb admiring *dyfalu* the poet contemplates its unimpeded freedom to traverse the world. 'The Star' is not in a strict sense a *llatai* poem: in praising the Star whose light illumined his journey to Morfudd, Dafydd is inspired to flights of imaginative *dyfalu* which far outdistance any conventional framework. In two poems Dafydd has a vision of his sweetheart in a dream; in the first his pursuit of love is symbolized as a hunt and the visionary hounds are described as his *llateion*, in the second it is the Dream itself which carries the sleeping poet to a girl whom he has loved at some former time, and abusive *dyfalu* is heaped upon the striking clock which shattered his sleeping vision. The poem to the river Dyfi in spate is a kind of reversed *llatai* poem: here the poet beseeches the turbulent wave to stop impeding his passage to Llanbadarn and to Morfudd's home, and promises, if it will do so, to employ all his skill in composing *dyfalu* in its praise. Dafydd's eloquent prayer to St Dwynwen, the patron saint of lovers, though to the modern mind it may appear an exotic and even bizarre adaptation of the *llatai* convention, would not have seemed profane or extraordinary to Christian believers of an earlier age, whose security in their faith enabled them to approach the very borders of blasphemy with relative impunity—compare 'Paying Love's Debt' (no.10) where Morfudd is said to be named at the end of every prayer, and above all 'The Woodland Mass' (no.24). In these poems there is no ridicule of sacred subjects, but rather a borrowing of sacred formulas to give poignancy to the secular matter.

Section V 'Love's Frustrations' gives a series of brief episodes in which Dafydd narrates his misadventures in the pursuit of love, and his attempts, too often frustrated, to hold trysts with various girls. It may be that 'Journeying for Love', with its detailed pointers to still-existing places in the neighbourhood of Dafydd's early home, comes closer than any other poem in this section to giving an account of the poet's genuine experiences. The ironic employment of the well-worn poetic epithets for a girl's beauty (bright as the sun, and with hair like gossamer) and the names of the traditional heroines is at its most incisive in the poem in which Dafydd remonstrates with a girl who shows too great a propensity to prefer a soldier as a lover rather than Dafydd—a mere poet—himself. 'The Goose Shed' and 'Trouble at an Inn' narrate episodes which are much in the style of the ribald international *fabliaux*. It is difficult to believe that Dafydd did not know of these foreign models, and therefore it seems most probable that fantasy is in the ascendant here over whatever nucleus of fact there may possibly once have been. Yet both in these *fabliaux* and in the two poems which reflect the continental forms of the *sérénade* and the *aube*, Dafydd adapts the continental models to his own purposes in so individual a manner as utterly to transform them. The section ends with the defence of his chosen mode of life which Dafydd makes to a Franciscan friar to whom he imagines himself as coming to make his confession.

Section VI 'Addresses to Friends' gives two of Dafydd's seven praise-poems to Ifor Hael ('the Generous'), a friend and patron who may be assumed to have played fully as important a part in providing intellectual stimulus for the poet as had his uncle Llywelyn in his early years. The four *cywyddau* which (in addition to *awdlau* and *englynion*) Dafydd addressed to Ifor not only illustrate the poet's concept of the independent and mutually beneficial relationship which he enjoyed with his patron, but also demonstrate the fusing and blending of two traditions—the heroic concepts and imagery of Dafydd's professional bardic predecessors with the new, more relaxed and personal expression of human relationships which became possible for poets in the new age of the *cywydd*. Examples follow of Dafydd's 'mock' elegies to men who were still alive at the time when they were composed: to his fellow-poets Gruffudd ab Adda and Madog Benfras, and to his neighbour in Ceredigion, the distinguished *uchelwr* Rhydderch ab Ieuan Llwyd. They illustrate the poet's relationships with certain of his contemporaries, and offer a measure of genuine insight into his feelings towards them.

The final Section VII assembles a mixed collection of poems in widely differing moods, in which the poet considers himself and his life and confronts the thoughts of old age and death. Awareness of loss and life's impermanence are evoked by man-made objects in 'The Ruin' and 'The Haycock'; 'Despondency' gives Dafydd's most pessimistic assessment of his years of fruitless devotion to Morfudd, while in his 'Recantation' he prays for divine forgiveness. But Dafydd contemplates himself in an altogether lighter vein in 'The Mirror' and 'His Shadow' and indicates in 'Love's Tribulation' that all is not lost in spite of old age advancing upon him. The concluding poem 'A Prayer' is one of the small group of poems which express Dafydd's intense religious devotion. It differs metrically from all the other poems in this book in that it is composed in a sequence of *englynion*, and is a reminder that the poet could excel in the older traditional metres no less than in the *cywydd*. The religious poems form an essential counterbalance to the more frivolous aspects of Dafydd's subject-matter, and must be represented in order to give complete and balanced expression to the depth and versatility of his genius.

The Translation

In undertaking the daunting task of translating a selection of Dafydd ap Gwilym's poems my purpose has been two-fold: firstly, to aid the interested student, who may have 'little Welsh' or none, to understand and appreciate the originals; and secondly, hopefully, to introduce some English readers who may have been barely aware of Dafydd ap Gwilym's existence, to a distinguished European poet who lived and composed his poetry in this island, and whose achievement fully deserves their sympathetic interest and attention. The purpose of the translations is to subserve the original text, since some measure of appreciation of the musical effects of *cynghanedd* is possible even for those who are without an extensive understanding of the vocabulary and structure of Welsh. It is a general belief that poetry is untranslatable except at the cost of so great a loss as to call in question the reasons for ever attempting it. Dafydd ap Gwilym's poetry is an extreme example of the validity of this interdiction, since his *awdlau* and *cywyddau* made their primary appeal to the ears of their original audiences: rarely—if ever—did these audiences see his poems in writing. Such impact as his poetry made upon their understanding must have been made at levels which varied according to the circumstances and capacity of the individual listeners: for instance, it has been observed that the device of *dyfalu* presupposes an audience familiar with this convention. By intricate innuendo and often by intentional ambiguity arising from the nuances of his traditional vocabulary, and by his figurative use of the new words of French origin which in his day were flooding into the language, Dafydd evolved for himself a poetic medium of a degree of complexity never previously envisaged in Welsh, and one which by its very nature defies all attempts at adequate paraphrase, let alone the far more difficult task of transposition into another language. It follows that very often there is no single 'right' meaning for a line or a passage, and since the full range of meaning possessed by the words in any one language does not hold the same nuances as the words which come nearest in meaning to it in another language, the translator is too often obliged to opt for a single meaning out of a choice of equally valid but never completely satisfactory alternatives.

Any attempts to translate Dafydd's *cywyddau* must come to terms with two main problems, the difficulties presented by his syntax, and the straight-jacket which the requirements of *cynghanedd* imposed upon his choice of vocabulary. Dafydd inherited from his professional predecessors a traditional syntax which belonged essentially to poetry. This was highly condensed and often imprecise, admitting of an inverted word-order which allowed for ambiguities in the relationship of substantives to each other, made frequent new compounds (both of nouns and adjectives), could on occasion dispense with pronouns, prepositions, and conjunctions, and even with certain forms of the verb 'to be'; and which frequently employed 'verb-nouns' (i.e. nouns denoting the verbal act, a characteristic feature of the Celtic languages) in place of the more precise finite verbal forms. The frequent counterpointing interjections enshrined in Dafydd's *sangiadau* further enhance the difficulties for the translator. The device of the *sangiad* was itself a partial answer to the demands of *cynghanedd*, since *cynghanedd* restricted the choice of words to those which contained the requisite consonants in the right order, or the necessary rhymes in the right place. Hence the tendency to formulaic repetition in the *sangiadau* (*gwn gyni*, *gwn gannoch*, *gwn ganclwyf* and the like), and the use of compounds whose lack of precision means that they contribute little, if anything, to the total meaning, but must nevertheless be translated, and if possible by a word of equivalent 'weight', i.e. degree of precision, or of the lack of it. A selection of words of this kind of which Dafydd was most fond would necessarily include the following: *gwiw*, *gwych*, *glwys*, *gloyw*, *gwyn/gwen*, *claer*, *hoyw*, *lliw*.

Inspite of all arguments advanced by those who regard verse as the only acceptable medium for translating verse, I have had no hesitation in adopting straight prose for my translation, since this is the only means of conveying any approximation to the meaning of the original. Verse translations of a number of Dafydd's *cywyddau* have been attempted at various times, and some readers may prefer these. They include some interesting recent attempts to conform with the syllabic length and a-symmetrical rhyme scheme of the *cywydd*, a medium which sits somewhat uneasily in English, but which is certainly preferable to the octosyllabic couplets favoured by earlier translators. A free prose translation is subject to none of the restrictions necessitated by meeting self-imposed metrical requirements, so that it is possible to strive for the maximum degree of accuracy consistent with the linguistic difficulties of the original which I have outlined above. I believe that straight prose has been the most successful medium employed by translators of Celtic poetry, both Welsh and Irish, in the present century—for Irish metrics are no less intricate than those of Welsh. Early in the century the tradition was inaugurated by that most gifted of translators of early Irish poetry, Kuno Meyer. He attempted neither rhythm nor rhyme, and yet his translations have since come to be regarded as classics in their own right, and his path has been successfully followed by a number of others, and in both languages—a single example among many is Kenneth Jackson's *A Celtic Miscellany*. I have aspired no higher than to provide a serviceable translation in what I hope is good and readable English (in so far as this is consistent with accuracy), and one which will assist the reader towards the interpretation and appreciation of the originals. I have adopted Meyer's arrangement of printing the translation in lines corresponding to those of the Welsh text, in order to indicate the structure of the *cywyddau*. Where the translation is not line for line, I have endeavoured to contain the meaning within the couplet, except in the occasional cases in which this is not possible owing to the presence of *sangiadau*, which have to be unravelled in order to disentangle the syntax. Round brackets or dashes are used for the *sangiadau*, which represent the poet's own interpolations. To distinguish my own from his I have employed square brackets for words not actually included in the text but which are essential to express in English what I conceive the poet's meaning to be: these include such 'fillers' as 'then, there, yet, not even' which may sometimes be required to point the emphasis.

Finally, I know of no better way in which to introduce my attempts to render Dafydd ap Gwilym into English than by quoting the words with which A.T. Hatto prefaced his translation of another mediaeval classic poem—Gottfried von Strassburg's *Tristan:*

'After enjoying (this poem) for thirty years I would never have dared to translate it but for the unending pleasure, despite the incalculable loss, which translations of otherwise inaccessible masterpieces have given me, even renderings that were manifestly poor or misconceived. I know from this experience that it is possible to succeed whilst failing; and how grateful a reader can be for a translator's courage, or maybe rashness.'

R.B.

Recommended for Further Reading:

Thomas Parry (trans. H. I. Bell) *A History of Welsh Literature* (Oxford, 1955).

A. O. H. Jarman and Gwilym Rees Hughes (eds.) *A Guide to Welsh Literature*, vol.2 (Swansea, 1980).

R. Bromwich *Dafydd ap Gwilym* ('Writers of Wales' series, Cardiff, 1974).

Poetry Wales (Special Dafydd ap Gwilym number) 1973.

ABBREVIATIONS

B	*Bulletin of the Board of Celtic Studies.*
BD	Henry Lewis, *Brut Dingestow* (Caerdydd, 1942).
BDG	*Barddoniaeth Dafydd ap Gwilym* O grynhoad Owen Jones (Myfyr) a William Owen (Pughe), (London, 1789).
BT	*The Book of Taliesin* (facsimile ed. J. G. Evans, Llanbedrog, 1910).
CA	*Canu Aneirin* ed. Ifor Williams (Caerdydd, 1938).
CD	J. Morris-Jones, *Cerdd Dafod* (Oxford, 1925).
CLIH	*Canu Llywarch Hen* ed. Ifor Williams (Caerdydd, 1935).
ChO	*Chwedlau Odo* ed. Ifor Williams (Wrexham, 1925; Caerdydd 1957).
Chotzen	Th. M. Chotzen, *Recherches sur la Poésie de Dafydd ap Gwilym* (Amsterdam, 1927).
DGG²	*Cywyddau Dafydd ap Gwilym a'i Gyfoeswyr*, ed. Ifor Williams and T. Roberts (Caerdydd, 1935).
EEW	T. H. Parry-Williams, *The English Element in Welsh* (London, 1923).
Fr.	French.
G	J. Lloyd-Jones, *Geirfa Barddoniaeth Gynnar Gymraeg* (Caerdydd, 1931-63).
GDG	Thomas Parry, *Gwaith Dafydd ap Gwilym* (Caerdydd, 1952).
GDG²	ibid. Ail Argraffiad (second edition, 1963).
GDG³	ibid (third edition, 1979).
GLM	Eurys I. Rowlands, *Gwaith Lewys Môn* (Caerdydd, 1975).
GMW	D. Simon Evans, *A Grammar of Middle Welsh* (Dublin, 1964).
GP	G. J. Williams and E. J. Jones, *Gramadegau'r Penceirddiaid* (Caerdydd, 1934).
GPC	*Geiriadur Prifysgol Cymru: A Dictionary of the Welsh Language* (Caerdydd 1950-).
H	J. Morris-Jones and T. H. Parry-Williams, *Llawysgrif Hendregadredd* (Caerdydd, 1933).
HGCr	Henry Lewis, *Hen Gerddi Crefyddol* (Caerdydd, 1931).
HRB	*Historia Regum Britanniae* by Geoffrey of Monmouth.
HW	J. E. Lloyd, *A History of Wales* (London, 1911).

IGE[2]	*Cywyddau Iolo Goch ac Eraill* ed. Henry Lewis, T. Roberts and Ifor Williams (Caerdydd, 1937).
Ir.	Irish.
LBS	S. Baring-Gould and J. Fisher, *Lives of the British Saints.*
LlC	*Llên Cymru.*
MA[2]	*The Myvyrian Archaiology of Wales* (second edition, Denbigh, 1870).
OBWV	*The Oxford Book of Welsh Verse.*
OED	*The Oxford English Dictionary.*
PKM	Ifor Williams, *Pedeir Keinc y Mabinogi* (Caerdydd 1930; ail argraffiad, 1951).
RBP	J. G. Evans (ed.) *The Poetry from the Red Book of Hergest* (Llanbedrog, 1911).
Rep.	J. G. Evans, *Report on Manuscripts in the Welsh Language* (London, 1898-).
SC	*Studia Celtica.*
TC	T. J. Morgan *Y Treigladau a'u Cystrawen* (Caerdydd, 1952).
THSC	*Transactions of the Honourable Society of Cymmrodorion.*
Tradn. and Innov.	R. Bromwich, *Tradition and Innovation in the Poetry of Dafydd ap Gwilym* (Cardiff, 1967, 1972).
TW.	Thomas Wiliems, Latin-Welsh Dictionary.
TYP	R. Bromwich, *Trioedd Ynys Prydein: The Welsh Triads* (Cardiff, 1961, 1978).
WM	*The White Book Mabinogion* ed. J. G. Evans (Pwllheli, 1907; ail argraffiad, Caerdydd, 1977).
YB	*Ysgrifau Beirniadol* ed. J. E. Caerwyn Williams (Dinbych, 1956 -).

I. LOVE AT ALL SEASONS (1-7)

1 May and January

Greetings, splendid greenwood choir,
Summer's May month—since for that I long—
strong horseman, lover's recompense,
4   with a green fetter mastering the wild forest,
the friend of love and friend of birds;
lovers are mindful of him, their kinsman he is,
ambassador for nine score lovers' trysts
8   for honourable, loving dialogue.
By Mary, it is a delightful thing
that May, the perfect month, is on the way,
intent—in ardent affirmation of his rank—
12   upon the conquest of each verdant glen.

In a dense screen, the clothing of the high-roads,
he has dressed all places in his web of green.
When there comes, after battle with the frost,
16   the tent of thick leaves to invigorate the fields,
green will be the paths of May
succeeding April (birds' chirping is my faith);
on topmost branches of the oak will come
20   the singing of the new-fledged birds,
and the cuckoo high over each land,
and a songster; with a long and joyful day,
and white mist-haze after the wind
24   protects the middle of the valley,
and sky at afternoon is clear and glad
with green trees and fresh gossamer,
and crowds of birds upon the trees,
28   and fresh leaves on forest saplings,
and Morfudd my golden girl, will come to [my] mind
with all love's seven-times-nine tumultuous turns.

All unlike to the sad black month
32   which rebukes everyone for loving,
and brings short days and depressing rain,
and wind that will despoil the trees,
and weakness—terrifying frailty—
36   a trailing cloak with rain and hail,
incitement to high tides, and colds,
grey flooding water-courses down the valleys,
rivers in spate with raucous noise,
40   and day-time sad and wearisome,
skies overcast, sombre and chill,
their hue hiding from us the moon.
Let there come to him—threat that's easy to predict—
44   evil two-fold for his boorishness!

Mis Mai a Mis Ionawr (69)

Hawddamor, glwysgor glasgoed,
Fis Mai haf, canys mau hoed.
Cadarn farchog serchog sâl,
4   Cadwynwyrdd feistr coed anial;
Cyfaill cariad ac adar,
Cof y serchogion a'u câr;
Cennad nawugain cynnadl,
8   Caredig urddedig ddadl.
A mawr fydd, myn Mair, ei fod,
Mai, fis difai, yn dyfod,
A'i fryd, arddelw frwd urddas,
12   Ar oresgyn pob glyn glas.

Gwasgod praff, gwisgiad priffyrdd,
Gwisgodd bob lle â'i we wyrdd.
Pan ddêl ar ôl rhyfel rhew,
16   Pill doldir, y pall deildew—
Gleision fydd, mau grefydd grill,
Llwybrau Mai yn lle Ebrill—
Y daw ar uchaf blaen dâr
20   Caniadau cywion adar;
A chog ar fan pob rhandir,
A chethlydd, a hoywddydd hir;
A niwl gwyn yn ôl y gwynt
24   Yn diffryd canol dyffrynt;
Ac wybren loyw hoyw brynhawn
Fydd, a glwyswydd a glaswawn;
Ac adar aml ar goedydd,
28   Ac irddail ar wiail wŷdd;
A chof fydd Forfudd f'eurferch,
A chyffro saith nawtro serch.

Annhebyg i'r mis dig du
32   A gerydd i bawb garu;
A bair tristlaw a byrddydd,
A gwynt i ysbeilio gwŷdd;
A llesgedd, breuoledd braw,
36   A llaesglog a chenllysglaw,
Ac annog llanw ac annwyd,
Ac mewn naint llifeiriant llwyd,
A llawn sôn mewn afonydd,
40   A llidio a digio dydd,
Ac wybren drymled ledoer,
A'i lliw yn gorchuddio'r lloer.
Dêl iddo, rhyw addo rhwydd,
44   Deuddrwg am ei wladeiddrwydd.

2 May Month

God knew the richness of fresh growth
would well become the beginning of May,
that without fail new shoots would grow
4   upon the Calends of the gentle month of May.
Unwithered tips of boughs retarded me—
yesterday great God gave May.
The poets' treasured jewel would not deceive me,
8   good was the life I had upon the coming of May.

It is a fair and handsome youth who has enriched me:
a generous prodigal nobleman is May.
He had sent to me honest currency,
12   pure green leaves of the tender hazels of May.
Florins of the tree-tops, they brought me no grief,
Fleurs-de-lys riches of the wealth of May.
He guarded me secure from treachery
16   beneath the leafy mantles of the wings of May.
Yet I am full of grief because he may not stay
for ever (how is it for me?), the month of May.

I tamed a girl who greeted me:
20   a gentle seemly lass beneath the choir of May.
The foster-father of fine poets, who has honoured me,
[and] of gentle lovers is May.
A god-child of the perfect Lord
24   (fine greenery), great is the honour of May.
He who would purify me came
from Heaven to the world—my life is May.

Green are the slopes, joyous the messengers of love,
28   long is the day in the fresh woods of May.
Verdant—for they do not hide themselves—
hill-sides and tops of undergrowth in May.
The night is short, no journey burdensome,
32   splendid the hawks and blackbirds are in May.
Joyful the nightingale where she would warble,
garrulous are the little birds in May.
He has taught me swift activity:
36   there is no great majesty but May.

Peacock of green wing of town-houses,
Which one of a thousand! Chief of all is May.
Who could build it out of leaves
40   within the month, but only May?
it fostered green battlements,
fresh gleaming hazels of the slender leaves of May.
Winter with its puddles, best if it did not come,
44   tenderest of all the months is May.

Mis Mai (23)

Duw gwyddiad mai da y gweddai
Dechreuad mwyn dyfiad Mai.
Difeth irgyrs a dyfai
4 Dyw Calan mis mwynlan Mai.
Digrinflaen goed a'm oedai,
Duw mawr a roes doe y Mai.
Dillyn beirdd ni'm rhydwyllai,
8 Da fyd ym oedd dyfod Mai.

Harddwas teg a'm anrhegai,
Hylaw ŵr mawr hael yw'r Mai.
Anfones ym iawn fwnai,
12 Glas defyll glân mwyngyll Mai.
Ffloringod brig ni'm digiai,
Fflŵr-dy-lis gyfoeth mis Mai.
Diongl rhag brad y'm cadwai,
16 Dan esgyll dail mentyll Mai.
Llawn wyf o ddig na thrigai
(Beth yw i mi?) byth y Mai.

Dofais ferch a'm anerchai,
20 Dyn gwiwryw mwyn dan gôr Mai.
Tadmaeth beirdd heirdd, a'm hurddai,
Serchogion mwynion, yw Mai.
Mab bedydd Dofydd difai,
24 Mygrlas, mawr yw urddas Mai.
O'r nef y doeth a'm coethai
I'r byd, fy mywyd yw Mai.

Neud glas gofron, llon llatai,
28 Neud hir dydd mewn irwydd Mai.
Neud golas, nid ymgelai,
Bronnydd a brig manwydd Mai.
Neud ber nos, nid bwrn siwrnai,
32 Neud heirdd gweilch a mwyeilch Mai.
Neud llon eos lle trosai,
Neud llafar mân adar Mai.
Neud esgud nwyf a'm dysgai,
36 Nid mawr ogoniant ond Mai.

Paun asgellas dinastai,
Pa un o'r mil? Penna'r Mai.
Pwy o ddail a'i hadeilai
40 Yn oed y mis onid Mai?
Magwyr laswyrdd a'i magai,
Mygr irgyll mân defyll Mai.
Pyllog, gorau pe pallai,
44 Y gaeaf, mwynaf yw Mai.

Gone is the spring—that did not trouble me—
refined gold ore is the gold wealth of May;
the birth of brilliant summer would disperse it,
48   it raises tears; beautiful is May.
I would be dressed in leaves of hazels with green bark—
a good life to me is the coming of May.
Great and wise God has so ordained.
52   with Mary to observe the month of May.

3 Summer

Woe to us, Adam's feeble breed
for Summer's shortness (surge of blessing);
by God, it is in truth most odious
4   that Summer comes [at all] since it must end—
with gentle and unclouded sky,
and joyful, summer-splendid sun,
and still and tranquil firmament:
8   delightful the whole world is in the Summer.

Good crops, unblemished in their flesh,
in Summer come from the old earth.
Summer was bestowed to cause to grow
12   comely green leaves upon the trees,
so that I laugh to see how fine
the lively birch grows hair upon her head.
To Paradise it is I sing:
16   who would not laugh when Summer is so fair?
With dedicated strength I sing its praise,
and with sweet satisfaction: what a gift is Summer!

Of the foam's hue is the girl I love
20   under the trees, her boldness is of Summer.
The Cuckoo lovingly will sing
if I request it, in the early summer sun,
a fair grey bird, [whom] I will gracefully dispatch
24   [to be] the vesper-bell at midsummer;
eloquent is the voice of sweetest Nightingale
sleek and emboldened, under Summer's awning;
the Cock-Thrush, with Summer's lively chatter
28   —I must retreat from competing with him.
Poet of Ovid, in the fine long days,
(a daring pledge) in summer-time I go and come;
the Jealous Husband, Adam's bastard son,
32   need not be anxious till the Summer come:
Winter was given for those of his like age,
the gift to lovers is the summer-time.

Deryw'r gwanwyn, ni'm dorai,
Eurgoeth mwyn aur gywoeth Mai;
Dechrau haf llathr a'i sathrai,
48 Deigr a'i mag, diagr yw Mai.
Deilgyll gwyrddrisg a'm gwisgai,
Da fyd ym yw dyfod Mai.
Duw ddoeth gadarn a farnai
52 A Mair i gynnal y Mai.

Yr Haf (24)

Gwae ni, hil eiddil Addaf,
Fordwy rhad, fyrred yr haf.
Rho Duw, gwir mai dihiraf,
4 Rhag ei ddarfod, dyfod haf,
A llednais wybr ehwybraf
A llawen haul a'i lliw'n haf,
Ac awyr erwyr araf,
8 A'r byd yn hyfryd yn haf.

Cnwd da iawn, cnawd dianaf,
O'r ddaear hen a ddaw'r haf.
I dyfu, glasu glwysaf,
12 Dail ar goed y rhoed yr haf.
Gweled mor hardd, mi chwarddaf,
Gwallt ar ben hoyw fedwen haf.
Paradwys, iddo prydaf,
16 Pwy ni chwardd pan fo hardd haf?
Glud anianol y'i molaf,
Glwysfodd, wi o'r rhodd yw'r haf!

Deune geirw dyn a garaf
20 Dan frig, a'i rhyfyg yw'r haf.
Y gog serchog, os archaf,
A gân, ddechrau huan haf,
Glasgain edn, glwys ganiadaf
24 Gloch osber am hanner haf.
Bangaw llais eos dlosaf
Bwyntus hy dan bentis haf.
Ceiliog, o frwydr y ciliaf,
28 Y fronfraith hoywfabiaith haf.
Dyn Ofydd, hirddydd harddaf,
A draidd, gair hyfaidd, yr haf.
Eiddig, cyswynfab Addaf,
32 Ni ddawr hwn oni ddaw'r haf.
Rhoed i'w gyfoed y gaeaf,
A rhan serchogion yw'r haf.

7

Under the birches I have no desire
36 in houses of the glade for aught but Summer's robes,
to dress myself in a pure woven web,
the splendid mantle of Summer's brave 'hair':
I untwine the ivy-leaves—
40 no cold will come in the long summer days.
if I entreat a gentle girl
glad keeping will she get at Summer's height.

Satire succeeds not, saddest portent,
44 to deny Summer to the sprightly poet;
wind does not allow (I can wear a cloak)
trees in good state: woe yesterday for Summer!
I do not deny the longing that there is
48 for Summer's sunshine in my heart.
If with Autumn, or with Winter,
snow and ice come to dispel the Summer—
woe's me, to Christ it is I ask
52 if He dispel it so soon—'Where is the Summer?'

4 Praise of Summer

You, Summer, father of proud arrogance,
begetter of luxuriant shady trees,
fair wood-ward, master of thick forest-slope,
4 you are a tower above us all, the thatcher of each hill;
it is you who bring about (a pledge of [your] virility
[as] perfect lord) the world's re-birth.
It is you who are—a cause of wondering utterance—
8 the homestead of each growing herb,
a balm for growing—a matter of double growth—
and ointment for trystings in the woods.

Your hand, by God who's loved, is well able
12 to make the green-wood branches grow;
best impulse of the earth's four quarters.
Also by your grace so wonderfully grow
birds and the crops of the fair earth,
16 and flocks [of birds] in flight,
the light hay on the meadows glassy-topped,
bee-hives and noble swarms of bees,
You are the foster-father—prophet of the highways—
20 of the earth's heaped burden, the garden's load of green;
you are the builder of my lovely bower—
fair leafy grafting from a web of leaves.
And it is an eternal grief
24 by night or day, how nearly August comes,
and to know that you, golden abundance,
from the prolonged defection, would depart.

Minnau dan fedw ni mynnaf
36 Mewn tai llwyn ond mentyll haf.
Gwisgo gwe lân amdanaf,
Gwnsallt bybyr harddwallt haf.
Eiddew ddail a ddadeiliaf.
40 Annwyd ni bydd hirddydd haf.
Lledneisferch os anerchaf,
Llon arail hon ar ael haf.

Gwawd ni lwydd, arwydd oeraf,
44 Gwahardd ar hoywfardd yr haf.
Gwynt ni ad, gwasgad gwisgaf,
Gwŷdd ym mhwynt, gwae ddoe am haf!
Hiraeth, nid ymddiheuraf,
48 Dan fy mron am hinon haf.
O daw, hydref, ef aeaf,
Eiry a rhew, i yrru'r haf,
Gwae finnau, Grist, gofynnaf,
52 Os gyr mor rhyfyr, 'Mae'r haf?'

Mawl i'r Haf (27)

Tydi'r Haf, tad y rhyfyg,
Tadwys coed brwys caead brig,
Teg wdwart, feistr tew goedallt,
4 Tŵr pawb wyd, töwr pob allt.
Tydi a bair, air wryd,
Didwn ben, dadeni byd;
Tydi y sydd, berydd barabl,
8 Tyddyn pob llysewyn pabl,
Ac eli twf, ddeudwf ddadl,
Ac ennaint coedydd gynnadl.

Da y gŵyr, myn Duw a gerir,
12 Dy law cadeiriaw coed ir.
Hoff anian pedwar ban byd,
Uthr y tyf o'th rad hefyd
Adar a chnwd daear deg
16 A heidiau yn ehedeg,
Bragwair gweirgloddiau brigwydr,
Bydafau a heidiau hydr.
Tadmaeth wyd, proffwyd priffyrdd,
20 Teml daearlwyth, garddlwyth gwyrdd.
Impiwr wyd i'm pur adail,
Impiad gwiw ddeiliad gwe ddail.
A drwg yw yn dragywydd
24 Nesed Awst, ai nos ai dydd,
A gwybod o'r method maith,
Euraid deml, yr aut ymaith.

'Tell me, Summer—this is wrong—
28   and I would like to ask of you
to what region or what kingdom
or what country, by wise Peter, do you go?'

'Quiet, praise-poet, with your careful verse,
32   quiet, master of enchanting vaunt,
it is my fate—an omen of might—
I am a prince'(—the Summer sang)
'that I should come here for three months and make to
grow
36   materials for a multitude of crops
and when roof-tree and leaves have finished
with their growing, and branches finished weaving,
to escape the wind of Winter
40   to Annwfn from the world I go.'

May the blessings of the world's poets
and their hundred greetings go with you.
Farewell, king of the splendid weather.
44   farewell, our ruler and our lord,
farewell, the young cuckoos,
farewell, June's fair-weather slopes,
farewell, the sun on high
48   and the plump cloud, a white-bellied ball.
Lord of an army, in truth you will not be
so high, with hill of drifting snow above
until there comes—the fair garden unveiled—
52   once more the Summer with his splendid slopes.

5 The Leafy Hut

You splendid poets, [give] blessing to the lovely lass—
my matchless golden girl, [who has] the region's loveliness—
who welcomed me
4   amidst birch and hazel, the mantles of May,
shining in fervent pride above the slope's confines
(good place to praise a maiden's countenance)
true furnishing of unfrequented citadel:
8   a living-room is better if it grows.

If my darling, shy and slender, comes
to the house of leaves that God the Father made,
her recompense will be the comely trees;
12   without soot will be her house today,
with no excess of work beneath its vaulted roof
(Holy God's workmanship is not less good).
Of like mind am I with my girl:

Manag ym, haf, mae'n gam hyn,
28 Myfy a fedr d'ymofyn,
Pa gyfair neu pa gyfoeth,
Pa dir ydd ei, myn Pedr ddoeth.

'Taw, fawlfardd, tau ofalfydr,
32 Taw, fost feistrawl hudawl hydr.
Tynghedfen sy'm, rym ramant,
Tywysawg, wyf,' tes a gant,
'Dyfod drimis i dyfu
36 Defnyddiau llafuriau llu;
A phan ddarffo do a dail
Dyfu, a gwëu gwiail,
I ochel awel aeaf
40 I Annwfn o ddwfn ydd af.'

Aed bendithion beirddion byd
A'u can hawddamor cennyd.
Yn iach, frenin yr hinon,
44 Yn iach, ein llywiawdr a'n iôn,
Yn iach, y cogau ieuainc,
Yn iach, hin Fehefin fainc,
Yn iach, yr haul yn uchel
48 A'r wybren dew, bolwen bêl.
Deyrn byddin, dioer ni byddy
Yn gyfuwch, fryn wybrluwch fry,
Oni ddêl, digel degardd,
52 Eilwaith yr haf a'i lethr hardd.

Y Deildy (121)

Heirdd feirdd, f'eurddyn diledryw,
Hawddamor, hoen goror gwiw,
I fun lwys a'm cynhwysai
4 Mewn bedw a chyll, mentyll Mai,
Llathr daerfalch uwch llethr derfyn
Lle da i hoffi lliw dyn;
Gwir ddodrefn o'r gaer ddidryf,
8 Gwell yw ystafell os tyf.

O daw meinwar fy nghariad
I dŷ dail a wnaeth Duw Dad,
Dyhuddiant fydd y gwŷdd gwiw,
12 Dihuddygl o dŷ heddiw.
Nid gwaith gormodd dan gronglwyd,
Nid gwaeth deiliadaeth Duw lwyd.
Unair wyf i â'm cyfoed,

11

16 we can in the forest there
    together listen to the talk of birds
    —the woodland's poets, whom the bright dawn loves—
    to their *cywyddau* in the weaving branches
20 —the privileged children of the leaves—
    a kindred with an unembittered tale,
    the fledgling minstrels of the oak-tree citadel.
    This [house] will have Saint David's bold blessing,
24 May's handicraft will erect it—
    his plumb-line the calm cuckoo,
    his set-square the woodland Nightingale,
    his house-timbers the long summer-day,
28 his laths the pangs of love-sickness,
    love's altar is the forest glade
    —with cunning—and his hatchet am I.

    Now at the year's beginning
32 no longer do I have the house:
    far is it from my mind to give rewards
    to a hag from an old sunken hovel
    I will not search—I am alluding to [her] malice—
36 [for such a one] to guard the building I have [now] abandoned.

6 Love's Husbandry

    I loved, despite the suffering,
    and love still more, or twice as much again,
    conserving my domesticated love
4 crippled by care, fresh brood of memory;
    and have preserved within my heart
    love, the deceiver, one who gnaws the flesh.
    It is augmenting in my breast
8 which has known grief (mother of treachery)
    sooner than growth, a strong creation,
    a powerful shoot, branch of a planted tree.
    To seek the proper harvest of my love
12 has been always my intent.

    Winter-tilth, a pang of care,
    I have made (due pay for passion's grief),
    in harbouring, while nourishing a hidden woe
16 my love for Morfudd through dead January:
    my breast was ploughed bravely in depth
    with a single deep furrow at a blow (?)
    and a sharp finely-fashioned plough [was used]
20 to open up my breast upon the other side.
    The plough-share pierced into my heart
    with love's coulter up over the heights,
    and in the right breast, a conspicuous wound,

16 Yno y cawn yn y coed
   Clywed siarad gan adar,
   Clerwyr coed, claerwawr a'u câr;
   Cywyddau, gweau gwiail,
20 Cywion priodolion dail;
   Cenedl â dychwedl dichwerw,
   Cywion cerddorion caer dderw.
   Dewi yn hy a'i dawnha,
24 Dwylo Mai a'i hadeila,
   A'i linyn yw'r gog lonydd,
   A'i ysgwîr yw eos gwŷdd,
   A'i dywydd yw hirddydd haf,
28 A'i ais yw goglais gwiwglaf;
   Ac allor serch yw'r gelli
   Yn gall, a'i fwyall wyf fi.

   Ni chaf yn nechrau blwyddyn
32 Yn hwy y tŷ no hyd hyn.
   Pell i'm bryd roddi gobrau
   I wrach o hen gilfach gau,
   Ni cheisiaf, adroddaf drais,
36 Wrth adail a wrthodais.

Hwsmonaeth Cariad (87)

   Caru y bûm, cyd curiwyf,
   A mwy neu ddeufwy ydd wyf.
   Cyfragod cariad tradof,
 4 Crupl y cur, croyw epil cof.
   Cadw a orwyf i'm ceudawd
   Cariad, twyllwr, cnöwr cnawd.
   Cynyddu, cwyn a wyddiad,
 8 Y mae i'm bron, mam y brad,
   Cynt no thyfiad, cread craff,
   Cangen o blanbren blaenbraff.
   Ceisio heiniar o garu
12 Yn briod fyth i'm bryd fu.

   Gaeafar, gwayw o ofal,
   A wneddwyf, dolurnwyf dâl;
   Rhwng deiliadaeth, cawddfaeth cudd,
16 Y marwfis a serch Morfudd
   Arddwyd y fron ddewrlon ddwys
   Onengyr ddofn yn ungwys,
   Ac aradr cyweirgadr call
20 I frynaru'r fron arall.
   Y swch i'm calon y sydd,
   A chwlltr y serch uwch elltydd.
   Ac i'r fron ddeau, glau glwyf,

13

24   sowed and harrowed passion's growth.
      And for three months, bright wisdom's choice,
      of spring-time—pang of deceptive sleeplessness—
      the travail took its root in me,
28   [the making of] the enclosure killed me, dalliance of passion.
      For naught but strife I get from my great love:
      no one will understand love's urgency.

      On May-day, lest through any negligence
32   my wealth (should suffer) by my will,
      with sprightly resolve I built a hedge
      around this foolhardy crop (I am a solitary man).
      While this bountiful girl's love
36   in a disabling manner, through my breast
      was an active fair growth, I did not care,
      and (when there was) a ripe and great increase
      I came and went, made no delay in hire
40   arranging for the reaping of my grief.

      Grievous the utter loss of all the corn
      disastrous the destruction (?) of a world,
      for the wind veered, far-journeying thunderbolt
44   from the south, cleaving the heart in two,
      and in my head—the affliction of a lover—
      there darkened those two stars of love
      the posterns of the sad harvest of tears—
48   the eyes; swimming with passion
      they looked on Morfudd's form beneath the flood,
      upon my gentle golden girl,
      being louvers for the deluge of water,
52   unhappy and laborious torrents (from my eyes).
      This heart has been wasted away tonight
      by freshly-flowing water, sorrow's fastening.
      Beneath my heart is grief pent up:
56   my eyes do not leave dry a [single] sheaf.

      Bad weather, from the fury of the west,
      is harmful to the stubble, load of grief;
      and there comes great dreary steady rain
60   upon the cheeks from out the eastern sky;
      and copious tears for her of Eigr's hue,
      because of the spoiled crop, let no sleep to my eye.
      Alas for love, too easily deceptive seeds
64   after the torment, woe to all your care
      that I could not (betrayal of deep pain)
      succeed in harvesting you [even] between two showers.
      Blighted has been my long and prosperous love—
68   I have been disappointed of my sustenance.

24   Hëu a llyfnu llifnwyf.
     A thrimis, befr ddewis bwyll,
     Gwanhwyndymp, gwayw anhundwyll,
     Cadeiriodd ynof ofid,
28   Coetgae a'm lladd, cytgam llid.
     Ni chaf eithr sias o draserch,
     Ni chred neb brysurdeb serch.

     Calanmai rhag cael unmodd
32   Seguryd i'm byd o'm bodd
     Caeais, hoywdrais ehudrwyf,
     Yn ei gylch, dyn unig wyf.
     Tra fu serch yr haelferch hon,
36   Trefn efrydd, trwy fy nwyfron
     Yn hoywdeg hydwf, ni'm dawr,
     Ac yn aeddfed gynyddfawr,
     Treiddiais, ni ohiriais hur,
40   Trefnau medelau dolur.

     Trwm fu gyfrgoll yr hollyd,
     Trallod yw byth trylliad byd.
     Tröes y gwynt, bellynt bollt,
44   O ddeau'r galon ddwyollt,
     A thywyllawdd, gawdd gordderch,
     Yn fy mhen ddwy seren serch,
     Llidiardau dagrau digrwyf,
48   Llygaid, nofiaduriaid nwyf;
     Edrychasant, lifiant lun,
     Ar Forfudd, araf eurfun;
     Lwferau dwfr lifeiriaint,
52   Lafurus annawnus naint.
     Curiwyd y fron hon heno
     Â dwfr glas, edifar glo.
     Dan fy mron y mae'r gronllech,
56   Ni ad fy nrem seldrem sech.

     Drwg yw ar sofl, gofl gofid,
     Drycin o orllewin llid;
     A daw prif wastadlaw prudd
60   O ddwyrain wybr ar ddeurudd.
     Hydr ddeigr am ne Eigr ni ad,
     Heiniar lwgr, hun ar lygad.
     Oio gariad, had hydwyll,
64   Gwedy'r boen, gwae di o'r bwyll,
     Na ellais, braisg oglais brad,
     Dy gywain rhwng dwy gawad.
     Syrthiodd y cariad mad maith;
68   Somed fi am osymaith.

7 The Holly Grove

Grove of Holly, a fair armful's load,
fortress of sunny aspect, coral-coloured fruit,
a comely choir that no man will uproot,
4   a bower whose roof is watertight, a house for two,
tower for a gentle girl to give me care,
spikes and spurs are on its leaves.

I am a man who wanders by the hill-side
8   beneath the woods (fine hair of gentle trees),
grace will protect an edifice so fair!
I walked in leafy fields and woods.
Who in the midst of winter ever found
12   May month dressed in livery of green?
I shall remember how I found today
a holly-grove on a spur of the hill.
Just such a bower of love, with hosts [of leaves]
16   I had, [dressed] in the same livery as in May.
A woodland bower where organ (music) can be had,
fine mansion on a column of fresh green,
store-house of song above the hostile snowy hollow,
20   a pent-house, God's hand painted it.

God the pre-eminent did his fair part
twice better than did generous Robert:
Hywel Fychan of generous conduct
24   profound in poetry (he knows how to choose form),
he praised (it is not villainous)
a woodland angel in a handsome bed,
splendid branches on the road-sides' edge,
28   thick short hair on the green-tabarded lad.
Chamber of birds from land of Paradise,
round temple of green gleaming leaves,
not like an old cabin, ravenous for the rain—
32   beneath it two nights' stay is watertight,
unwithered are the holly's leaves, unless it be by chance,
and they are edged with steel.
From here to Severn there's no goat will chew
36   a load of this, nor any old buck.
An iron muzzle, when the night is long,
and frost on each valley and moor,
the fair tree will not lose its tithe
40   inspite of the cry of the cold bleak wind of spring
Genuine *chamelot* of fresh green leaves
united near the summit of the hill.

Y Llwyn Celyn (29)

Y celynllwyn coel iawnllwyth,
Caer araul ffriw, cwrel ffrwyth,
Côr gweddaidd nis diwraidd dyn,
4 Clos to diddos, tŷ deuddyn.
Tŵr i feinwar i'm arail;
Pigau, ysbardunau dail.

 Gŵr wyf yn rhodio ger allt
8 Dan goedydd, mwynwydd manwallt;
Rhad a geidw, rhydeg adail,
Rhodiais wŷdd, dolydd a dail.
Pwy mewn gaeaf a gafas
12 Mis Mai yn dwyn lifrai las?
Cof y sydd, cefais heddiw
Celynllwyn yn nhrwyn y rhiw.
Un gadair serch, un gadoedd,
16 Un lifrai â Mai ym oedd.
Cadeirgoed lle cad organ;
Cadrblas uwch piler glas glân.
Pantri cerdd uwch pant eiry cawdd;
20 Pentis, llaw Dduw a'i peintiawdd.

 Deuwell y gwnâi Dduw diwael
Rhyw bart teg no Rhobert hael.
Hywel Fychan hael fuchedd,
24 Geirddwys gwawd, gŵyr ddewis gwedd,
Moli a wnaeth, nid milain,
Angel coed yng ngwely cain.
Hardd osglau wrth ffiniau ffyrdd,
28 Tew byrwallt was tabarwyrdd.
Trefn adar gwlad Baradwys,
Teml gron o ddail gleision glwys.
Nid fal henfwth, lle glwth glaw,
32 Diddos fydd dwynos danaw.
Dail ni chrinant ond antur
Celyn un derfyn â dur.
Ni chny gafr hyd yn Hafren
36 Un baich o hwn, na bwch hen.
Penfar heyrn, pan fo'r hirnos
A rhew ymhob glyn a rhos,
Ni chyll pren teg ei ddegwm,
40 Er llef gwanwynwynt oer llwm,
Siamled gywir ddail irion
Gysylltiedig ger brig bron.

Notes

1

Many poets down the ages have contrasted the months of May and January to typify the marriage of a young woman with an old man; the OED cites examples from Chaucer's Merchant's Tale onwards (cf. Ll.C.V, 125). Though Dafydd does not explicitly make the comparison, he dwells elsewhere on *Yr Eiddig*'s preference for the winter months; cf. no.3 (GDG 24), ls.31-4.

1. *glwysgor.* The metaphor of *côr* 'choir' for the forest trees recurs in no.2 (GDG 23), l.20 and in no.7 (GDG 29), l.3. It recalls the 'bare ruined choirs where late the sweet birds sang' of Shakespeare's forty-second sonnet.

13. *gwasgod.* See n. to no.50, l.13.

16. *pill doldir. Pill* 'refuge, strength, branch'; but also 'tune, snatch of song', perhaps an intentional ambiguity.

22. *a chethlydd. Cethlydd* occurs as early as CLIH VI, 10a with specific reference to the cuckoo, *kethlyd kathyl uodawc . . . coc vreuer* 'songster of continuous song . . . the loud cuckoo'. Elsewhere it is used of any song-bird: Dafydd employs it of the lark in no.23, l.26, as well as in reference to his fellow-poet Gruffudd Gryg, GDG 20, l.63. An *englyn* in the Bardic Grammar applies it to the nightingale, (GP 7). Ifor Williams suggested that a distinction is intended in the present passage between *cog* and *cethlydd* (Ch.O.60), but it is difficult not to take *cethlydd* otherwise than as referring to the *cog* of the previous line. *Cethlydd y gog* (in Dyfed *gwas y gog*) is a meadow pipit, a bird who is closely connected with the cuckoo—its nest being the most sought-after repository for the cuckoo's eggs.

31. *mis dig du.* Dr Parry points out that *an miz du* signifies November in Breton and Cornish; so also *an mios dubh* in Sc. Gaelic. References by Welsh poets show clearly, however, that for them it is the month of January; see B.IX, 40-2; XIII, 204-5.

44. *ei wladeiddrwydd.* Winter, like Summer, is personified in the last two lines. *Gwladaidd, gwladeiddrwydd* 'churlishness, discourtesy' are popular words with Dafydd, and are used by him of *Yr Eiddig* who is *Iddew gwladaidd* 'a churlish Jew' (GDG 76, l.4). He also uses the word of Death's rapacity in carrying off each one of his fellow-poets Gruffudd ap Adda, no.47 (GDG 18), l.48; Madog Benfras, no.48 (GDG 19) l.44, and Gruffudd Gryg (GDG 20, l.6). The opposite adjective *diwladaidd* 'urbane, courteous' appears for the first time in a verse in the Bardic Grammar (GP 12) at a date not far removed from that of its appearance in Dafydd's poetry (GDG 74, l.2). For *diwladeiddrwydd* 'urbanity, politeness' cf. IGE² 61, l.1.

2

This poem and the following one are the only compositions which Dafydd bases on a monorhyme: in this instance each couplet ends with the word *Mai*, and I have preserved this feature in the translation. The poet's necessity to find a series of di-syllabic words to rhyme with *Mai* is responsible for the sequence of verbs ending in 3 sg. imperfect in -*ai.* Since the choice of tense has been so strongly conditioned by metrical requirements, I have varied the translation of these verbs within the range of meanings of the imperfect, according to what seemed required by the context; e.g. in l.7 I have chosen the conditional 'would not' but this could as well be translated 'did not'. The poem is analysed in detail by Eurys Rowlands, *LL.C.*V. (1958), 1-25. He lays emphasis on the poet's employment of *geiriau mwys* or intentional ambiguities in both vocabulary and syntax. Among the numerous secondary meanings proposed, those of *mwyn* are especially significant throughout the poem: as an adj. 'gentle, tender', as a noun 'wealth, richness, (mineral) ore'—this latter meaning underlies the money imagery which characterizes ls.9-18. In offering a single interpretation, my translation unavoidably omits a number of variant possibilities.

1. *gwyddiad*. Old ending of the 3 sg. imperfect; cf. GMW 122. Alternatively 'God would know'.

4. *Duw Calan*. The Calends or 1st May (Irish *Beltaine*) was traditionally the beginning of summer in early Celtic belief. Various rites were connected with May-day in the Middle Ages all over Britain, such as dressing in leaves (cf. l.49 and ls.36-8 in the following poem), and the bestowal of garlands of leaves and flowers by one lover on another; cf. Dafydd's frequent references to the *cae bedw* or garland of birch-twigs. May-day has always held erotic connotations in European literature: for some relevant Welsh literary parallels see A. and B. Rees, *Celtic Heritage* (1961), 285-7.

7. *Dillyn beirdd*. A reference to the fact that greetings to May have always been a popular theme among poets; cf. l.21-2 below.

8. The line is repeated, with change of *oedd* to *yw*, l.50 below.

11. *iawn fwnai*. *Mwnai* 'money' is a borrowing from E. *moneye*, *monaye*. The fourteenth century saw a spread and increase of a money economy in Wales, gradually replacing barter; cf. RBP 1031, ls.22-3 *kyfnewit Seis ac aryant* 'the Englishman traffics in money'.

13-14. *Ffloringod brig . . . Fflŵr-dy-lis*. The young leaves are compared to golden florins. The florin was first minted in Florence in 1252 and it bore on its obverse the fleur-de-lis, which was the heraldic device of the city of Florence (as well as of the kings of France), and this device was retained on all florins subsequently minted in other European countries. The only florin to be minted in England was the gold florin of Edward III, valued at 6 shillings, which was minted only between January and August 1344, and subsequently withdrawn from circulation as a base coin, because its gold value fell short of its nominal value in silver. It was replaced by the gold noble, worth 6s 8p. In 'Gold Coins in Mediaeval English Literature', *Speculum* 36 (1961), 282-4, D.C. Baker shows that references in mediaeval literature, including those by Chaucer, are normally to the Italian florin which enjoyed widespread currency over all Europe; cf. GDG 44, ls.22-4, *Fflwring aur . . . da lun ar ddail fflŵr-dy-lis . . . o gaer Baris*, and GDG 70, l.37 where the moon is called *fflwring*. Often 'florin' was simply a term for money in general. Since this Italian florin was 'the standard gold coin of the Middle Ages', I feel reluctantly unable to accept the argument advanced by D.Stephen Jones 'Fflwring Aur Dafydd ap Gwilym', B.XIX (1961), 29-34, that Dafydd's 'pejorative' references to the gold florin in this poem and his more neutral references elsewhere can have any specific topical reference to Edward III's base coin. Unfortunately this necessitates the rejection of the *terminus a quo* in 1344 which the writer advocates for the composition of the poem. I would myself regard the pejorative comparison of the gold coin with the fresh leaves of May as but one facet of the constant *leitmotif* underlying Dafydd's poetry: the exaltation of nature's riches as preferable to all human artefacts. In any case the fleur-de-lis design is much more prominent on the continental coins, where it forms the single device on the obverse, whereas on Edward III's florin the flowers, reduced in size, merely fill in the background to the design of the enthroned king. Both *fflwring* and *fflŵr-dy-lis* are first attested in Welsh in the poetry of Dafydd ap Gwilym and Iolo Goch.

15. *diongl rhag brad*. The apprehended treachery is presumably the unwelcome interference of *Yr Eiddig*. Dafydd uses *diongl* elsewhere for

the Wind, no.29 (GDG 117), l.12, lit. 'without angles'—it has been suggested that in the present instance *diongl* may hold an allusion to 'clipped' coinage, (B. XXV, 20). The subject of *a'm cadwai* may be either *Mai* (understood) or *cyfoeth* (l.14, i.e. the wealth of leaves), but *Mai* is certainly the subject of *na thrigai* in l.17.

16-17. *Beth yw i mi!* lit. 'what is it to me?'. This *sangiad* refers to the previous line: the poet contemplates the impermanence of his own life, and of all human mortality.

20. *dan gôr Mai.* On *côr* see n. to previous poem, l.1.

27-35. The series of descriptive statements in *neud* recalls the early 3-line gnomic and proverbial *englynion* descriptive of nature, RBP 1028-1034; see K. Jackson, *Early Celtic Nature Poetry* and *Early Welsh Gnomic Poems.* These were undoubtedly a significant element in Dafydd's inheritance from earlier Welsh poetic tradition.

37. *Paun.* The personification of May changes abruptly from that of a *gŵr mawr hael* (l.10) to that of a peacock: 'it' refers to the luxurious growth of verdure and trees; the underlying thought is probably of a peacock's tail castellated or spread out to display its rich colouring.

41. *magwyr laswyrdd* 'green battlements'; cf. the *bwlch dail* 'battlements of leaves', of no.25 (GDG 63), l.6. The forest is a fortified defence to the poet's imagined secret retreat.

47. *dechrau haf llathr.* Perhaps the month of June is intended, though May is usually regarded as the beginning of Summer.
a'i sathrai. Sathru is cognate with Ir. *sernaid* 'scatters, disposes' etc. This indicates the meaning in the present instance.

48. *deigr a'i mag.* Alternatively 'tears nurture it' (DGG² 207) or 'it' (May's departure) has fostered tears. *Deigr* 'tears' are presumably raindrops; in fact the April showers which traditionally precede the beginning of May.

52. *a Mair.* May is intimately associated with the Virgin in Catholic theology, though the association is of uncertain antiquity. Cf. G. M. Hopkins's poem 'The May Magnificat' 'May is Mary's month', etc.

3

With the monorhyme in *haf* sustained throughout the poem cf. the monorhyme in *Mai* in the previous poem, and introductory note. In this case the rhyme is responsible for the numerous 1sg. pres. indic. endings in *-af* and superlative adjs. in *-(h)af.* The first and last lines suggest that a wet summer is the immediate occasion for the reflections which follow on the transitoriness of the season and, by extension, on the impermanence of human life.

3. *gwir mai dihiraf.* lit. 'true that it is most wretched'. *Mai* could alternatively denote 'May' rather than 'is'.

17. *glud* 'glutinous, tenacious, assiduous' etc.; *anianol* 'innate, natural, strong, lively'. Reversing the order of these two adjs., I translate *anianol* as if it were a noun. As adjs. the two do not go easily together in English, so that a slight latitude is unavoidable in order to convey the meaning.

23. *glwys ganiadaf.* The syntax is not clear; I follow Dr Parry in taking *gloch osber* in l.24 to be the object of *caniadaf.* Alternatively 'I will send a grey bird *at the time of* vespers at midsummer . . . the Nightingale . . .' Or the Nightingale may be intended as the *cloch osber;* cf. GDG 25, l.35 where she is called *cloch aberth y serchogion* 'the sanctus-bell of lovers'.

25. *bangaw* 'eloquent, melodious', used of the Nightingale in two other of Dafydd's poems, GDG 25, l.37; and no.24 below (GDG 122), l.27.

26. *pentis* from mediaeval English *pentis* 'pent-house'. Used also by Dafydd of the Holly Grove, no.7 (GDG 29), l.20.

29. *Dyn Ofydd* means Dafydd himself, and the idea of his freedom to indulge in loving beneath the summer foliage is paralleled in the previous poem, ls.15-16. On Ovid see n. to no.28, l.3, below.

36. *mentyll haf.* Cf. n. to previous poem, l.4.

38. A *cwnsallt* was 'a loose garment worn over the armour and covering the horse as well', perhaps derived from Fr. *ca(i)nsil;* R.L.Thomson. *Owein or Chwedyl Iarlles y Ffynnawn* (Dublin, 1968),54.

42. *ar ael haf.* lit. 'on the brow of summer'.

43. *Gwawd* as used by Dafydd commonly means 'a poem of praise'; see the exx. listed in GDG and GPC. But the later meaning 'satire' is clearly present in GDG 152, ls.34, 60, and since *gwawd* in this line is paralleled by *arwydd oeraf* it seems most probable that 'satire' rather than 'praise' is also the meaning here. Although the two opposite meanings are not recorded as overlapping before the sixteenth century, it would seem that both were known to Dafydd. Cf. n. to no.8, l.57 on *gwawdrydd.*

4

2. *caead brig. Caeadfrig* 'thick-branched, shady'; here the second element is left unlenited.

3. *Teg wtwart,* E. *wode-ward* (EEW 65). The 'woodward' was the official keeper of a forest, who had charge of the growing timber. Both the name and the office go back to Anglo-Saxon times.

5-6. For these two lines I have adopted the reading of the majority of MSS (which is also that of DGG², XLII). This means that I have rejected the ingenious emendation proposed by W. J. Gruffydd, B VIII, 301 of *a bair* to *yw pair* and of *Didwn* to *Annwn.* (The second of these emendations is however rejected in GDG², see Dr Parry's note p.556). Gruffydd saw in the lines an allusion to the *pair dadeni* of *Mabinogi Branwen* which (like Summer in the poem) had the property of restoring the dead to life—*dadeni byd* is in fact referred to elsewhere by the poet, GDG 134, l.28. But he was unjustified in confusing the *pair dadeni* with the *pair pen Annw(f)n* which 'does not boil the food of a coward' of an early poem, BT 55, ls.2-3. No doubt he did this under the influence of the allusion to *Annwfn* in l.40 below, but in favour of retaining the reading of the MSS is the fact that *didwn* 'unbroken, perfect' is a word employed elsewhere by the poet, no.14 (GDG 79) l.47. *Pen* 'lord, chief' rather than 'head' seems probable in the context, however. My interpretation of the lines is therefore a simpler one than the elaborate mythological interpretation advocated by Eurys Rowlands, Ll.C.V (1959),126-30.

8. *eli* 'ointment, balm' in the sense of 'encouragement for growing'.

11. *Da y gŵyr.* For *gwybod* in the sense of 'to be able' see GPC 1687.

20, 26. *teml, euraid deml.* Davies gives *templum, fanum* for *teml,* but an older meaning was 'pile, mound'; cf. CA 244-5. In the second instance it is used figuratively 'abundance'.

33. *rym ramant.* Davies gives *auspicium, omen* for *rhamant;* it is a borrowing from French or English, which developed secondary meanings in Welsh.

34. *tes a gant. Tes* 'warm weather', i.e. 'summer' is the subject of the verb *cant;* cf. DGG² 202.

36. *Defnyddiau* 'substance, materials', i.e. the crops.

40. *Annwfn.* Cf. no.28, 42; no.36, 44. In PKM 99-101 Ifor Williams cited these three allusions by Dafydd ap Gwilym as clear indications that by *Annw(f)n* the poet had in mind the pagan Celtic Otherworld. This was conceived of as lying *beneath* the ground, according to a ninth century (?) poem, BT 20, ls.8-9, which contrasts *yn annwfyn is eluyd, yn awyr uch*

eluyd 'in Annwfn beneath the earth, in the air above the earth'. He understood the meaning of the word to be 'the In-world', from *an* meaning 'in' and *dwfn* 'world', an element present in a number of Gaulish personal names, such as *Dumno-rix* 'king of the world', etc. (see D.Ellis Evans, *Gaulish Personal Names*, 196-7). He compared the Irish concept of the Otherworld as situated beneath the ground and approached by entering one of the *sídhe* or 'fairy mounds' of Ireland, and as a Welsh parallel to these he noted the *gorsedd Arberth* in the *Mabinogi*, which is repeatedly the centre of magical happenings in the tales. Dafydd employs *dwfn* 'world' elsewhere, in his elegy on his uncle, GDG 13, l.17.

49. *Deyrn byddin.* i.e. the Sun. *Teyrn* is here mono-syllabic, though commonly di-syllabic.

5

1. *Heirdd feirdd.* This is apparently a direct address to the audience: for similar instances cf. below no.13, l.56; no.22, l.22, and GDG 51, l.51. *Hawddamor* 'good luck, blessing' goes with *i fun lwys* in l.3: this has necessitated a slight re-arrangement in the translation.

2. *hoen goror gwiw.* Elsewhere Morfudd is described as *eiry goror* (GDG 43, l.34) '(with beauty like) a snowy slope'. But *goror* can also have the meaning 'region, district, surroundings', and this is how it should probably be interpreted here.

4. *mentyll Mai.* The same phrase occurs in no.2, l.16 above; cf. also *mentyll haf* no.3, l.36.

7-8. *o'r gaer ddidryf.* The forest retreat is envisaged first as a citadel, cf. the *magwyr laswyrdd* 'green battlements' of no.2, l.41 above (see n.), and in the ensuing lines as a dwelling which has none of the smoky disadvantages which must have beset the mediaeval housewife in an ordinary house.

24. *Dwylo Mai.* lit. 'May's hands'. *Yn gall* (l.30) refers back to this line, and completes its sense.

25-30. These lines contain a series of technical words for a builder's tools and materials. I take *ais* l.28 as the pl. of *asen* 'lath', i.e. the small strips of wood used in roofing; *llinyn* is a plumb-line (a string with a ball of lead at the end, used for testing the perpendicularity of a wall, etc.), and *ysgwir* a craftsman's set-square (a triangular plate for drawing angles). With Dafydd's fondness for the figurative use of terms from carpentry; cf. no.48 below, lines 25-6, and n.

34. *i wrach o hen.* With *gohen* 'oldish, aged' cf. WM 146,33, *gwreic ohen a gwreic ieuanc.* Lines 33-4 are paralleled in no.30, lines 5-7 below, in which the poet re-iterates his unwillingness to bribe an old hag as his love-messenger.

6

Many years ago the Dutch scholar Th.M.Chotzen in his *Recherches sur la Poésie de Dafydd ap Gwilym* (1927), 331-2 showed that the extended 'husbandry' image developed in this poem finds a striking parallel in the 13th century French poem *Le Roman de la Rose* (ed. F.Lecoy, Paris 1965, lines 3932-42). Presenting himself as a disappointed lover, the poet here compares his plight to that of a farmer who watches his seed grow and prosper, until at the moment when it is ripe for harvest it is destroyed by a sudden storm. The *Roman* enjoyed a wide literary influence in France and England, and there is evidence that it was known in Glamorgan shortly before the time of Dafydd ap

Gwilym, since the existence of a copy is recorded among the confiscated possessions of Llywelyn Bren, who was executed as the result of the part which he played in the revolt of 1317 (Chotzen, 110; G.J.Williams, *Traddodiad Llenyddol Morgannwg*, 146). Yet as Chotzen wisely remarks 'Source studies rarely lead to absolute truths, and the best established parallels are often illusory owing to our ignorance of intermediate forms which have been irrevocably lost.' The final lines suggest that some genuinely painful experience underlies this poem: possibly this may have been Morfudd's marriage. Dafydd shows a remarkable and sensitive understanding of a farmer's anxieties in watching over his growing crops.

12. *yn briod*. Deliberately ambiguous, since *priod* 'proper' also means 'married'.

16. *y marwfis*, i.e. the month of January; B.ix, 40.

17. *y fron* means both 'breast' and 'slope, hillside'; obviously both meanings are here present.

18. *onengyr*. No other instance of this word has been recorded. Dr Parry suggests 'blow'.

20. *I frynaru*. *Braenaru* is to fallow, to open up the soil.

24. *llifnwyf*. *Llif* 'flood, deluge' here used figuratively for the seeds of love; hence 'growth', to follow the metaphor.

27. *cadeiriodd*. *Cadeirio* is used of both trees and wheat taking root; B.ix, 41.

28. *a'm lladd* is figurative, as 'kill' in modern usage.

32. *byd* can mean not only 'world, life, wealth' etc but also 'darling'.

33. I am indebted to Dr Parry for my rendering of this couplet. Among the various meanings of *rhwyf* 'pride, excess, satisfaction' is also 'harvest'; DGG[2] 189; GDG 513. The double meaning is probably present here.

42. *trylliad*. No other instance of this word has been recorded.

47. *dagrau digrwyf*. 'Harvest' is here the most appropriate meaning for *rhwyf*.

51. *Lwferau*. From English *louver*, a primitive kind of vent over mediaeval halls for the purpose of letting out smoke; GDG 513.

55. *cronllech*. This is the only recorded instance in GPC: 'pent up with grief or sorrow'.

61. *Eigr*. The mother of Arthur according to the literary tradition represented in *Brut y Brenhinedd*; see TYP 366. Eigr is the most frequently cited by Dafydd ap Gwilym of all the traditional heroines of romance.

7

The authenticity of this *cywydd* was questioned in the 18th century by Dafydd Jones of Trefriw who attributed it to Dafydd ab Edmwnd, but quoted the authority of Dr Davies, Mallwyd that it is by Dafydd ap Gwilym. On balance, Dr Parry chose to retain it (GDG 470,n.). It contains several rare words which are found in others of Dafydd's poems (lines 19, 20); the personification of the tree (l.28) is characteristic of the poet; and it contains an allusion (l.35) which is taken up by Gruffudd Gryg in one of his two supposed *marwnadau* to Dafydd ap Gwilym (see n.).

3. *Côr*. For other instances in which Dafydd employs the metaphor of 'choir' for trees see n. to no.1, line 1 above (GDG 69, l.1).

8. *manwallt*. The 'hair' of the trees—particularly birch-trees—is also an image used frequently by Dafydd; cf. no.3, ls.13-14 (GDG 24).

15. *cadoedd*. 'armies, multitudes', here presumably used fig. for leaves.

19. *pantri*. A borrowing from English or French, first recorded in English in 1330 (OED), and meaning a room used for the storing of provisions. Other instances: no.29 (GDG 117), 1.6; GDG 134, 1.23.

20. *pentis* 'penthouse' from E. *pentis*, first recorded in 1325 (OED). Cf. no.3, 1.26 above.

21-6. A series of obscure and hitherto unexplained allusions, since there seems little chance of identifying men bearing names of such common occurrence. Lines 23-6 imply that *Hywel Fychan* was a poet, and ls.21-2 suggest that *Robert hael* may have been a painter, whose work is compared unfavourably with that of God.

28. *tabarwyrdd*. From Ml.E *tabard*, Fr. *tabart* 'a loose upper garment without sleeves, formerly worn out-of-doors by the lower classes, monks, and foot-soldiers' (OED).

29. *trefn*. Here 'room, chamber'. With *adar gwlad Baradwys* cf. Dafydd's two descriptions of the Thrush, nos.20, 1.30; 21, 1.48 below. (GDG nos.28, 123).

35. *Ni chny gafr*. In *Yr Ywen uwchben Bedd Dafydd* (GDG p.429) Gruffudd Gryg gives the same property to the Yew-tree above the poet's grave, *Geifre ni'th lwgr, nac afrad/Dy dwf yng ngwedre dy dad* 'A herd of goats will not consume you, nor will your growth be unseemly in your father's land' (DGG[2] 82, ls.29-30). The allusion seems unmistakable to the present poem.

37. *Penfar*. Dr Parry (GDG 471) records the word as used in Arfon for a leather muzzle with spikes sticking out, which is put on a calf's mouth to stop him sucking his mother; Davies's Dictionary gives *capistrum*, *fiscella*.

39. *ei ddegwm*. The tree's 'tithe' is its evergreen leaves.

41. *Siamled* is from Ml.E. *chamelot*, a costly material of eastern origin, made of a mixture of silk and camel's hair, and used for cloaks (OED).

II. MORFUDD, DYDDGU, AND OTHERS
(8-19)

8 Morfudd like the Sun

    I woo a softly-spoken girl,
pale as fine snow on the field's edge;
God sees that she is radiant
4   and brighter than the crest of foam,
white as the glistening garrulous wave's edge,
with the Sun's splendour; gracious is she.
She knows the way to win a love-song from my lips—
8   the Sun's excelling glory near a cloud.
The peoples' princess, in cloak of fine fur
(she knows how to deride [her] ugly husband).
Lovely Morfudd, woe to the weak idle poet
12 who loves her—handsome, gracious, gentle girl—
a web of gold [her hair]—alas for anyone in shape of man,
comely of form, who cries out in his woe.

    Skilled is she in deception, and her wiles
16 exceed all measure—yet she is my dear.
At one time my fair girl appears
in church and court; another time
[like] someone on proud lime-washed castle's battlements
20 bright, sparkling Morfudd disappears,
like to the Sun, a vital succour to the land,
the one who nurtures and entices warmth.
Praiseworthy is her excellent work,
24 huckstress of the brilliance of May.
Great is the expectancy for splendid Morfudd,
bright image of noble Mary's excellence.

    To the earth's wide circumference
28 the Sun descends, like to my bright-complexioned girl;
[she is] the unique being of the day-time,
the shepherdess of the sky, from end to end.
When there comes, great monstrous war,
32 across her face some heavy cloud,
when there is—and we may feel great pain—
need for the Sun, which dazzles our sight,
under the cover of darkness she escapes;
36 there is a feeling of sad pain, when the night comes:
the dark blue firmament will be filled
with semblance of sadness in the planet's place.
Unlikely then it is for anyone to know
40 (God's orb she is) where she is gone.
No hand has the ability to touch her
nor to seize hold upon her brow.
Next day she will rise again
44 and from Heaven afar will brighten the whole world.

Morfudd fel yr Haul (42)

Gorllwyn ydd wyf ddyn geirllaes,
Gorlliw eiry mân marian maes;
Gwŷl Duw y mae golau dyn,
4 Goleuach nog ael ewyn.
Goleudon lafarfron liw,
Goleuder haul, gŵyl ydyw.
Gŵyr obryn serchgerdd o'm pen,
8 Goreubryd haul ger wybren.
Gwawr y bobl, gwiwra bebyll,
Gŵyr hi gwatwaru gŵr hyll.
Gwiw Forfudd, gwae oferfardd
12 Gwan a'i câr, gwen hwyrwar hardd.
Gwe o aur, llun dyn, gwae ef
Gwiw ei ddelw yn gwaeddolef.

Mawr yw ei thwyll a'i hystryw,
16 Mwy no dim, a'm enaid yw.
Y naill wers yr ymddengys
Fy nyn gan mewn llan a llys,
A'r llall, ddyn galch falch fylchgaer,
20 Yr achludd gloyw Forfudd glaer,
Mal haul ymylau hoywles,
Mamaeth tywysogaeth tes.
Moliannus yw ei syw swydd,
24 Maelieres Mai oleurwydd.
Mawr ddisgwyl Morfudd ddisglair,
Mygrglaer ddrych mireinwych Mair.

Hyd y llawr dirfawr derfyn
28 Haul a ddaw mal hoywliw ddyn
Yn deg o uncorff y dydd,
Bugeiles wybr bwygilydd.
Gwedy dêl, prif ryfel praff,
32 Dros ei phen wybren obraff,
Pan fo, poen fawr a wyddem,
Raid wrth yr haul a draul drem,
Y diainc ymron duaw,
36 Naws poen ddig, y nos pan ddaw.
Dylawn fydd yr wybr dulas,
Delw *eilywed*, blaned blas.
Pell i neb wybod yna,
40 Pêl yw i Dduw, pa le'dd â.
Ni chaiff llaw yrthiaw wrthi,
Nac ymafael â'i hael hi.
Trannoeth y drychaif hefyd,
44 Ennyn o bell o nen byd.

Not unlike [it brings me grief]
Morfudd's sunset towards me
when she has come, as from the air above
48   beneath a sun-lit sky, to journey below,
[then like the Sun] she sets (even her scowl is fair)
beneath the lintel of her dreary husband's door.

I pursued passion in the glade
52   of Penrhyn, love's abode.
Daily in that place is seen
my sweet sparkling girl, nightly she flees.
No easier is it in the middle of a hall
56   to lay a hand on her [I have been slain]
than is it—dazzling maiden, freely praised—
for anybody's hands to grasp the Sun.
No more joyful splendid form
60   has the flaming Sun than she.
If [of the two] there be a fairer one this year
the fairer is *our* Sun, [a girl] of noble race.

Why should not [a desirable step]
64   the one take over a nightly display,
and the other, with her splendid warmth
and excellent light, illuminate the day?
If these two beauties were to alternate
68   orbiting the four corners of the world
it were a wonder, in the stiff leaves of a book
if in the maiden's life-time night should ever come.

9 The Spear

I saw a girl with hair of burnished gold
[and] sprightly as the dancing shallow waves,
all golden was she from her head to foot,
4   a maid twice comparable to dayspring's hue
yesterday listening in Deinioel's choir
at Bangor to the mystery play (?) of Noah's Ark,
there was sufficient beauty there for the whole world—
8   Fflur's loveliness, a double pang, and onrush of treachery
to see that supremely lovely girl:
alas for such a blessing! heavy wounds were mine.

Pierced was I by a seven-sided spear
12   with consciousness of grief—[a matter for] seven songs.
I know I languish from a poisoned barb,
it was the wish of envious rivals from the land of Môn,
a barb which is transfixed within my heart,

Nid annhebyg, ddig ddogni,
Ymachludd Morfudd â mi;
Gwedy dêl o'r awyr fry,
48 Dan haul wybr dwyn hwyl obry,
Yr ymachludd teg ei gwg
Dan orddrws y dyn oerddrwg.

Erlynais nwyf ar lannerch
52 Y Penrhyn, esyddyn serch.
Peunydd y gwelir yno
Pefrddyn goeth, a pheunoeth ffo.
Nid nes cael ar lawr neuadd
56 Daro llaw, deryw fy lladd,
Nog fydd, ddyn gwawdrydd gwiwdraul,
I ddwylo rhai ddaly yr haul.
Nid oes rhagorbryd pefrlon
60 Gan yr haul gynne ar hon.
Os tecaf un eleni,
Tecaf, hil naf, ein haul ni.

Paham, eiddungam ddangos,
64 Na ddeaill y naill y nos,
A'r llall yn des ysblennydd,
Olau da, i liwio dydd?
Ped ymddangosai'r ddeubryd
68 Ar gylch i bedwar bylch byd,
Rhyfeddod llyfr dalensyth
Yn oes bun ddyfod nos byth.

Y Gwayw (111)

Y ferch dan yr aur llathrloyw
A welais, hoen geirwfais hoyw,
Yn aur o'r pen bwy gilydd,
4 Yn rhiain wiw deuliw dydd,
Yn gwarando salm balchnoe
Yng nghôr Deinioel Bangor doe.
Digon i'r byd o degwch,
8 Deugur, bryd Fflur, a brad fflwch,
Weled y wenferch wiwlwys,
Wi o'r dawn! mau wewyr dwys.

Â seithochr wayw y'm saethawdd,
12 A seithwawd cymhendawd cawdd.
Gwenwyn awch, gwn fy nychu,
Gwyn eiddigion gwlad Fôn fu,
Nis tyn dyn dan wybr sygnau,

16 no man beneath the starry Heaven can draw it forth.
    No smith it was who beat out this,
    no grinding done by hand created it,
    unknown the colour—fitting to be praised in song—
20 nor yet the shape of the sharp weapon which has smitten
                                                        me:
        subdued my splendid energy and all my looks—
        crazy I am for Gwynedd's candle.
        Woe to me! these shafts will long afflict me,
24 Good luck to me! her beauty is like Mary's.
    Grievous eighteen-fold my weakness from the spear
    has made me a sad youth with furrowed cheek;
    sorely it smarts, poison which repays,
28 a whetted shaft, a skewer of care.
    She of Esyllt's form gives it to me
    this shaft within my shattered breast.

        Sad to me is it to hold it so long,
32 the auger of my shivered breast is wasted,
    the [piercing] awl of love [is] instrument of pain,
    and treason's foster-brother the arrow's triple pang.

10 Paying Love's Debt

    Cywyddau, burgeoning of splendid intellect,
    fine burden, output of a cultured poet,
    there never was—[this is] the point of my complaint—
4   any organ that so much resounds.
    Love's prison, its mother and its father,
    my breast is, and it has betrayed me.
    All that is within the hoary robber's scope
8   was given birth to by himself.

        I gave her, as pertaining to my office,
        eloquent praise out of my store,
        sound of harp and striking clock
12 (too great a gift, a drunken man has given it).
    Like a mad lover I have sown
    her praise throughout Gwynedd's extent:
    it sprang up into splendid growth
16 with lusty sprouts—a fair sowing that was.
    The girl is famed afar (she does not lack discretion)
    all know it, every tender generous girl.
    All followed me, with lively questioning,
20 'Who is it?' was heard in every street;
    a paternoster without cease
    by all who pluck harp's deepest string
    her song of praise, [made] splendid for her sake,

30

16 I mewn y galon y mae.
Nis gorug gof ei guraw,
Nis gwnaeth llifedigaeth llaw.
Ni wŷs na lliw, gwiw gwawdradd,
20 Na llun y dostarf a'm lladd.
Gorwyf, o'm gwiwnwyf a'm gwedd,
Gorffwyll am gannwyll Gwynedd.
Gwae fi! gwewyr a'm hirbair;
24 Gwyn fy myd! ail gwiwne Mair.
Gwydn ynof gwayw deunawnych,
Gwas prudd a wnâi'r grudd yn grych.
Gwynia'n dost, gwenwyn a dâl,
28 Gwayw llifaid, gwäell ofal.
Esyllt bryd a'i dyd er dig,
Aseth cledr dwyfron ysig.

Trwm yw ynof ei hirgadw,
32 Trwyddew fy mron friwdon fradw.
Trefnloes fynawyd cariad,
Triawch saeth fydd brawdfaeth brad.

Talu Dyled (34)

Cywyddau, twf cywiwddoeth,
Cofl hardd, amdwf cathlfardd coeth,
Ni bu ag wynt, pwynt apêl,
4 Un organ mor annirgel.
Maendy serch, unfam, undad
Yw fy mron, a wnâi fy mrad.
Holl gwmpas y lleidrwas llwyd
8 O'r un oll yr enillwyd.

Rhoais iddi, rhyw swyddau,
Rhugl foliant o'r meddiant mau,
Gwrle telyn ac orloes,
12 Gormodd rhodd, gŵr meddw a'i rhoes.
Heais mal orohïan
Ei chlod yng Ngwynedd achlân.
Hydwf y mae'n ehedeg,
16 Had tew, llyna head teg.
Pellwawd yw'r ddyn nid pwyllwael,
Pawb a ŵyr, pob dyn hwyr hael.
Pybyr fu pawb ar fy ôl,
20 A'u 'Pwy?' oedd ymhob heol.
Pater noster annistaw
Pawb o'r a gant llorfdant llaw
Ymhob cyfedd, ryfedd ri',

24 in every feast, a wonderful excess.
My tongue has spread her praise
(sweet is her smile), the *Amen* of all praise,
since at the end of every prayer
28 a true remembrance, she is named.
She is the sister, hue of radiant warmth,
to Gwgon's daughter, horsewoman.

    Where she might stand, I have only one voice,
32 like to the cuckoo, paid serving-maid of May.
It is her nature that she does not know
in her grey mantle, any speech but one.
The cuckoo does not cease from clamour
36 but stutters between rock and sea,
she sings no song—a quiet asseveration—
and has no other note except 'Cuckoo'.
It is known in Môn that [like] a servant to the monks
40 my burden ever was too much for me,
for such a one, stout-hearted, does not do
aught but one single task—yet two sneezes are good.

    With tireless purpose I pursued
44 my sincere plaint, as though drawing breath.
Farewell, it is no longer possible
to conceal anything concerning her.
I have employed to honour her
48 my most profound resources of song.
If she is thrifty with them she has a store
(and if they are set up on fertile ground);
seven *cywyddau* to slender Morfudd
52 (gay form erect) and seven score.
Because of love for her I am a wretch,
Let her take all—for I am free of guilt.
Perfect love extorts no pay
56 nor has she henceforth [further] claim on me.

11 Love Kept Secret

    I learned to act quickly in my love,
in manner courteous, stealthy, at high cost;
[for] it is best with rightly-chosen words
4 to tell the tale of secret love;
so unreliable is a confidant
that a man's love is best kept secret;
while we two together were in crowds
8 my love and I, dissolute pair,
[there was] no one—comment without spite—
[able] to guess at our familiarity.

24 Yw ei cherdd yn wych erddi.
    Tafod a'i tyfodd canmawl,
    Teg ei gwên yw, Amên mawl,
    Cans ar ddiwedd pob gweddi,
28 Cof cywir, y'i henwir hi.
    Chwaer ydyw, tywynlliw tes,
    I ferch Wgon farchoges.

      Unllais wyf, yn lle y safai,
32 Â'r gog, morwyn gyflog Mai.
    Honno ni feidr o'i hannwyd
    Eithr un llais â'i thoryn llwyd.
    Ni thau y gog â'i chogor,
36 Crygu mae rhwng craig a môr;
    Ni chân gywydd, lonydd lw,
    Nag acen onid 'Gwcw'.
    Gwŷs ym Môn mai gwas mynaich
40 Fûm i yn ormodd fy maich,
    Yr hwn ni wna, da deutrew,
    Lafur ond un, lawfron dew.

      Dilonydd bwyll, ddidwyll ddadl,
44 Dilynais fal dal anadl.
    Yn iach bellach heb allel
    Na chudd amdanai na chêl.
    Defnyddio i'w hurddo hi
48 Defnyddiau cerdd dwfn iddi.
    Talm sydd iddi, os tolia,
    Ac o dodir ar dir da:
    Saith gywydd i Forfudd fain
52 Syth hoywgorff a saith ugain.
    Adyn o'i chariad ydwyf,
    Aed ag wynt, dieuog wyf.
    Ni ddeily cariad taladwy,
56 Ni ddyly hi i mi mwy.

Y Serch Lledrad (74)

    Dysgais ddwyn cariad esgud,
    Diwladaidd, lledradaidd, drud.
    Gorau modd o'r geiriau mad
  4 Gael adrodd serch goledrad.
    Cyfryw nych cyfrinachwr,
    Lledrad gorau cariad gŵr,
    Tra fuom mewn tyrfaau,
  8 Fi a'r ddyn, ofer o ddau,
    Heb neb, ddigasineb sôn,
    Yn tybiaid ein hatebion.

Because of our confidence we were for long
12 enabled to have dalliance together.
Now it is more difficult for us
because of slander, to exchange three words.
Perdition to the one with evil tongue
16 through knot of suffering—with bad fortune's mark—
rather than that he should cast words of calumny
upon us two, who were of spotless name.
Most pleased he was if he might get [word of] warning
20 while we in hiding kept our secret hid.

I walked, while leaves were green, and gave
my worship to my darling's leafy home.
It was sweet, my love, a while
24 to live our life beneath the grove of birch,
more sweet was it fondly to embrace
together hid in our woodland retreat,
together to be wandering on the ocean's shore,
28 together lingering by the forest's edge,
together to plant birches—task of joy—
together weave fair plumage of the trees,
together talk of love with my slim girl,
32 together gaze on solitary fields.
It is a blameless occupation for a girl
to wander through the forest with her lover,
together to keep face, together smile,
36 together laugh—and it was lip to lip—
together to lie down beside the grove,
together to shun folk, together to complain,
to live together kindly, drinking mead together,
40 to rest together and express our love,
maintaining true love in all secrecy:
there is no need to tell any more.

12 A Girl's Enchantment

Garlands, binding chains of love
and praise in poetry, sprightly girl,
and gold—I know how I can please you—
4 I have given you in your court.
Nothing but sleeplessness, fair lovely maid,
sickness, weak tears—O lively glancing one—
my payment was; bold questioners
8 came as my enemies, in constant crowds.
I called you 'Countess of the snow's bright hue'
to fair parchment likening your face;
with dire opprobrium, to my face

Cael, herwydd ein coel, hirynt
12 A wnaetham ymgytgam gynt.
Bellach modd caethach y cair
Cyfran, drwy ogan, drigair.
Difa ar un drygdafod
16 Drwy gwlm o nych, dryglam nod,
Yn lle bwrw enllib eiriau
Arnam, enw dinam, ein dau.
Trabalch oedd o chaid rhybudd,
20 Tra gaem gyfrinach trwy gudd.

Cerddais, addolais i ddail,
Tref eurddyn, tra fu irddail.
Digrif fu, fun, un ennyd
24 Dwyn dan un bedwlwyn ein byd.
Cydlwynach, difyrrach fu,
Coed olochwyd, cydlechu,
Cydfyhwman marian môr,
28 Cydaros mewn coed oror,
Cydblannu bedw, gwaith dedwydd,
Cydblethu gweddeiddblu gwŷdd.
Cydadrodd serch â'r ferch fain,
32 Cydedrych caeau didrain.
Crefft dddigerydd fydd i ferch—
Cydgerdded coed â gordderch,
Cadw wyneb, cydowenu,
36 Cydchwerthin finfin a fu,
Cyd-ddigwyddaw garllaw'r llwyn,
Cydochel pobl, cydachwyn,
Cydfod mwyn, cydyfed medd,
40 Cydarwain serch, cydorwedd,
Cyd-ddaly cariad celadwy
Cywir, ni menegir mwy.

Hudoliaeth Merch (84)

Caeau, silltaerynnau serch,
A gwawd y tafawd, hoywferch,
Ac aur, gwn dy ddiheuraw,
4 I'th lys, a roddais i'th law.
Anhun, wych loywfun, a chlwyf,
A deigrnych, drem edegrnwyf,
Fy ngelynion, holion hy,
8 Fedel aml, fu dâl ymy.
Yn iarlles eiry un orlliw
Y'th alwn, gwedd memrwn gwiw;
Yn herlod salw y'm galwud

12   you named me 'vilest wretch' continually.
Fair web of silk I gave
to please you, hue of falling snow,
but not the slightest thing, for me
16   would you give, lass with whitest teeth.
Love's pangs, worse than [the sufferings of] holy men,
were mine through sore affliction.

    You are a fine girl, [but like] Gwaeddan, I
20   fare worse and worse in passion's interchange,
for on a like path you have driven me
as Gwaeddan once, in pursuit of his cap:
by magic and by agitating change
24   and by enchantment still deceiving me.
You disappoint me by your conduct of deceit
and by [your] frequent discourtesy.
Bright girl, endowed with nature's gifts,
28   blameless is your deceit, [since] of Dyfed you are.
There is not any school of wizardry
nor practice of deceit, a constricted argument,
nor Menw's magic, nor frequent desire,
32   nor treachery to men, nor splendid fight,
terrible mastery, nor furious intent
but your own magic and your own address.

    Three warriors—it brings me riches—
36   knew well enchantment before this:
battle-experienced, the first upholds his name—
the gentlest of the three was Menw;
the second's name (good day for understanding)
40   is Eiddilig the Dwarf, a wily Irishman;
third was, beside the seas of Môn,
Math, lord of splendid kind, and Arfon's king.

    At festival time I walked
44   equipped with full poetic art—more sorry the exchange—
for rarely do you keep a single tryst,
it is like the confusion of Llwyd, Cel Coed's son.

    Well you deserve, fair girl discreetly wise,
48   a silver harp, deception's string;
your name will be, as long as man may last
'Enchantress of the lively Harp'.
Famous you will be made, a weighty word,
52   [false] prophesy, harpist in deceit:
the harp was built
to passion's tune—you are a golden girl—
there is on it the mark of agitation's scale (?)
56   and carving of deceit and of pretence:
its frame (?) not made of forest wood

12 I'm gŵydd drwy waradwydd drud.
   A gwe deg, liw'r gawad ôd,
   O sirig a rois erod;
   Ni roud di erof fi faint
16 Y mymryn, gwenddyn gwynddaint.
   Gwewyr serch gwaeth no gwŷr saint
   A gefais drwy ddigofaint.

   Gwiwddyn wyd, Gwaeddan ydwyf,
20 Gwaethwaeth newidwriaeth nwyf.
   Gyrraist fi yn un gerrynt
   Gwaeddan am ei gapan gynt,
   O hud a rhyw symud rhus,
24 A lledrith yn dwyllodrus.
   O ddyad twyll ydd wyd di,
   Anfoes aml, yn fy siomi.
   Dyn gannaid, doniog annwyd,
28 Ddifai dwyll, o Ddyfed wyd.
   Nid dim ysgol hudoliaeth,
   Na gwarae twyll, cymwyll caeth,
   Na hud Menw, na hoed mynych,
32 Na brad ar wŷr, na brwydr wych,
   Uthr afael, wyth arofun,
   Eithr dy hud a'th air dy hun.

   Tri milwr, try ym olud,
36 A wyddyn' cyn no hyn hud—
   Cad brofiad, ceidw ei brifenw,
   Cyntaf, addfwynaf oedd Fenw;
   A'r ail fydd, dydd da dyall,
40 Eiddilig Gor, Wyddel call.
   Trydydd oedd, ger moroedd Môn,
   Math, rhwy eurfath, rhi Arfon.

   Cerddais ar holl benceirddiaeth
44 Cyfnod gŵyl, cyfnewid gwaeth;
   Anaml y cedwy unoed,
   Ail rhyfel Llwyd fab Cel Coed.

   Da dlyy, wen gymhenbwyll,
48 Delyn ariant, tant y twyll.
   Henw yt fydd, tra fo dydd dyn,
   Hudoles yr hoyw delyn.
   Enwog y'th wnair, gair gyrddbwyll,
52 Armes, telynores twyll.
   Y delyn a adeilwyd
   O radd nwyf, aur o ddyn wyd;
   Mae arni nadd o radd rus,
56 Ac ysgwthr celg ac esgus.
   Ei chwr y sydd, nid gwŷdd gwŷll,

but conjured by Virgilian art.
Its column strikes me down stone dead
60   from true magic and from poignant longing;
its pegs are a deception
made up with falsehood, flattery and change.
The value of two strips of gold
64   are your two hands, plucking the string;
alas the feeble song, maid fair as dawn,
that you can make from measure that is good.

Better is artistry, they say, than wealth:
68   girl of bright seagull's hue and long enchantment;
receive from me—traitor to a host, with snow-like

beauty,

candle of Camber's land, and fortune's gift,
a girl gently to be honoured,
72   swan-coloured—an engagement for the feast.

13 Dyddgu

(an address to her father)

Ieuan, lord of noble ancestry and flaming spear,
true son of Gruffudd, inciter of battle,
son of Llywelyn Llwyd, with fair fortress stocked with wine,
4   a chieftain are you, leader on the field of war:
in vigorous mood, the other night
I was at your house—long recompense be yours—
since then until today [such] great excitement [has been mine]
8   no easy matter has it been for me to sleep.
Your wealth I had, a free and gracious gift,
your sparkling wine, your joyfulness,
your fresh mead poured unstintingly for poets,
12   your bragget with its dark brown crest of foam.

I know your daughter will accept no wooing:
fair slender maid in mansion built of stone;
I have not slept a wink, nor had a scrap of it,
16   I have composed no song [but have felt] grievous ill.
Holy God, who will make me calm?
nothing finds entrance to my heart
except [the thought of] her inestimable love:
20   if that were given me, could I need aught else?
But sickness wastes me, for she loves me not,
allowing me no sleep, were old age to allow it me.

Rome's Wise Men would have marvelled at it—
24   the wonder of my slender darling's grace,

O ffurf celfyddyd Fferyll.
Ei llorf a'm pair yn llwyrfarw
60 O hud gwir ac o hoed garw.
Twyll yw ebillion honno
A thruth a gweniaith a thro.
Deulain o aur a dalant
64 Y dwylo tau er daly tant.
Wi o'r wangerdd, wawr wengoeth,
A fedry di o fydr doeth.

Gwell yw crefft, meddir, hir hud,
68 Ne gwylan befr, no golud.
Cymer, brad nifer, bryd nyf,
Gannwyll Gwlad Gamber, gennyf,
Lawrodd ffawd, lariaidd ei pharch,
72 Le yr ŵyl, liw yr alarch.

Dyddgu (45)
merch Ieuan ap Gruffudd ap Llywelyn

Ieuan, iôr gwaywdan gwiwdad,
Iawnfab Gruffudd, cythrudd cad,
Fab Llywelyn, wyn wingaer,
4 Llwyd, unben wyd, iawnben aer,
Y nos arall, naws arial,
Y bûm i'th dŷ, bo maith dâl;
Nid hawdd er hyn hyd heddiw,
8 Hoen wymp, ym gaffael hun wiw.
Dy aur a gawn, radlawn rydd,
Dy loyw win, dy lawenydd,
Dy fedd glas difaddau i glêr,
12 Dy fragod du ei friger.

Dy ferch, gwn na ordderchai,
Feinwen deg o feinin dai.
Ni chysgais, ni weais wawd,
16 Hun na'i dryll, heiniau drallawd.
Duw lwyd, pwy a'm dilidia?
Dim yn fy nghalon nid â,
Eithr ei chariad taladwy;
20 O rhoid ym oll, ai rhaid mwy?
Ni'm câr hon, neu'm curia haint,
Ni'm gad hun, o'm gad henaint.

Rhyfedd gan Ddoethion Rhufain
24 Rhyfedded pryd fy myd main,

for she is fairer than the snow in spring—
I am bereft of love from the sweet girl.
Pale is the brow beneath her head-dress (?)
28 black is the hair, the maid is chaste.
More black the hair (straight as a tree)
than blackbird or than clasp of jet (?)
unsullied whiteness on her smooth skin
32 makes dark her hair, all fitting to be praised.

Her kind of beauty—[and] it is her poet who speaks—
is not (genial day) unlike
to that [possessed by] that gentle girl,
36 (mine is the grief!) on whom a warrior long since set his love,
Peredur, looking for deep agony,
the son of Efrog, a strong modest knight,
when he gazed in the bright light
40 upon the snow, eagle-like lord
—an azure mantle beside Esyllt's grove—
proud path where the wild hawk had been
killing a blackbird—no one hindered it—
44 proud maid, [the hawk was] in the wrong.
There lay rightly all the evidence:
(is not such painting as hers worthy of God?)
upon the level snow, burdensome drift,
48 which had the likeness of her brow (her people will confirm)
[and like] the wing of the swift blackbird
was her eyebrow—it bred enchantment—
[while like] the bird's blood, after it had snowed,
52 with sun-like splendour, were her cheeks.

Such is the gold-encircled head
of Dyddgu, with her gleaming dark hair.
I used to be a judge, running my course,
56 now let the crew of judges over there
judge if my life can prosper for me when such great desire
oppresses me [with longing] for my darling?

14 Morfudd and Dyddgu

I am misery's very image
because, alas, ere she reached marriageable age
I did not learn to love, without delay,
4 a slender, worthy, gentle girl,
fulfilled of all endowments, true and wise,
dear, cultured, expert in all skills,
and, in a word, inheritress of land,
8 impetuous (?), pampered, a truth-speaking girl,
round and plump and unperturbed,

40

Gwynnach nog eiry y gwanwyn;
Gweddw wyf o serch y ferch fwyn.
Gwyn yw'r tâl dan wialen,
28 Du yw'r gwallt, diwair yw gwen.
Duach yw'r gwallt, diochr gwŷdd,
No mwyalch neu gae mywydd.
Gwynder disathr ar lathrgnawd
32 Yn duo'r gwallt, iawnder gwawd.

    Nid annhebyg, ddiddig ddydd,
Modd ei phryd, medd ei phrydydd,
I'r ferch hygar a garawdd
36 Y milwr gynt, mau lwyr gawdd,
Peredur ddwysgur ddisgwyl
Fab Efrog, gwrdd farchog gŵyl,
Pan oedd yn edrych, wych wawl,
40 Yn yr eiry, iôn eryrawl,
Llen asur ger llwyn Esyllt,
Llwybr balch lle y buasai'r gwalch gwyllt
Yn lladd, heb neb a'i lluddiai,
44 Mwyalch, morwyn falch, ar fai.
Yno'r oedd iawn arwyddion
(Pand Duw a'i tâl paentiad hon?)
Mewn eiry gogyfuwch, luwch lwyth,
48 Modd ei thâl, medd ei thylwyth;
Asgell y fwyalch esgud
Megis ei hael, megais hud;
Gwaed yr edn gwedy r'odi,
52 Gradd haul, mal ei gruddiau hi.

    Felly y mae, eurgae organ,
Dyddgu a'r gwallt gloywddu glân.
Beirniad fûm gynt, hynt hyntiaw,
56 Barned rhawt o'r beirniaid draw
Ai hywaith, fy nihewyd,
Ymy fy myw am fy myd.

Morfudd a Dyddgu (79)

Ochan fi, drueni drum,
Heb ohir, na wybuum
Garu cyn oedran gwra
4 Hocrell fwyn ddiell fain dda,
Gywair o ddawn, gywir, ddoeth,
Gynilgamp, gu, anwylgoeth,
Gair unwedd etifedd tir,
8 Gorwyllt foethusddyn geirwir,
Yn gronfferf, yn ddiderfysg,

replete with learning and all gifts,
pure and fair, with Indeg's sprightliness
12 (like a steer on untilled land I am),
a sweetheart of unvacillating love,
a golden wand, with shining brow.
Such a one—entitled to widespread praise—
16 is Dyddgu of the gentle dark-hued eyebrow.

Morfudd is not like that:
but thus she is, a glowing red ember,
loving those who rebuke her,
20 a stubborn lass, always exasperating,
possessing—matter fitting for respect—
a house and husband: lovely indeed she is.

Not less frequently did I flee
24 at midnight, for her sake,
away from the girl, from her glass-windowed home,
than [I did so] by day—I am a leaper bold—
and her persistent husband, with his foolish shout
28 clapping one hand against the other hand,
perpetually making outcry, with quick-awakened lust,
and shout at the abduction of his children's mother.

The puny weakling, making such a clamour
32 to the devil let him go, why should he weep?
alas, woe to him, his incessant wail
calling on God; is there a spell on him?
an impudent beast with an unceasing cry,
36 deceiving him is but a foolish task—
wonderful how cowardly he behaved
to cry out about the sprightly slender maid—
he will waken all the south country
40 with his yelling, will this kite of girls.
It is unpleasing, nor does it become,
ugly it is to listen to—not good—
a bawling man, like to a rowdy horn,
44 crying as it were a raven for his brother.

The man with the nightmarish shout
false-lipped, was a bad one for lending,
were I to buy—bright perfect idea—
48 in my lifetime a wife, deceptive step,
so that I might [but] get an hour of peace,
I would give her to this angry fornicator,
so inept is he—the surly man—
52 at [love's] play, his fate [will be] the woe of widowhood.

I have no hesitation in my choice:
I will love Dyddgu, if she may be had.

Yn gyflawn o'r dawn a'r dysg,
Yn deg lân, Indeg loywnwyf,
12 Yn dir gŵydd (enderig wyf),
Yn gariad dianwadal,
Yn lath aur, yn loyw ei thâl,
Mal y mae, mawl ehangddeddf,
16 Dyddgu â'r ael liwddu leddf.

Nid felly y mae Morfudd,
Ond fel hyn, farworyn rhudd:
Yn caru rhai a'i cerydd,
20 Rhywyr fun, a rhyir fydd;
Yn berchennog, barch uniawn,
Tŷ a gŵr, yn ddyn teg iawn.

Nid anfynychach ym ffo
24 Am hanner nos am honno
Rhag dyn o'i phlas dan laswydr
No'r dydd, wyf llamhidydd hydr;
A'r gŵr dygn, a'r gair digall,
28 Dan guraw y llaw'n y llall,
Llef beunydd a rydd, rwyddchwant,
A bloedd am ddwyn mam ei blant.

Eiddilwr, am ei ddolef
32 I ddiawl aed; pam ydd ŵyl ef,
Och, gwae ef, ddolef ddylyn,
Hyd ar Dduw, o hud ar ddyn?
Llwdn hirllef llydan haerllug,
36 Llafur ffôl yw llyfr ei ffug.
Llwfr a rhyfedd y gwneddyw,
Llefain am riain fain fyw.
Y Deau ef a'i dihun
40 Dan ddywedyd, barcud bun.
Nid dawnus, nid dianardd,
Nid teg gwarandaw, nid hardd,
Gŵr yn gweiddi, gorn gwaeddawd,
44 Ar gân fal brân am ei brawd.

Ys drwg o un anhunfloedd,
Finffug ŵr, am fenffyg oedd.
Pei prynwn, befr didwn bwyll,
48 Wraig o'm hoedl, rhyw gam hydwyll,
Caliwr dig, er cael awr daw,
Rhan oedd, mi a'i rhown iddaw,
Rhag dryced, weddw dynged wae,
52 Y gŵr chwerw, y gŵyr chwarae.

Dewis yr wyf ar ungair
Dyddgu i'w charu, o chair.

15 Choosing One from Four

A girl bestowed her love on me:
star of the neighbourhood of Nant-y-Seri,
a fine maid, not in judgement false,
4   generous Morfudd, great [my] thoughts [of her].
Though by some dire activity I lose,
my booty was a just abduction,
though our exchange was valuable
8   she was a property of value also to her husband.
Lest he displease—condition terrible—
God above [in heaven]—she [stays] impenitent
after her lover—the dread was a betrayal—
12   moon of the world, swore that he would desist.

If therefore I [then] cast my love
half-trusted, on that bald merchant's wife
hunch-backed, with his pseudo-retinue,
16   wife of a certain burgher, Robin Nordd,
Elen, avid [as she is] for wealth,
my darling with persistent alien speech,
queen, lady of the wool,
20   [and] of warehouses, land [ready] for gorse-firing,
there was need there for a lover—
and woe to me if such one were not I!
She—form of the fair wave—will not accept
24   a song for free, a powerful point of honour:
[and thus] with ease I get an entire load
of stockings of good quality; nothing easier.
and if I get from her of fairest gossamer hue
28   [but] motley ones, she will [yet] make me content.

I am not—carefree vivacity—
by God, without obtaining some reward:
whether it be chosen words of praise,
32   or else in planning some sweet melody,
or else in gold, though I excuse myself,
or in some other thing, for I am eloquent.
Also, though my tongue may be
36   to Dyddgu weaving words of praise,
there is no other office left me, by my God,
but that of tracing her inconstancy.

The kingdom's princess, she who rules its nurture,
40   the fourth is, as everyone well knows:
from my lips, discreet and wise
not she—the wave's vivacity—nor any other will obtain
her name, nor name of country whence she comes,
44   deserving all praise—nor which one she may be.

Dewis Un o Bedair (98)

Ei serch a roes merch i mi,
Seren cylch Nant-y-seri,
Morwyn wych, nid ym marn au,
4 Morfudd ŵyl, mawr feddyliau.
Cyd collwyf o wiwnwyf uthr
Fy anrhaith a fu iawnrhuthr,
Cyd bai brid ein newid ni,
8 Prid oedd i'r priod eiddi.
Eithr rhag anfodd, uthr geinfyw,
Duw fry, diedifar yw,
Gwedy i'w chariad, brad fu'r braw,
12 Lloer byd, roi llw ar beidiaw.

O cherais wraig mewn meigoel,
Wrth hyn, y porthmonyn moel,
Gwragennus, esgus osgordd,
16 Gwraig ryw benaig, Robin Nordd,
Elen chwannog i olud,
Fy anrhaith â'r lediaith lud,
Brenhines, arglwyddes gwlân,
20 Brethyndai, bro eithindan,
Dyn serchog oedd raid yno,
Gwae fi nad fyfi fai fo!
Ni chymer hon, wiwdon wedd,
24 Gerdd yn rhad, gwrdd anrhydedd.
Hawdd ym gael, gafael gyfa,
Haws no dim, hosanau da;
Ac os caf, liw gwynnaf gwawn,
28 Fedlai, hi a'm gwna'n fodlawn.

Nid ydwyf, nwyf anofal,
Rho Duw, heb gaffael rhyw dâl:
Ai ar eiriau arwyrain,
32 Ai ar feddwl cerddgar cain,
Ai ar aur cyd diheurwyf,
Ai ar ryw beth, arab wyf.
Hefyd cyd bo fy nhafawd
36 I Ddyddgu yn gwëu gwawd,
Nid oes ym, myn Duw, o swydd,
Ond olrhain anwadalrhwydd.

Gwawr brenhiniaeth, maeth a'i medd,
40 Y byd ŵyr, yw'r bedwaredd.
Ni chaiff o'm pen cymen call,
Hoen geirw, na hi nac arall
Na'i henw, na'r wlad yr hanoedd,
44 Hoff iawn yw, na pha un oedd.

There is no sprightly burgher's wife
nor [wife of] any man that I may love so much
as the bright lass of the lime-washed fortress's zone;
48   Goodnight to her, she thanks me not for it.
Word may be had of loving fruitlessly—
I'll not withhold it, I will be repaid.
If she, who is a man's hope, were to know
52   that thus it were concerning her
it were to her as bad—slim maiden ruddy-fair—
as for her to be hanged—a powerful curse (?).
The greater the importance, cruel pain is mine,
56   that I should praise her, Nia's loveliness,
of shapely form, all Gwynedd praises her,
and blessed indeed is he who can possess her!

16 Her Beauty Spoiled

The girl I used to call my golden sweetheart
and my fair darling, gracious and serene,
I have it in my mind—a grievous, just decision
4   by God's strength, a struggle from deceit—
[and] I have thought—the world demands it of me—
to give her up (the birch-grove calls for her).
What payment have I had from following her?
8   It were high time to have done with the girl.

Spoiled—a grievous wrong—has been
the girl's complexion, now this long time since.
Not I, nor any power avails
12   that may improve the colour of the girl.
I do believe, mine is the grief,
that I know, greater is my pain,
the outrage that, with its increase,
16   is harming the beauty of her cheeks.
Gentle Enid, it is the Jealous One's breath
from his black lips creating woe
when that tiresome man lets fall
20   (a wicked trick, for she had Eigr's fairness)
his breath, like murky smoke from peat
about her: why does the lass not cleanse herself?
it is a sorrow like a fetter's bond
24   to leave that monster with the girl.

A varnished image made of alderwood
of English workmanship, fit offering for a lord,
in bad keeping, treated wrongfully

Nid oes na gwraig benaig nwyf,
Na gŵr cymin a garwyf
Â'r forwyn glaer galchgaer gylch;
48   Nos da iddi, nis diylch.
Cair gair o garu'n ddiffrwyth,
Caf, nid arbedaf fi, bwyth.
Pei gwypai obaith undyn
52   Mai amdeni hi fai hyn,
Bai cynddrwg, geinwen rudd-deg,
Genthi â'i chrogi, wych reg,
Mwy lawnbwys, mau elynboen,
56   Moli a wnaf hi, Nyf hoen,
Hoyw ei llun, a holl Wynedd
A'i mawl; gwyn ei fyd a'i medd!

Llychwino Pryd y Ferch (81)

Y ferch a alwn f'eurchwaer,
A'm annwyl eglurwyl glaer,
Mae i'm bryd, enbyd iawnbwyll,
4   Trwy nerth Duw trin i wrth dwyll,
Bod i'm cof, byd a'm cyfeirch,
Beidio â hi, bedw a'i heirch.
Ba dâl *a*'m bu o'i dilyn?
8   Boed awr dda beidio â'r ddyn.

Llygru a wnaeth, gaeth gerydd,
Lliw'r dyn er ys llawer dydd.
Ni allaf, nerth ni pherthyn,
12   Ni ellir da â lliw'r dyn.
Meddylio'r wyf, mau ddolur,
Myfi a'i gwn, mau fwy gur,
Y chwaen gyda'r ychwaneg
16   A ludd ei deurudd yn deg.
Enid leddf, anadl Eiddig
O'i enau du a wna dig,
Gwedy gollyngo, tro trwch
20   Y gŵr dygn, bu Eigr degwch,
Anadl fal mwg y fawnen
Yn ei chylch (pam nas gylch gwen?)
Gofal yw fal rhwym gefyn
24   Gadu'r delff i gyd â'r dyn.

Delw o bren gwern dan fernais,
Dogn benrhaith o saerwaith Sais,
Drwg gadwad, dygiad agwyr,

47

28 a swinging lantern can spoil utterly;
and English fur, sufficiently fine
will be destroyed by smoke from a peat fire;
fog will utterly absorb
32 the fair Sun's brightness in the sky;
the spreading branches of an oaken groyne
will wither when they are beside the sea.

I roamed—abduction joyous and prolonged (?)—
36 each of the girl's homes while she was fair.
[It was but] stewardship of a captive love,
so long as her beauty might last, no certain home.
Well does he know how to deface her beauty
40 yet she was [formerly] my darling love.
The wretched Jealous One prefers it thus,
the black dog, that she should no more be fair.
Polluted has the dirt from off his lips
44 the bright complexion of my sweetheart's hue.
By God and Cadfan, there were need
that grace preserve [her]: she was very beautiful.

17 Morfudd Ageing

God grant life and grace unstinted
to that virtuous stray crow, the straggling hairy friar.
No peace do they deserve who do revile
4 the friar whose form is as a shadow
of that lord who is honoured in Rome,
he is a man bare-foot, whose hair is like a nest of thorns.
His coat is ragged as he walks the world,
8 a kind of a cross-beam of spiritual grace.

Confessor, craftsman of wise words,
well does he sing, the kite of noble God,
much privileged the charter of his home:
12 a ram he is, from out the roof of Heaven.
Eloquent the wise words from his mouth,
long life [coming] from the lips of Mary's wizard!
He said (severe discretion's praise)
16 about the hue of her who does not often deceive:

'Dress yourself, lord of a throng of lords,
in shift of cambric, and in shining white,
Put on, without discarding for a week,
20 a costly mantle for the wearisome flesh.
A well-born girl—a second Deirdre's tale—
it will become more black, and twice alas for me!'

28 Llugorn llon a'i llwgr yn llwyr.
   Y pân Seisnig da ddigawn
   A fydd drwg ym mwg y mawn.
   Nïwl a ddwg yn awyr
32 Gan yr haul wiw ei lliw'n llwyr.
   Cadeirgainc dderw, coed argor,
   A fydd crin ym min y môr.

   Tramwyais, hoywdrais hydreg,
36 Trefi y dyn tra fu deg.
   Ystiwardiaeth gaeth gariad,
   Ond tra fo teg, nid tref tad.
   Da y gŵyr beri digaru
40 Ei phryd, fy anwylyd fu.
   Gorau gan Eiddig oeryn,
   Gi du, na bai deg y dyn.
   Llychwinodd llwch o'i enau
44 Lliw'r dynyn mireinwyn mau.
   Rho Duw a Chadfan, rhaid oedd
   Rhad a geidw; rhydeg ydoedd.

Morfudd yn Hen (139)

Rhoed Duw hoedl a rhad didlawd,
Rhinllaes frân, i'r rhawnllaes frawd.
A geblynt, ni haeddynt hedd,
4 Y brawd o gysgawd gosgedd
Nêr a rifer o Rufain,
Noeth droed, ŵr unwallt nyth drain.
Rhwyd yw'r bais yn rhodio'r byd,
8 Rhyw drawsbren, rhad yr ysbryd.

   Periglor gerddor geirddoeth,
   Barcutan, da y cân, Duw coeth.
   Mawr yw braint siartr ei gartref,
12 Maharen o nên y nef.
   Huawdl o'i ben gymhennair,
   Hoedl o'i fin, hudol i Fair.
   Ef a ddywawd, wawd wydnbwyll,
16 Am liw'r dyn nid aml ar dwyll:

   'Cymer dy hun, ben cun cant,
   Crysan o'r combr a'r crisiant.
   Gwisg, na ddiosg wythnosgwaith,
20 Gwasgawd mwythus lyfngnawd maith.
   Dirdras fun, chwedl ail Derdri;
   Duach fydd, a dwyoch fi!'

The bald grey friar, with ever-ready warning,
24   the gloomy friar spoke thus of my girl's loveliness.
I would not give up Morfudd, [even] were I Pope
so long as I remained a sprightly youth;
but now—vexations and complaint—
28   the Creator has disfigured her
till there is not in proper healthy state
one single tress of grey that more lacks lustre—
a treacherous provision for an emaciated face;
32   my girl's beauty will not last like gold.
Queen of the land of sleeplessness,
her beauty and her form were ample treachery
to men: for one a life-time's sleeplessness—
36   it is a dream, how swiftly passes life!
A broom upon an earthen floor,
of elder [now] half-withered and grey.

Tonight I may not sleep—for I am wounded, sick—
40   one wink, unless I may be over there:
it is the stunning blow of love for yonder girl,
a nightmare in the guise of a familiar robber.
She was created magically [once],
44   an enchantress, now a grey-haired thief,
the bent stick of an Irish mangonell,
a chilly shieling: [yet] she was lovely once.

18 A Stubborn Girl

As I was going on my way
over the mountain, men of holy faith,
in summer's longing, wearing my gay clothes
4   as though I were a husbandman;
see before me on the moor
a stripling maid awaiting me.
I thought her gentle as a swan
8   and greeted her, sensible and gentle girl,
she made in answer to her poet
response of love, or so it seemed to me.

The frigid lass would not consent
12   to go with me as maidens go in May:
straightforward was I with the comely girl
but not straightforward with a kiss was she.
I praised her for her sparkling eyes—
16   all the handsome chief poets praise her.
I asked if she, before the wars should come
could fancy me, for she was Heaven to me.

Foel-llwyd ddeheuwawd frawd-ddyn,
24 Felly'r brawd du am bryd dyn.
Ni pheidiwn, pe byddwn Bab,
Â Morfudd tra fûm oerfab.
Weithion, cyhuddeidion cawdd,
28 Y Creawdr a'i hacraawdd,
Hyd nad oes o iawnfoes iach
Un lyweth las anloywach,
Brad arlwy, ar bryd erlyn;
32 Nid â fal aur da liw'r dyn.
Brenhines bro anhunedd,
Brad y gwŷr o bryd a gwedd,
Braisg oedd, un anun einioes,
36 Breuddwyd yw; ebrwydded oes!
Ysgubell ar briddell brag,
Ysgawen lwydwen ledwag.

Heno ni chaf, glaf glwyfaw,
40 Huno drem oni fwyf draw.
Hyrddaint serch y ferch yw ef,
Henlleidr unrhyw â hunllef.
Hudolaidd y'i hadeilwyd,
44 Hudoles ladrones lwyd.
Henllath mangnel Wyddeleg,
Hafod oer; hi a fu deg.

Merch Gyndyn (41)

Fal yr oeddwn yn myned
Dros fynydd, gwŷr crefydd Cred,
A'm hoyw dudded amdanaf
4 Fal amaeth, mewn hiraeth haf,
Nycha gangen ar y rhos
O forwyn i'm cyfaros.
Cyfarch, meddwl alarch mwyn,
8 Gwell iddi, ddyn gall addwyn.
Ateb a wnaeth ei phrydydd,
Ateb serch o'm tyb y sydd.

Cydgerdded fal merched Mai,
12 Ac oerddyn ni chydgerddai.
Gosyml fûm am forwyn lân,
Gosyml ni bu am gusan.
Canmol ei llygaid gloywon,
16 Canmolid prifeirdd heirdd hon.
Gofyn cyn dêl rhyfeloedd
A fynnai fi; fy nef oedd.

'Country-boy, you will not get
20 an answer, for I do not know as yet:
let us on Sunday to Llanbadarn church
or to the tavern, you forward man,
there to arrange a trysting place
24 in the greenwood, or yet [perhaps] in Heaven.
Lest I should be defamed, I would not want
my presence in the birch-grove to be known.'

'I am judged cowardly for love of you,
28 [but yet] your wooer is a valiant man.
Do not avoid me, [girl of] high-born stock
on account of that woman's trouble-making,
I know a mansion in the greenwood
32 (no second person ever knew of it),
one which the Jealous One will not find out
so long as [leafy] mantle tops the trees.
My farewell to you, girl, who are
36 both thief and guardian of the grove.

The perverse hussy, cuckoo's niece,
performed not in accordance with her word:
a reckless promise [having] made me glad,
40 her 'tryst' turns out to be a promise made in wine.

19 Wooing the Nuns

Be pacified, my busy messenger,
since it is May, go yonder from the March;
you left me, you departed, by the Lord,
4 [but] now, [however], I have need of you.
Gentle requests, a blameless enterprise
—you did well in the place you know, before.

You gained me [once] a girl by but one word,
8 gain for me [now] that I may see the girls of Mary.
Go to proud Llanllugan, choose the form
of one, where there are many as pale as lime.

Seek in the church, and give a greeting
12 to that great gaoler, overseer of girls.
Say this to the gaoler: the insistent claim
of poets—that is [my kind of] psalm.
Lament the heaviness of my complaint
16 and win for me the nuns.
The saints on every side deny me,
within their sleeping-quarters, these fair holy ones,
white as the snow, or like the gossamer's edge;

'Ni chai, fab o ael y fro,
20   Un ateb; na wn eto.
Down i Lanbadarn Ddyw Sul,
Neu i'r dafarn, ŵr diful;
Ac yno yn yr irgoed
24   Neu'n y nef ni a wnawn oed.
Ni fynnwn, rhag cael gogan,
Wybod fy mod mewn bedw mân.'

'Llwfr iawn y'm bernir o'th serch,
28   A dewrddyn yw dy ordderch.
Nac eiriach, diledach do,
Er cynnen y wraig honno.
Mi a wn blas o lasgoed,
32   A'r ail nis gwybu erioed,
Ac nis gwybydd dyn eiddig
Tra fo llen ar bren a brig.
Cymryd fy nghennad, forwyn,
36   Ceidwades, lladrones llwyn.'

Ni wnâi hocrell afrywiog
A wnaeth â'i gair, nith y gog.
Addaw ffôl a'm gwnâi'n llawen,
40   Addewid gwin fydd oed gwen.

Cyrchu Lleian (113)

Dadlitia'r diwyd latai,
Hwnt o'r Mars dwg hynt er Mai.
Gedaist, ciliaist myn Celi,
4   Arnaf y mae d'eisiau di.
Dof holion, difai helynt,
Da fuost lle y gwyddost gynt.

Peraist ym fun ar ungair,
8   Pâr ym weled merched Mair.
Dewis lun, dos i Lan falch
Llugan, lle mae rhai lliwgalch.

Cais yn y llan ac annerch
12   Y sieler mawr, selwr merch.
Dywed, glaim diwyd y glêr,
Hon yw'r salm, hyn i'r sieler.
A chŵyn maint yw'r achwyn mau.
16   A chais ym fynachesau.
Saint o bob lle a'm gweheirdd
Santesau hundeiau heirdd,
Gwyn eiry arial gwawn oror,

20   they are swallows, dwellers in the convent's choir,
     [and yet] god-sisters are they every one
     to Morfudd, to my gentle golden girl.

     Your two feet are good implements:
24   bring from the choir some sweet girl to the wood
     [you are] the one can do it—[to] our bower—
     a black-robed nun into the leafy grove.
     If from the frater's care I may entice
28   a girl with forehead manifest
     (friend of some sixty other darlings),
     seek [even] the chantress from the choir:
     if she, bright hue of snow, to win her fame
32   for all your asking, will not come,
     try then to entice the abbess
     sweet glow of warmth, before the summer moon.

20 Gwenoliaid, cwfeiniaid côr,
     Chwiorydd bedydd bob un
     I Forfudd, araf eurfun.

     Da ddodrefn yw dy ddeudroed,
24 Dwg o'r côr ddyn deg i'r coed,
     Un a'i medr, einym adail,
     A'r lleian du i'r llwyn dail.
     Or caf finnau rhag gofal
28 O'r ffreutur dyn eglur dâl,
     Câr trigain cariad rhagor,
     Cais y glochyddes o'r côr.
     Oni ddaw, er cludaw clod,
32 Hoywne eiry, honno erod,
     Cais frad ar yr abades,
     Cyn lleuad haf, ceinlliw tes.

Notes

8

Like 'Love's Husbandry' (No.6) this poem belongs to the small group of Dafydd's compositions in which a single metaphor is sustained throughout. There is a helpful analysis of the poem by John Rowlands, *YB* VI (1971),16-44, from which I have adopted the suggestions made in the notes to ls.13, 19 below.

1. *geirllaes*, 'slow of speech, of gentle speech, drawling' (GPC). Dr Parry now accepts this rendering (GDG³) as against his earlier 'parablus, llac ei hymadrodd', and advocates the translation 'soft-spoken'. The same phrase occurs GDG 125, l.4 *yn gorllwyn fy nyn geirllaes*, and—again in reference to a girl—by Gruffydd Gryg, DGG² LXXV, l.72.

3. *dyn*. Dr Parry restores the syntactically correct *dyn* in place of *ddyn*, the reading of nearly all the MSS. *Dyn* is ambiguous as to gender.

8. *wybren* can mean both 'cloud' as here and in l.32, and 'sky' as in l.37.

9. *gwawr*. The original meaning is 'dawn', but GPC lists a number of figurative usages, including 'lady, princess'.

10. *gŵr*. Since the poet describes himself in l.14 as 'of comely form' the allusion here is clearly to Morfudd's husband, as is indeed confirmed by the allusion to him in ls.49-50.

11. *oferfardd* 'frivolous' or (in some instances) 'scurrilous bard'. For instances see TYP 21-2. CF. *oferwaith* no.53 (GDG 90), l.9, and n.

13. *gwe o aur*. Perhaps with a side-glance at the fact that a spider's web can also ensnare.

19. *bylchgaer*. The explanation of this image is that Morfudd appears and disappears alternately, like someone walking along the parapet of a castle, and seen between the gaps in the battlements—just as the Sun appears and disappears behind the clouds.

21. *ymylau*. Dr Parry points out to me that from its original meaning of 'edge, border', *ymyl* developed in some instances that of 'land, country': a semantic development which is paralleled in the words *ardal, goror* which from their original meaning 'border' came to be used for 'district', as is pointed out by Ifor Williams, B.iv,139. (For *goror* with the meaning of 'region' cf. no.5, l.2 above).

hoywles. 'lively/active' and 'benefit/succour'. An alternative meaning for *lles* was proposed by W.J.Gruffydd, B.viii,304 in discussing a line from *Cywydd y Sêr*, DGG² XL; where he understands it as meaning a legal 'lease'. D.J. Bowen would extend this meaning to the present instance, *LL.C.* VII, 205 n. In a figurative sense the Sun's 'rays' would then correspond to the illuminated lettering on a legal document. Cf. l.69 below.

22. *mamaeth tywysogaeth tes*. The literal meaning is 'the one who nurtures the enticement of warmth'. *Tywysogaeth* 'the act of leading or enticing'; *tywys* 'to lead, entice'; *tywysog* 'leader'. Cf. no.41 (GDG 89),12 below where Morfudd is described as *mamaeth tywysogaeth twyll* 'mistress of the enticement of deceit'.

23-6. *ei syw swydd*. Alternatively 'its . . . work', referring to the Sun. These lines virtually equate Morfudd with the Sun: *maelieres* 'female merchant, huxtress' could denote either the one or the other (though the parallelism with *bugeiles* l.30 favours personification of the Sun, and though *haul* is masc. in MW, it is treated as fem. in ls.41, 42 below). This ambivalence—no doubt fully intentional—somewhat mitigates the near blasphemy of the comparison of Morfudd with the Virgin Mary in l.26.

34. *a draul drem*. lit. 'which expends sight'.

37-44. An interesting presentation of pre-Copernican astronomy, in which it is the Sun which turns from the world, rather than the opposite. These lines invite comparison with *Y Seren*, no.30 (GDG 67), ls.31-2, in which the Star (the Sun's replica) is in like manner described as above and beyond the reach of human hand; cf. ls.57-8 below.

38. *eilywed*. Dr Parry's emendation. The MSS read *Eluned* and *Elfed*, which in the context are clearly meaningless. *Planed* (E.'planet') here denotes the Sun.

52. *Penrhyn*. It is tempting to see here a reference to the village of Penrhyn-coch, only a mile or two from Dafydd's birth-place at Brogynin. Dr Parry however expresses caution (GDG xxxiv,xlv), pointing out that *penrhyn* 'headland' is a very common element in place-names.

57. *gwawdrydd*. Dafydd employs *gwawd* on occasion in each of its two contrasting meanings of 'praise' and 'satire' (for an unmistakeable instance of the latter cf. GDG 152, ls.34, 60), though 'praise' is his most frequent meaning. There is therefore an element of ambiguity here: 'freely mocking' is as likely to be the poet's epithet for Morfudd as 'freely praised'. In *gwiwdraul* the meaning of *traul* is as in l.34 above (see n.); the two epithets together could mean 'freely expending mockery'.

63. *eiddungam*. In this *sangiad*, *cam* can mean either 'crooked, false, deceitful', etc. or 'leap, degree, progress', etc. Alternatively, therefore 'a deceptive desire'.

64. *na ddeaill*. The old meaning of *deall* was 'grasp, take possession of' see CLIH 121-2; G.sv. *dyall*[2].

69. *llyfr dalensyth*. i.e. it would be hard to believe even if it were to be attested in some written document.

9

This poem with its emphasis on the wounds inflicted (metaphorically) on the poet by the 'spears' of love has been regarded as the immediate occasion of the poetic contention between Dafydd and Gruffudd Gryg (GDG nos.147-154). Morfudd's name, however, is not given, though in GDG 147 it is she who is named as the cause of Dafydd's sufferings through the 'spears' or pangs of love. Both here and in the Contention there is play upon the double meanings of *gwayw*, *gwewyr* 'spear(s)' and also 'pang(s)'. The scene is Bangor cathedral, founded in the sixth century by St Deinioel (cf. l.6).

5. *salm balchnoe*. Two closely contemporary references establish beyond doubt the fact that 'Noah's Ark' was the meaning of *balchnoe* in the fourteenth century: Gruffudd ap Maredudd RBP 1220, ls.24-6 (see B.iv,344); Peniarth MS.V,29b-30a (cited GPC 251). Iolo Goch employs the form *alch Noe* (IGE[2] XXV,16) with similar meaning. A further instance from a sixteenth-century source confirms this meaning (B.iv,223). The word derives from Lat. *barca* which gave W. *barc(h)* and then *balch* through dissimilation of *r* and *l*. The story of the Deluge was a popular subject for miracle plays in Britain, so that the allusion here could well be to a dramatic presentation of some kind in the cathedral. Elsewhere Dafydd employs *salm* in the general sense of 'poem, (religious) song', see GDG index. The occurrences of the word referred to above render superfluous Saunders Lewis's over-ingenious suggestion (*Ll.C.* ii, 204, cited GDG[2] 558) that the allusion is to the so-called 'Noeane system' of chanting psalms. On the symbolical meaning of *arch Noa* as denoting the church of Christ, and the reasons for believing that this meaning was recognised in Wales, see J. E. Caerwyn Williams, *Y Traethodydd* CXXXIV (1979), 139-41.

8. *fflwch* is from E. 'flush', i.e. an outpouring. *Fflur*: a traditional heroine loved by Caswallawn fab Beli; TYP 352.

14. *Gwyn eiddigion.* Dr Parry hesitates between *gwyn* and *gŵyn* as the meaning here. The two come close together, since both include 'desire, lust' among their meanings, but the first offers the alternative of 'wish, desire' and the second that of 'pain' and 'jealousy'. I adopt the first. Perhaps, as D.J.Bowen suggests (Ll.C. VIII, 9n.) the poet Gruffudd Gryg may be one of the *eiddigion* or jealous rivals intended in the allusion.

20. *Lladd* has the two meanings of 'to pierce, strike' and 'to kill'.

22. *am gannwyll Gwynedd. Cannwyll* is used figuratively for the girl. Cf. no.12, l.70 and Gruffudd ap Maredudd's *eurgannwyll Bentraeth* for Gwenhwyfar of Môn, RBP 1319, l.1.

26. *yn grych* i.e. his cheek is wrinkled by tears.

29. *Esyllt*; a traditional heroine loved by Drystan (Tristan); TYP 349. *aseth* '(sharp-pointed) spar', especially for fastening thatch on a roof: so here the vital pin or peg which holds together the framework of rafters supporting a roof.

30. *cledr dwyfron* 'breastbone'. Used with intentional ambiguity, since *cledr* also means 'laths, rafter, beam', etc.

33. *trefnloes.* From *trefn* + *gloes* 'pain, pang'; hence 'causing (lit, 'arranging') pain'.

mynawyd. (shoemaker's) awl.

10

This poem is possibly to be linked to the previous one owing to the references to Môn which occur in both. But although Morfudd is named in l.51, as Dr Parry points out, there is no certainty that she is also the girl celebrated in *Y Gwayw.*

1. *Cywyddau, Cywydd* both here and in l.51 is used in its primary meaning of 'song, poem'; similarly in no.43, l.27 below.

5. *maendy*, lit. 'stone house'. But cf. the *llestyr maen* in which Luned was imprisoned, *Owein* l.694.

7. *y lleidrwas llwyd*, i.e. love itself.

11. *orloes* is a clock (Fr. *horloge*, E.*orloge*; EEW 212-3). Both here and in two other instances in which Dafydd employs the word, no.47, l.8 and GDG 142, l.27 it is clear that he is referring to a loud (and in this case a repetitive) noise, and this is also how the word is used by Chaucer, 'The kok, that orloge is of thorpis lyte' (*Parlement of Foules*, 350). Other poets similarly combine *gwrle(s)* with *orloge*, IGE[2] 100, l.18; 230, l.14.

13-16. With the image of 'sowing praise' cf. no.6 above, and no.44, l.36 below.

18. *dyn* is here entirely ambiguous, as is frequently the case. But in the present context 'girl' seems more probable than 'man'.

21-5. *Pater noster* is the beginning of the Lord's Prayer and *Amen* its end; thus Morfudd is the beginning and the end of all prayer.

22. *llorfdant.* This is the longest string on a harp, nearest to the column and furthest from the player; it makes the deepest sound.

30. *I ferch Wgon farchoges.* The allusion is totally obscure, except that Gwgon Gleddyfrudd 'of the red sword' is referred to in GDG 46, ls.67-8, and he was apparently a local hero of Ceredigion; see TYP 389-90.

34. *a'i thoryn llwyd.* The phrase is strongly reminiscent of a ninth-century Irish 'hermit' poem in which the cuckoo is similarly described as *hi mbrot glass* 'in a grey cloak'; G.Murphy, *Early Irish Lyrics* 4-5; K.Jackson, *Early Celtic Nature Poetry*, no.II.

39. *gwas mynaich*. As Ifor Williams pointed out DGG² 170, this does not mean that Dafydd is claiming to have ever been employed as a servant in a monastery, but it seems rather to be an innuendo against the idleness of such servants. The idleness of monastic servants seems indeed to have become proverbial by the time of the Reformation.

40. *yn ormod fy maich*, i.e. the burden of his songs to Morfudd. In the Contention, GDG 152, ls.39-50, Dafydd speaks of the welcome he would receive in Môn for his poetry, since his reputation there is as high as that of Gruffudd Gryg himself.

41. *da deutrew*. A proverb is given in Davies's Dictionary, *Nac untrew na dau, ni nawdd rhag angau* 'Neither one nor two sneezes, there is no deliverance from death'. One sneeze is said to bring ill-luck, and Ifor Williams suggests (GDG² 170), that the opposite may also have been the case, and that two sneezes may have been supposed to be fortunate. This would fit well with the allusion here. (cf. BBC 82).

43. *diddwyll ddadl*. Dadl here has a legal flavour, which is further upheld by the use of *dyly* in l.56 as 'having a claim to', a sense which is frequently exemplified in the Laws. This instance is cited as an example of the legal usage, B.VII,364-6.

51-2,55-6. These lines occur in identical form in one of the apocryphal poems, DGG², XX1, *Y ferch a wnaeth gwaew dan f'ais*. On Dr Parry's reasons for rejecting this poem's authenticity see GDG clxxxv—vi, and for a contrary argument which favours its restoration to the canon, see D.J.Bowen. Ll.C. VIII. 20.

55. *Ni ddeily*. GPC 881 cites this line as an e.g. of *dal* in the infrequent sense of 'to ask a price or payment for'.

11

2. *Diwladaidd*. Lit. 'unrustic'. Both this word and its positive form *gwladaidd* 'rustic, churlish' were popular with Dafydd ap Gwilym, as H.I.Bell pointed out, *Fifty Poems of Dafydd ap Gwilym* (London, 1942), 36. Dafydd may have adopted *diwladaidd* from its earlier occurrence in an example of the measure *awdl gywydd* cited in the Bardic Grammar as it occurs in the Red Book of Hergest (see GP 12 and YB X,173).

3. *o'r geiriau mad*. Lit. 'goodly words'. The meaning seems to be, however, that love is best concealed by dissembling it, uttering nothing but conventional commonplaces.

8. *ofer o ddau* 'a dissolute pair' (Dr Parry's interpretation). With *ofer* cf. n. to *oferwaith* no.53,9 below, and the triad *Tri Oferfeirdd*, TYP no.12 and n.

10. *atebion*. Lit. 'our answers' or 'responses'.

12. *ymgytgam*, from vb. *cytgamaf* 'to jest, sport, play, dally'.

15. *un drygdafod*. Chotzen 285 discusses this passage in relation to the role of the *lausengier* or *mesdisant*, generally an anonymous slanderer or envious rival, in the poetry of *amour courtois* in Provençal and French. As in the present instance, the nature of the slanderer's accusations is rarely elucidated in the continental poems.

16. *dryglam nod*. Or, as we might put it 'through a chapter of accidents'.

29. *Cydblannu bedw*. Presumably a reference to a popular lovers' custom.

12

The general tenor of this poem suggests that it is a 'Morfudd' poem, though her name is not mentioned. The refs in lines 44, 72 seem to indicate that this poem was composed upon the occasion of some particular *gŵyl* or festival.

4. *llys*. The girl's 'court' is her home.

10. *gwedd memrwm gwiw*. Cf. *lliw papir* 'colour of paper' for a girl's beauty, no.43, l.22 (see n.). Most of the comparisons Dafydd employs for this purpose are strictly conventional, and such comparisons with paper and parchment are uncommon.

19-22. *Gwaeddan*. Nothing is known of this character, or his story. His *capan* may have been either his cap or his cloak.

28. *Dyfed*. In *Mabinogi Manawydan* the enchantment placed on the seven *cantrefi* of Dyfed by Llwyd fab Cilcoed (cf. l.46 below) caused it to become a 'Waste Land', deprived of all vegetation and of all animal life.

31. In the tale of *Culhwch ac Olwen* and in *Trioedd Ynys Prydein* Menw fab Teirgwaedd figures as an enchanter, capable of making himself and his companions invisible; TYP 457-8.

35-42. *Tri milwr*, etc. See the three variant versions of this triad, TYP nos.27,28 and in *Pedwar Marchog ar Hugain Llys Arthur* (TYP Appendix IV, no.4) and notes.

30. *cymwyll caeth*. Cf. no.29 (GDG 117),19 *gam gymwyll*, and n.

46. *Llwyd fab Cel Coed*. The latter's name is *Kil Coet* in PKM 64,5-6, but is spelled *kelcoet* in the text of *Culhwch ac Olwen*, WM 466, l.1; RM 110, 8.

52. *armes*, a prophecy (frequently of disaster). Ifor Williams quotes these lines in his discussion of the meaning of *armes*, *Armes Prydein* (Cardiff, 1955),xxxv.

54-5. *gradd* lit. 'dignity, worth, merit', or 'scale' in musical terminology (GPC). The ambiguity is presumably intentional in l.55.

58. *Fferyll*, i.e. Virgil, who was regarded as a magician in the Middle Ages.

67. *Gwell yw crefft*, etc. A traditional proverb, such as Dafydd was fond of quoting; exx: GDG 72, ls.17-18 and ls.25-6; 115, ls.53-4, etc. All the proverbs quoted by Dafydd are cited by John Davies and are given at the end of his dictionary (1632).

69. The object of *Cymer* is *le yr ŵyl*, l.72, i.e. an engagement to play the harp at the feast (cf. l.43 above) (Dr Parry's interpretation). The girl is a 'harpist' (l.52), even if the description is merely intended metaphorically.
bryd nyf. *Nyf* is frequently ambiguous in poetry, since it can either mean 'snow' or be an allusion to the heroine *Niamh* in the Irish Ossianic Cycle; see n. to no.15, l.56 below.

70. *Gwlad Gamber*, i.e. Wales. According to the 'geography' of Geoffrey of Monmouth, reproduced in the Welsh *Brut y Brenhinedd*, the eponymous Camber was one of the sons of Brutus, the legendary first ruler of Britain. With *cannwyll* cf. *cannwyll Gwynedd* for the girl praised in no.9, l.22.

13

1-2. *gwaywdan, cythrudd cad*. As elsewhere in his praise-poetry, Dafydd here employs the conventional warlike images of bardic encomium inherited from the Gogynfeirdd, however inappropriate these may have been at times to the altered circumstances of the 14th century. *Gwiwdad* 'of noble ancestry' (Dr Parry's rendering).

1-4. Dr Parry observes (GDG xliv, GDG² xxv) that the names of Dyddgu's forebears are too common to admit of identification. Owing to the tmesis in these lines, *llwyd* is as likely to be an epithet for Ieuan himself as for his grandfather.

11. *clêr*. See n. to no.43, l.29 below.

22. i.e. though old age is not the reason (for his insomnia).

23. *Doethion Rhufain*. The oldest text of the *Chwedleu Seith Doethon Rufein* or 'Seven Sages of Rome' (ed. H.Lewis, Cardiff 1958, 1967) is mid 14th century, but the individual tales may have enjoyed previous circulation by oral channels in Wales. Dafydd may therefore have known of these traditional Wise Men, or he may here be referring to those other *Doethion Rhufain* who interpreted to the emperor Maxen his dream in the tale of *Breuddwyd Maxen*, (WM 183,18-23).

27. *gwialen*. The translation is conjectural, since the usual meaning of *gwialen* is 'twig, sapling', etc. It is derived from a Brittonic root meaning 'to turn, weave, bend' (GPC compares Lat. *vieo*), so that 'plait' or 'head-dress' seems appropriate in the context.

30. *mywydd* is unattested elsewhere. Several MSS offer various misspellings suggesting an original *muchudd* 'jet'. This is rendered the more probable as the original reading by the fact that *muchudd*, like *mwyalch* (see below on l.37) was a conventional colour-comparison for a girl's hair or brow; cf. Gruffudd Gryg *muchudd o liw* DGG[2] LXXII, l.19, and Chotzen, 210.

37. *Peredur*. In the *Historia Peredur fab Efrawc* (WM cols. 117-178) this incident is related with the only difference that in the romance the bird killed in the snow is a duck, while in Dafydd's version it is a blackbird, perhaps because the blackbird's hue was a conventional colour-comparison for a girl's beauty; cf. GDG 30 l.39 (*dyn*) *ael blu mwyalch*; Gr. ap Maredudd, *mwyalchliw ddwyael*, RBP 1318, l.31; and Chotzen 210 for further examples.

41. *llwyn Esyllt* like the similar phrase *cae Esyllt* 'E's chaplet' (GPC 382) probably denotes any treasure or valuable object; here used for the girl's hair. For Esyllt cf. no.9, l.29 above; TYP 349-50.

44. *morwyn* refers to the blackbird; cf. Dafydd's description of the cuckoo as *morwyn gyflog Mai* 'paid serving-maid of May', no.10, l.32.

46. *paentiad* is from earlier E. *peinte* 'paint' (EEW 195). The meaning seems to be that the girl's colouring, with its vivid black, white, and red, is worthy of God's own artistry as 'painter' of the colours in nature. *Talu* here means 'to deserve, be worthy of', cf. CA 70.

53. *organ*. Here used for a part of the body, i.e. Dyddgu's head.

56. *Barned rhawt*. Note the direct address to the audience.

14

8. *gorwyllt*. Usually 'wild', as in GDG 116, l.10, but also 'uncultivated' in reference to land; hence 'untamed'. Possibly 'virginal', cf. no.13, l.28 (of Dyddgu).

9. *yn gronfferf*. i.e. with a good figure. 'Round and plump' is Dr Parry's suggestion.

11. *Indeg*, daughter of *Garwy Hir*, a legendary heroine of whom very little is known, though her name in frequently cited as a standard of beauty by Dafydd and his successors; see TYP 412-3.

25. *dan laswydr*. Elsewhere Dafydd employs *ffenestr* for a window, GDG 64,20, *ffenestr wydrlen* GDG 40,9. *Gwydr* implies that the window was of glass, not just a wooden shutter. Glass windows were already known to Cynddelw Brydydd Mawr: *trwy ffenestri gwydyr yd ymgwelynt*, RBP 1425,25-6.
Dyn is ambiguous as to gender, (cf. no.10, l.18 and n.) but here refers to the girl, being contrasted with *gŵr* 'her husband' in l.26.

36. *llyfr ei ffug*. Lit. 'the book of his deceit'.

39. *Y Deau*, i.e. Deheubarth, South Wales.

40. *barcud* lit. 'kite, buzzard', but here used fig. for a snatcher, plunderer.

44. *Brân*, a raven (lit. crow). Alternatively a personal name, and this is not impossible here. According to Geoffrey of Monmouth's *Historia Regum Britanniae* III, ch.I ff. (followed in BD 33 ff.), Brân was a son of Dyfnwal Moelmud who conquered Rome and became emperor, with the help of his faithful friend and brother Beli; see TYP 132, 284.

46. *am fenffyg*. Benffyg is an old form of *benthyg* (from Lat. *beneficium*). Morfudd is of course the 'lending' here referred to. With the episode described cf. no.39 (GDG 126) below.

15

This is an enigmatic poem. After speaking of his love for Morfudd, for Elen, wife of Robin Nordd, and for Dyddgu, Dafydd refers obscurely to an un-named fourth girl—we are told only that she is *rhudd-deg* 'ruddy-fair' and that she belongs to Gwynedd. The necessity for secrecy in the affairs of love was one of the conventions of *amour courtois*, and is emphasized frequently by Dafydd; cf. no.11 above, and GDG 30, 1.20; 40, ls.31-2; 78, ls.1-2.

2. *Seren cylch Nant-y-seri*. This means Morfudd; see n. to no.34, 1.32 below. Cwmseiri lies a mile and a half from Capel Bangor, only a few miles from Brogynin. Since *nant* and *cwm* may be used interchangeably it is likely that this is the same place. On this see B.viii, 141.

6. *anrhaith* has the primary meaning of 'plunder, booty', but also 'treasure, darling'. The two meanings are present here, as in l.18.

7. *newid*, i.e. *cyfnewid* 'exchange, barter', here used figuratively; cf. no.14 above, 1.46 for the idea of Morfudd's husband 'lending' her to the poet.

9-12. These lines seem to mean that for fear of divine anger Dafydd has renounced his love for Morfudd, whatever the cost to himself, but that she does not repent her love. The clauses are inverted in such a way as to obscure the sense: the poet has desisted *in order that* he may not anger God.

14. *porthmonyn* from E. *port(h)mon* 'a burgher, one of a select number of citizens chosen to administer the affairs of a borough'—OED. Only in Welsh did the word develop the meaning 'merchant' (and later 'drover').

16. *ryw benaig*. Penaig = Pennaeth 'leading man' i.e. 'burgher', the equivalent of *porthmonyn* in its primary meaning; cf. 1.45 below. On *Robin Nordd* see B. VIII, 144-5; GDG xxxiv (GDG[2] xvi,xxix). 'Robert le Northern' was the name of a burgess of Aberystwyth who is listed in legal proceedings for the year 1342, when he is alleged to have had stolen from him a silver cup by a certain Hywel ap Gronw. *Robertus le Northern* is also listed as one of the bailiffs of Aberystwyth who swore allegiance to the Black Prince in 1343; B. XXV, 26-7.

18. *llediaith lud:* Elen and her husband were obviously both English.

28. *Medlai* 'variegated, motley'; cf. *mwtlai*, used of the Magpie's wings, no.25, (GDG 63), 1.57 below. From E. *mottelee*, first attested in Chaucer's *Prologue* 1.271, where interestingly enough, it is also used of a merchant's clothes: Dafydd's two instances are therefore older than any recorded in English. If *medlai* in 1.28 is to be taken as an adj. rather than a noun, the couplet could be rendered 'if I get motley cloth (in addition), she will make me satisfied'.

54. *gwych reg:* perhaps deliberately ambiguous, since it could as well mean 'an excellent gift'.

56. *Nyf hoen*. As Ifor Williams showed, this is the Irish heroine *Niamh* of the Ossianic Cycle, beloved by Oisín; see DGG[2], 187; IGE[2], 360, and cf. TYP lxxxii, n. (This name is now commonly rendered *Nia*, following T. Gwynn Jones's rendering of the story.) Cf. no.12, 1.69

above, and n., and Dafydd's single reference to the other Irish heroine *Deirdre*, no.17, l.21 below. Since *nyf* also means 'snow' it is often difficult to distinguish which meaning is intended by poets.

16

There is no certainty that this is a 'Morfudd' poem, though the content strongly suggests that this is so. Cf. the next poem, no.17, where Morfudd's name is given.

1. *f'eurchwaer*. *Chwaer* is not necessarily 'sister', but frequently denotes 'sweetheart, mistress'.

5. *byd* is ambiguous, since it can also mean 'darling', as in no.13, l.58 above. Alternatively, therefore 'my darling greets me'.

4. I understand *trin* as a verb-noun; hence the comma after 'strength'.

7. *a'm bu*. Dr Parry's emendation: the MSS all read *y'm bu*.

17. *Enid*. A legendary heroine; wife of Geraint fab Erbin in the Mabinogion romance which bears his name; TYP 347-8.

20. *Eigr*. Another legendary heroine, mother of Arthur according to *Brut y Brenhinedd*, rendering the story of Arthur's birth as told by Geoffrey of Monmouth, HRB VIII, chs.19-20, where the name is *Ygerna*. In the *Brut* she is said to be the daughter of *Amlawdd Wledig*; TYP 366. Dafydd cites Eigr as a standard of beauty more frequently than any other heroine.

25-34. I adopt Dr Parry's interpretation of the quadruple imagery in these lines (*Poetry Wales: Special Dafydd ap Gwilym number* (Spring, 1973), 41, and I take this oportunity to correct my earlier misinterpretation of these lines as one of the examples of Dafydd's use of triple images (*Tradn. and Innov.*, 47).

33. A 'groyne' is a timber palisade on the shore to stop the encroachment of the sea. This is the only example of *argor* cited in GPC, which compares *côr* as in *bangor, cored*.

35. *hydreg*. The translation is conjectural: no other instance of this word has been recorded.

38. *tref tad*. 'patrimony'. The contrast intended is probably that between Dafydd's conduct of love by stolen meetings, and the assured possession of the girl's husband.

45. *Cadfan*. A saint who was the traditional founder of the church at Tywyn, Meirionydd, and of Llangadfan, Powys; see Baring-Gould and Fisher, *Lives of the British Saints* ii, 1.

46. *Rhydeg ydoedd*. Cf. the last line of the following poem, *hi a fu deg*. Dr Parry cites both as examples of Dafydd's stylistic device of frequently closing a poem with a couplet of telling significance, often with a pronounced break in the middle of the last line (*Y Traethodydd* CXXXIII (Ebrill, 1978), 77-8).

17

This poem is one of four, GDG nos.136-9, in which Dafydd cites the critical advice allegedly given to him by a Friar; cf. no.43 below. There are many obscurities, some of which have been discussed by D.J.Bowen, Ll.C. VIII,231-5, and by Gwyn Thomas, *B*. XXVIII,405. I have adopted suggestions made by both in my rendering.

2. *Rhinllaes*. It is tempting to translate 'loose-virtued', but in view of the mock-complimentary description given to the Friar, this seems unlikely. Perhaps *llaes* 'loose, trailing' may refer to the customary widespread travels of the friars, referred to in l.7. In combination with *rhawn* ('horse-hair') *llaes* can hardly refer to the friar's hair, as he would have been tonsured (*foel-llwyd*, l.23). Perhaps he wore a rough hairy garment. There is a pun on the two meanings of *llaes* in the line.

4. *o gysgawd gosgedd*, obscure. If this is a close compound meaning 'of a shadowy form (appearance)' *gosgedd* should normally be lenited; see n. GDG p.541. I adopt the alternative of taking lines 4 and 5 together.

5. *Ner . . . o Rufain*, i.e. the Pope.

7. *Rhwyd* 'a net, snare'. Hence fig. for a ragged garment.

8. *Rhyw drawsbren*. A satirical expression for the Friar's role as spiritual mediator.

9. *Cerddor* is here 'craftsman, artificer', cf. GDG 143, l.10 *cerddor ystryw* 'craftsman of tricks, trickster'.

12. *Maharen* 'ram'. D.J.Bowen suggests that the ref. is to *Aries*, the first sign of the zodiac, which presides over the days from mid-March to mid-April: the combination with *nen* favours this interpretation.

16. *nid aml ar dwyll*. Ambiguous: either 'does not often deceive' or 'is not often deceived'. Since punctuation is not shown in the MSS. it is not absolutely certain whether the reference is to the Friar or to Morfudd. If the latter, the phrase can only be interpreted as ironical, in view of the frequent allusions to Morfudd's 'deceit'; exx: no.12, l.52; no.41, l.12.

17. *ben cun cant* is certainly ironical: something like 'my fine gentleman' conveys the nuance suggested.

18. *combr* 'fine line, cambric' (Fr. *cambrai*). This instance of the word, with two others by Dafydd, no.36, l.37; GDG 44, l.16; are the earliest recorded instances in Welsh.

20. *gwasgawd*. See n. to no.50, l.13. *Maith* 'long', but here 'tedious, wearisome'.

21-2. *dirdras fun*. GDG reads *fûm*, which makes it difficult to take the line otherwise than as intended to be spoken by Morfudd herself. However, Gwyn Thomas suggests reading *fun* (*bun* 'girl') for *fûm*, following the reading of two of the MSS. Dr Parry (in conversation) recommends the acceptance of this emendation, which I have made in the text accordingly. It makes the two lines an appropriate sequel to the Friar's previous words.

ail Derdri. This is Dafydd's single allusion to the tragic heroine of the Irish Ulster Cycle, and it bears witness to the knowledge of her story in Wales (cf. n. to *Nyf*, no.15, l.56 above). Her story told how she was betrothed to the aged king Conchobar, but eloped with her young lover Naoise, eventually dying for love when she dashed her head against a stone. The Friar's sardonic meaning in this passage appears to be that just as a shift of cambric will be soiled after a week's wear, so the girl's body (i.e. that of Morfudd) will decay and become even blacker (*duach*) and more corrupt than the soiled shift. This is the Friar's grimly repeated warning throughout the four poems, and it is a sentiment which was to be developed more fully by Siôn Cent. *Du* has an extremely wide range of meanings, 'black, sad, gloomy, angry, bitter, wicked,' etc., any or all of which may be intended here. The Friar hints at the likelihood of a similar fate for Morfudd to that of Deirdre, if she too prefers her lover (Dafydd) to her husband *Y Bwa Bach*.

24. *brawd du*. The *brodyr du* were the Black Friars or Dominicans, just as the *brodyr llwyd* were the Grey Friars or Franciscans. But this interpretation seems questionable in the present context, since the Friar has been called *llwyd* in the previous line, and GDG nos. 136 and 137 (no.43 below) are addressed to Grey Friars. I therefore render *du* here as 'gloomy'.

25-6. *Ni pheidiwn . . . â Morfudd*. These lines closely resemble those in an *englyn* in which Dafydd replies to another *englyn* by Gruffudd Gryg (GDG p.416) in which he suggests that Morfudd's husband had threatened to bring down the rigours of the law upon Dafydd.

26. *oerfab*. Used also by Rhys Goch Eryri, IGE[2] 301,7. The precise significance can only be guessed: 'foolish' is an equally likely alternative.

31. Lit. 'on a harassed complexion'. *Erlyn* 'persecution', etc. (GPC); the verbal adj. formed from the root of the verb *erlidiaf* 'follow, persecute, harass'.

35. *braisg*. Conjecturally, I take *braisg* as qualifying *brad*. But an alternative meaning 'pregnant' is recorded in GPC on the basis of *Morris Letters* ii, 323 where *braisg* is given as the SW equivalent of NW *beichiog*. Morfudd's pregnancy is alluded to in GDG 85,29-32, so the possibility of this meaning for *braisg* should here be kept in mind.

un anun. The 'one' who is rendered sleepless evidently means the poet.

37. *brag* 'malt liquor', used fig. for the best or most choice of anything.

42. *henlleidr*. Love is the 'old' and therefore 'accustomed, familiar' robber who steals the poet's sleep. Cf. *y lleidrwas llwyd*, no.10, l.7.

43-4. *Hudolaidd . . . Hudoles*. For Morfudd's 'enchantment' cf. no.12 above.

44. *llwyd* 'grey (haired)' seems appropriate in the context, though 'pale' is also possible.

45. *Henllath*. Dr Parry explains that a *llath* 'rod' was the bent stick which discharged the missile from the *mangonell*, a siege implement used for hurling stones (from Fr. and E. *mangonel(le)*, EEW 75), a thoroughly new and up-to-date weapon. *Gwyddeleg* 'Irish' may here be merely a term of opprobrium rather than an exact description; Dr Parry (p.542) cites similar instances from the poets in which 'Irish' is a derogatory term.

46. *Hafod*, a summer shieling where the cattle were kept.

18

This lively dialogue has been compared by a number of writers to poems conforming with the convention of the *pastourelle*, which flourished in the literature of northern France during the twelfth and thirteenth centuries. The *pastourelle* was a poem about the (usually unsuccessful) attempts to seduce a country girl by a man of superior birth or sophistication. For comment on the resemblance see Ifor Williams, THSC 1913-14, 120-1; P.Dronke in *Dafydd ap Gwilym a Chanu Serch yr Oesoedd Canol* (ed. J.Rowlands), 3. But the differences from the continental model are great: so that here, as in other instances, in which Dafydd may have been aware of the existence of a foreign literary convention, he treats it in so individual a fashion as virtually to parody it. Cf. nos.41 and 42 below.

2. *gwŷr crefydd Cred*. A direct address by the poet to his audience—here, apparently, a monastic audience. Other instances of direct address are no.5 (GDG 121), l.1; no.13 (GDG 45), l.56; no.22 (GDG 118), l.22; GDG 51, l.51.

4. *amaeth*, cf. *mab ael y fro* l.19. In the continental poems the man is always of superior station, never a countryman.

7. *alarch mwyn*. Gentleness is not a characteristic one would easily associate with a swan, but rather the opposite. The ambiguity (probably intentional) is reinforced by *call* in the following line, which can mean both 'wise, discreet, sensible', and also 'sharp, wily'.

11. *Cydgerdded*. The meaning of the innuendo is indicated by the use of the same word in no.11, l.34 above, where *cydgerdded coed a gordderch* is listed among the delights to be shared with Morfudd in the forest.

13. *gosyml*. Lit. 'foolish, simple, artless, honest'.

am forwyn lân. *Glân* can also mean 'uncorrupted, undefiled' so that it is intentionally ambiguous.

16. *Canmolid*. Old 3rd. sg. ending of the pres. indic.; GMW 119. Alternatively '[in turn] she praises handsome poets'.

17. There is no obvious explanation of the reference to the wars, unless it is here a side-glance at the role of knight as wooer in the *pastourelle*.

21. *Llanbadarn*. i.e. the church of the parish in which Brogynin is situated. Cf. no.38 below.

29. *diledach do*. Lit. 'generation of noble lineage'. Here used ironically.

30. *Er cynnen*, etc. This may merely signify idle gossip.

33. *dyn eiddig*. Probably this means any prying or interfering person, as *dyn eiddig* does not necessarily refer specifically to Morfudd's husband, but is frequently used in a more general sense.

37. *hocrell* is not necessarily pejorative; cf. no.14, l.4 above, but with *afrywiog*, 'hussy' seems justified in the context.

38. *nith y gog*. The only other recorded e.g. of this idiom is *Gwaith Lewis Mon* XCIV, 25, *Ni tharia gwen, nith i'r gog*. As in the present instance, the meaning seems to be 'fickle, volatile'.

19

This is, strictly speaking, a *llatai* or love-messenger poem: as such it would deserve a place in the next section, were it not that the messenger is nowhere identified. Since he is two-footed (l.23) it is fair to assume that the poet is giving his instructions to a boy or a bird. *Llanllugan* was a Cistercian nunnery in Powys on the Welsh Marches (*Mars*, 1.2), founded *circa* 1236 (HW 603).

1. *dadlitia*. 2 sg. imperative; the first of a series of injunctions to the messenger. On *llatai* see introduction p.xxiii above.

9-10. *i Lan falch Llugan*. An e.g. of *trychiad* or tmesis, a device favoured by the poets, particularly with proper names (CD 83).
rhai lliwgalch. Comparisons with the whiteness of lime, as Chotzen points out (*Recherches*, 203) is one of the conventional expressions for a girl's beauty which belongs in common to Irish and Welsh literature. See below on l.19.

12. *Y sieler*, i.e. the Abbess.

19. Comparisons with snow and with gossamer are stock comparisons for female beauty taken over from the Gogynfeirdd, who employ them frequently. To apply such terms to the beauty of nuns cannot but be lightly ironical, in view of the associations of the words: similarly, *lliwgalch* l.10, *hoyne eiry* l.32. (See Chotzen, 203ff., *Trad and Innov.* 18-19).

20. *Gwenoliaid*. In one of the poems of the *apocrypha* a nun is similarly compared to a swallow; DGG² XXV, 32; OBWV no.59, *fal gwennol ar fol gwaneg*.

19. *arial gwawn oror*. A desirable emendation would be to read *gwaun* for *gwawn* 'their nature white as snow on moorland's edge', but this lacks MS support.

22. The same phrase *araf eurfun* describes Morfudd in no.6, l.50 above.

27. *Or caf*. Dr Parry's emendation. For *o* with perfective *ry* followed by the radical see GMW 241.

28. *ffreutur*, from Fr. *fraitur* or E. *freitur* (EEW 172,191), the 'frater' or dining hall in a monastery or convent.
dyn eglur dâl. Certain poets of the period make jibes at nuns for exposing their foreheads. According to Coulton, *Medieval Panorama*

(Cambridge, 1938) 277, these ought to have been amply covered by the nuns' wimple. He refers to Chaucer's Prioress, *Prologue* lines 154-5, *But sikerly she had a fair forheed/it was almost a spanne brood, I trow*. Cf. also DGG[2] XXV, 13-16 (one of the apocryphal poems attributed to Dafydd), *A'i thâl . . . Och Dduw Tad, na chuddiwyd hwn! . . . mŷr eiry*, etc. *Eglur* combines the meanings of 'shining, bright' and 'evident, obvious, discernible'.

29. *Câr* combines the meanings of 'friend' and 'relative'.

30. *y glochyddes* fem. of *clochydd* 'sexton'; hence 'female sexton, songstress, chantress'.

III. BIRDS AND ANIMALS (20-28)

20 The Song Thrush

Yesterday I heard the cock Thrush
with loving song in pure and limpid tone
in diction fine and clear, auspiciously endowed;
4 from underneath the birch-trees came his voice.
What sweeter composition could there be
than his diminutive whistling?

For matins three lessons he reads
8 in our midst—feathers are his chasuble—
far off across the lands is heard
his voice from out the thicket and his clear loud shout.
He is the hill-side's prophet, longing's powerful author,
12 bright poet of passion in the wooded glen.
Each clear accent on the valley's brow
he sings, impelled by dear vivacity,
each happy song in poetry's art,
16 each stave of music, every tune,
each gentle melody to please a girl
debating over love's priorities.
He is a preacher, he reads lections,
20 sweet, pure, and undimmed is his inspiration.
He is the faultless poet of Ovid's craft of song,
a gentle primate of the great order of May.

I know him, from his birch-wood trysting place
24 he leads all woodland birds in song,
a joyful chorus from the lovely glade
of all the odes and measures that belong to love.
He is a merry bird who sings in hazel trees
28 in the fair forest, a winged angel—
it were a wonder if the expert birds
of Paradise who love him [could]
revolving memory's store with artistry
32 recite all the songs he sang.

21 The Mistle Thrush

Faultlessly punctual, every May there comes
to the topmost branches in the wood
to the shining hazel-fortress, a triumphant singer
4 —agile beneath his wings of grey—
the fine cock Thrush (gift greater than an organ):
by the law's authority he sings.

Assiduous preacher in all languages,
8 he was the chieftain of the woodland,
Sheriff he is amidst birch-woods in May,

70

Y Ceiliog Bronfraith (28)

Y ceiliog serchog ei sôn
Bronfraith dilediaith loywdon,
Deg loywiaith, doe a glywais,
4 Dawn fad lon, dan fedw ei lais,
Ba ryw ddim a fai berach
Plethiad no'i chwibaniad bach?

Plygain y darllain deirllith,
8 Plu yw ei gasul i'n plith.
Pell y clywir uwch tiroedd
Ei lef o lwyn a'i loyw floedd.
Proffwyd rhiw, praff awdur hoed,
12 Pencerdd gloyw angerdd glyngoed.
Pob llais diwael yn ael nant
A gân ef o'i gu nwyfiant,
Pob caniad mad mydr angerdd,
16 Pob cainc o'r organ, pob cerdd,
Pob cwlm addwyn er mwyn merch,
Ymryson am oreuserch.
Pregethwr a llywr llên,
20 Pêr ewybr, pur ei awen.
Prydydd cerdd Ofydd ddifai,
Primas mwyn prif urddas Mai.

Adwaen ef o'i fedw nwyfoed,
24 Awdur cerdd adar y coed,
Adlais lon o dlos lannerch,
Odlau a mesurau serch.
Edn diddan a gân ar gyll
28 Yng nglwysgoed, angel esgyll,
Odid ydoedd i adar
Paradwys cyfrwys a'i câr
O dro iawngof drwy angerdd
32 Adrodd a ganodd o gerdd.

Y Ceiliog Bronfraith (123)

Y mae bob Mai difeioed
Ar flaenau canghennau coed
Cantor hydr ar gaer wydr gyll,
4 Esgud dan wyrddion esgyll—
Ceiliog teg, rheg rhag organ,
Bronfraith drwy gyfraith a gân.

Pregethwr maith pob ieithoedd,
8 Pendefig ar goedwig oedd;
Siryf fydd ym medw-wydd Mai,

and would sing in seven score tongues,
a worthy Justice on the tip of twigs,
12   Steward of the Court (among) the matted leaves,
perpetual teacher of my fellowship
linguist on crest of mansion's planted trees,
a trusty lad on the green crests above
16   and my companion in the wood;
a singer of the noblest kind of song,
epitomizing wisdom and all eloquence.

     . . . by my faith in Creirwy
20   that the girl should go with me . . .
Bravely and with pride he flew
and with fair divinatory power
through his great love, from place to place,
24   from grove to grove, for the girl's sake
he learned to greet and to descend
where the girl was—and she was gentle [too].

     He fairly spoke my message
28   for he is a reliable and beneficial lord.
In his letter of authority he showed
the truth ([he was one of] a throng nurtured together),
his declaration he read out in verse
32   from his green shining house, fair comely [words of] praise.
In lengthy legal terms he summoned me
at summer's opening, from his parchment role.
I lost—I wished no bitterness—
36   the reward of [all my] work, a forfeit of disdain.
And though I lost, [there was], I know, a gain
[from] forfeits under the green trees:
the girl's exceeding love will not be lost to me
40   [with its] fair powers, nor my complaint to her.
If the messenger prove skilful
with wisdom he will manage to entice her.

     May God (her intent is concealed)
44   accomplish, for my sake and for that of fair [St] David,
an easy contract [with] my darling most wise
concerning the messenger, that superb champion,
to leave him [undisturbed] with his exquisite song,
48   the poet of love from Paradise,
a judge, fine patron of the month of May,
and famed for supreme wisdom; it befits him there.

Saith ugeiniaith a ganai;
Ustus gwiw ar flaen gwiail,
12 Ystiwart llys dyrys dail;
Athro maith fy nghyweithas,
Ieithydd ar frig planwydd plas;
Cywirwas ar friglas fry,
16 Cydymaith mewn coed ymy;
Ceiniad yw goreuryw gân,
A gynnull pwyll ac anian.

    mwy Creirwy cred
20 Am y fun a mi fyned
Hyder a balch ehedeg
A wnaeth â dewiniaeth deg;
O blas i blas drwy draserch,
24 O lwyn i lwyn er mwyn merch,
Dysg annerch a disgynnu
Lle'r oedd y fun; llariaidd fu.

    Dywad yn deg fy neges,
28 Diwyd fydd, pen-llywydd lles.
Dangos a wnaeth, cydfaeth cant,
Y gwir yn ei lythr gwarant.
Darlleodd ymadrodd mydr,
32 Deg lwyswawd, o'i dŷ glaswydr.
Gelwis yn faith gyfreithiol
Arnaf, ddechrau haf, o'r rhol.
Collais, ni ddymunais ddig,
36 Daered rym, dirwy dremyg.
Cyd collwn, gwn, o gynnydd,
Dirwyon dan wyrddion wŷdd,
Ni chyll traserch merch i mi,
40 Cain nerthoedd, na'm cwyn wrthi.
O bydd cymen y gennad
O brudd, ef a gais ei brad.

    Duw a wnêl, gêl ei gofeg,
44 Erof fi a Dewi deg,
Amod rhwydd, fy myd rhyddoeth,
Am y gennad, geimiad goeth,
Ei adel ef a'i lef lwys,
48 Brydydd serch o Baradwys,
Ynad, mygr gynheiliad Mai,
Enw gwiwddoeth; yno y gweddai.

22 The Seagull

Fair Seagull on the tide, in truth
your colour like the snow or the white moon;
unpolluted is your beauty,
4 a fragment of the sun, gauntlet of the salt sea.
You are light upon the ocean wave,
swift, proud, fish-eating bird.
Yonder you would ride at anchor
8 holding hands with me, sea-lily.
Like a [white] page of brilliant texture
a nun on the wave's crest you are.

[There is] a girl ripe for far-flung praise:
12 fly round the rampart and the castle
and look if you may see her, Seagull,
a girl of Eigr's form, on the fair fortress.
Tell her my message of desire:
16 Let her choose me: go to the girl,
if she's alone, be bold enough to greet her,
be skilful with the gently-nurtured girl
to win advantage; say that I cannot stay alive
20 —a kind and cultured youth—unless I win her.

I love her, with passion's full support;
ah, men, there never loved—
nor Myrddin with his goodly flattering speech,
24 nor [yet] Taliesin—one of fairer form.
a girl like Venus(?), copper-haired, contended for,
most perfect her surpassing form.
O Seagull, if [only] you could see
28 her cheek, who is the loveliest in the world,
unless I win a gentlest greeting [from her]
this girl will bring about my death.

23 The Skylark

Triumphant hours are the Lark's
who circles skywards from his home each day:
world's early riser, with bubbling golden song,
4 towards the firmament, guardian of April's gate.

Gracious of voice, disposing harmonies,
sweet is your labour on a joyful course,
making a poem above the hazel grove

Yr Wylan (118)

Yr wylan deg ar lanw dioer
Unlliw ag eiry neu wenlloer,
Dilwch yw dy degwch di,
4   Darn fel haul, dyrnfol heli.
Ysgafn ar don eigion wyd,
Esgudfalch edn bysgodfwyd.
Yngo'r aud wrth yr angor
8   Lawlaw â mi, lili môr.
Llythr unwaith llathr ei annwyd,
Lleian ym mrig llanw môr wyd.

    Cyweirglod bun, câi'r glod bell,
12   Cyrch ystum caer a chastell.
Edrych a welych, wylan,
Eigr o liw ar y gaer lân.
Dywed fy ngeiriau duun.
16   Dewised fi, dos at fun.
Byddai'i hun, beiddia'i hannerch,
Bydd fedrus wrth foethus ferch
Er budd; dywed na byddaf,
20   Fwynwas coeth, fyw onis caf.

    Ei charu'r wyf, gwbl nwyf nawdd,
Och wŷr, erioed ni charawdd
Na Myrddin wenieithfin iach,
24   Na Thaliesin ei thlysach.
Siprys dyn giprys dan gopr,
Rhagorbryd rhy gyweirbropr.

    Och wylan, o chai weled
28   Grudd y ddyn lanaf o Gred,
Oni chaf fwynaf annerch,
Fy nihenydd fydd y ferch.

Yr Ehedydd (114)

Oriau hydr yr ehedydd
A dry fry o'i dŷ bob dydd,
Borewr byd, berw aur bill,
4   Barth â'r wybr, brothor Ebrill.

    Llef radlon, llywiwr odlau,
Llwybr chweg, llafur teg yw'r tau:
Llunio cerdd uwchben llwyn cyll,

8 with the gentle feat of your grey wings.
You have a mind to preach
(dear office) and with language excellent,
a powerful song [that springs from] the source of faith
12 deep-seated privileges before the Lord.
Upwards you fly, with Cai's own attribute,
and upwards as you go you sing each song
a splendid charm near to the rampart of the stars,
16 a long-revolving journey to the heights.
Your feat [is now] accomplished, you have climbed high
enough,
you have indeed attained to your reward.

Let each fortunate creature praise
20 his Maker, the immaculate pure Ruler,
let him praise God, as was decreed,
a thousand hear it. He should be praised, do not desist.
Author of the ways of love, where are you?
24 with dear sweet voice, dressed in grey-brown,
pure and delightful is your song,
brown songster, one inspired,
a *cantor* from the chapel of the Lord
28 skilled are you, and your augury is good.
Completely privileged, with well-proportioned song,
your full head-dress is a crest of grey.
Make for the familiar firmament,
32 song-bearing, to that wild untrodden land.

Man sees you up aloft
in truth, when day is at its height;
when you may come [thus] to worship,
36 this gift God One and Three has given you:
no branch of tree high up above the world
sustains you—you have [your own] speech—
but the grace of the just Father
40 His abundant miracles and His design.

Teacher of praise, between the light and dark,
descend, may God protect your wings:
my fair brown bird, and brother in authority,
44 if you will go as my love-messenger,
carry a greeting to one fair of form,
brilliantly gifted, Gwynedd's moon.
Seek a kiss—or even two—from her
48 to bring back here to me [again].
King of the intricate waters of the sky,
go yonder to approach her court.
May I, one morning, be with her,
52 though it for ever will enrage the Jealous One.

76

8 Lledneisgamp llwydion esgyll.
   Bryd y sydd gennyd, swydd gu,
   A brig iaith, ar bregethu.
   Braisg dôn o ffynnon y ffydd,
12 Breiniau dwfn gerbron Dofydd.
   Fry yr ai, iawnGai angerdd,
   Ac fry y ceny bob cerdd;
   Mygr swyn gerllaw magwyr sêr,
16 Maith o chwyldaith uchelder.
   Dogn achub, digon uched
   Y dringaist, neur gefaist ged.

   Moled pob mad greadur
20 Ei Greawdr, pefr lywiawdr pur.
   Moli Duw mal y dywaid,
   Mil a'i clyw, hoff yw, na phaid.
   Modd awdur serch, mae 'dd ydwyd?
24 Mwyngroyw y llais mewn grae llwyd.
   Cathl lân a diddan yw'r dau,
   Cethlydd awenydd winau.
   Cantor o gapel Celi,
28 Coel fydd teg, celfydd wyd di.
   Cyfan fraint, aml gywraint gân,
   Copa llwyd yw'r cap llydan.
   Cyfeiria'r wybr cyfarwydd,
32 Cywyddol, dir gwyndir gŵydd.

   Dyn uwchben a'th argenfydd
   Dioer pan fo hwyaf y dydd.
   Pan ddelych i addoli,
36 Dawn a'th roes Duw Un a Thri:
   Nid brig pren uwchben y byd
   A'th gynnail, mae iaith gennyd,
   Ond rhadau y deau Dad
40 A'i firagl aml a'i fwriad.

   Dysgawdr mawl rhwng gwawl a gwyll,
   Disgyn, nawdd Duw ar d'esgyll.
   Fy llwyteg edn, yn llatai,
44 A'm brawd awdurdawd, od ai,
   Annerch gennyd wiwbryd wedd,
   Loyw ei dawn, leuad Wynedd.
   A chais un o'i chusanau
48 Yman i'w ddwyn ym, neu ddau.
   Dyfri yr wybrfor dyrys,
   Dos draw hyd gerllaw ei llys.
   Byth genthi bwyf fi a fydd,
52 Bâr Eiddig, un boreddydd.

So intricate [would be] the payment for your homicide
that no man dares to slay you.
Were he to try to do so—daring turmoil
56 and terror to the Jealous One—you would survive.
Enormous is the cage encompassing your perch:
so far you are from hand that draws a bow.
The bowman, trampling on the ground, is sad,
60 his great purpose will turn out clumsily,
his anger frustrate. Rise above his reach,
and let him with his arrow pass you by.

24   The Woodland Mass

I was in a happy place today,
under mantles of lovely green hazels,
listening, at dawn of day,
4 to the ingenious cock Thrush
singing a polished *englyn*
with portents and bright lessons.

[He is] a stranger, wise his nature,
8 a grey messenger who came here from afar:
he came from fair Carmarthenshire,
being thus requested by my golden girl.
With eloquence, though with no verbal warranty
12 his course is towards Nentyrch valley—
Morfudd [it was] who had commissioned him—
the fosterson of May, versed in the art of song.
He wore about him a vestment
16 of the flowers of May's sweet branches,
and his chasuble (one would suppose)
of the winged green mantles of the wind.

By great God, there was not there
20 as roofing to the chancel anything but gold.
I heard there, in language loud and clear
a chanting, long and without cease,
and the gospel read distinctly
24 to the parish—no unseemly haste.
There was raised upon a mound for us
a perfect leaf as consecrated wafer,
and the eloquent slender Nightingale
28 from the corner of the near-by thicket
(the valley's wandering poetess) rang out
the Sanctus bell to the assembly, with clear whistle,
and lifted up the consecrated Host

Mae arnad werth cyngherthladd
Megys na lefys dy ladd.
Be rhôn a'i geisio, berw hy,
56 Bw i Eiddig, ond byw fyddy.
Mawr yw'r sercl yt o berclwyd,
Â bwa a llaw mor bell wyd.
Trawstir sathr, trist yw'r saethydd,
60 Trwstan o'i fawr amcan fydd;
Trwch ei lid, tro uwch ei law
Tra êl â'i hobel heibiaw.

Offeren y Llwyn (122)

Lle digrif y bûm heddiw
Dan fentyll y gwyrddgyll gwiw,
Yn gwarando ddechrau dydd
4 Y ceiliog bronfraith celfydd
Yn canu englyn alathr,
Arwyddion a llithion llathr.

Pellennig, pwyll ei annwyd,
8 Pell ei siwrnai'r llatai llwyd.
Yma y doeth o swydd goeth Gaer,
Am ei erchi o'm eurchwaer,
Geiriog, heb un gair gwarant,
12 Sef y cyrch, i Nentyrch nant.
Morfudd a'i hanfonasai,
Mydr ganiadaeth mab maeth Mai.
Amdano yr oedd gasmai
16 O flodau mwyn gangau Mai,
A'i gasul, debygesynt,
O esgyll, gwyrdd fentyll, gwynt.

Nid oedd yna, myn Duw mawr,
20 Ond aur oll yn do'r allawr.
Mi a glywwn mewn gloywiaith
Ddatganu, nid methu, maith,
Darllain i'r plwyf, nid rhwyf rhus,
24 Efengyl yn ddifyngus.
Codi ar fryn ynn yna
Afrlladen o ddeilen dda.
Ac eos gain fain fangaw
28 O gwr y llwyn gar ei llaw,
Clerwraig nant, i gant a gân
Cloch aberth, clau ei chwiban,
A dyrchafel yr aberth

32   to the sky above the copse
with adoration to our Lord the Father,
with a chalice of ecstasy and love.

   I am well-pleased with this psalmody:
36   the gentle birch-tree thicket fostered it.

25   The Magpie's Advice

   I, sickened for I loved a sparkling girl,
[being] in a wood, making a charm of love
one day—it was a snatch of powerful song—
4   beneath a cloudless sky, when April came,
with the Nightingale among green branches
and the smart Blackbird on a leafy battlement
—a woodland poet, he lives in a forest house—
8   and the Thrush on a verdant tree-top
singing loudly before the rain
with golden notes, upon a tapestry of green;
and the Lark, with serene voice
12   dear, wise-voiced bird, with a grey head-dress,
ascending, in complete abandonment
with a song to the zenith of the sky
from the bare plain, a hovering prince
16   he climbs with backward turn.

   I, the poet of a lissom girl
in the greenwood, joyful enough
yet weary-hearted [from] remembering [her];
20   my spirit being refreshed within
for sheer joy of seeing the trees
with vital force, having donned new clothes,
and the shoots of vine and wheat
24   after the sun-shot rain and dew,
and the green leaves, on the valley's brow,
and the thorn-tree, fresh, white-nosed.
By Heaven, there was also
28   the Magpie, most cunning bird in the world
building—lovely stratagem—
in the tangled crest of the thicket's core
an ambitious tenement of leaves and clay and lime,
32   and her mate was helping her.

   The Magpie muttered—indictment of [my] anguish—
proud, sharp-beaked, upon the thorn-bush:
'Great is your fuss, a vain and bitter chant,

32 Hyd y nen uwchben y berth;
   A chrefydd i'n Dofydd Dad,
   A charegl nwyf a chariad.
   Bodlon wyf i'r ganiadaeth,
36 Bedwlwyn o'r coed mwyn a'i maeth.

Cyngor y Biogen (63)

A mi'n glaf er mwyn gloywferch,
Mewn llwyn yn prydu swyn serch,
Ddiwrnawd, pybyrwawd pill,
4 Ddichwerw wybr, ddechrau Ebrill,
A'r eos ar ir wiail,
A'r fwyalch deg ar fwlch dail—
Bardd coed mewn trefngoed y trig—
8 A bronfraith ar ir brenfrig
Cyn y glaw yn canu'n glau
Ar las bancr eurlais bynciau;
A'r ehedydd, lonydd lais,
12 Cwcyllwyd edn cu callais,
Yn myned mewn lludded llwyr
Â chywydd i entrych awyr,
(O'r noethfaes, edlaes edling,
16 Yn wysg ei gefn drefn y dring);
Minnau, fardd rhiain feinir,
Yn llawen iawn mewn llwyn ir,
A'r galon fradw yn cadw cof,
20 A'r enaid yn ir ynof
Gan addwyned gweled gwŷdd,
Gwaisg nwyf, yn dwyn gwisg newydd,
Ac egin gwin a gwenith
24 Ar ôl glaw araul a gwlith,
A dail glas ar dâl y glyn,
A'r draenwydd yn ir drwynwyn;
Myn y Nef, yr oedd hefyd
28 Y bi, ffelaf edn o'r byd,
Yn adeilad, brad brydferth,
Yn nhalgrychedd perfedd perth,
O ddail a phriddgalch, balch borth,
32 A'i chymar yn ei chymorth.

Syganai'r bi, cyni cwyn,
Drwynllem falch ar y draenllwyn:

'Mawr yw dy ferw, goeg chwerw gân,

36 old man, all by yourself,
      better it were for you, by Mary of eloquent fame,
      to be beside the fire, you old grey man,
      rather than here, amidst the dew and rain,
40 in the greenwood, in a chilly shower.'

      'Shut up, and leave me here in peace
      if only for an hour, until my tryst.
      It is my passion for a lovely, faithful girl
44 that causes me this tumult.'

      'It is but vain for you, servant of passion,
      despicable grey old man, half imbecile;
      —a foolish sign of the labour of love—
48 to rave about a sparkling girl.'

      'You, Magpie, black your beak,
      infernal, very savage bird,
      you have—vain [your] interference (?)—
52 long toil and [even] greater labour;
      your nest is like a gorse-bush,
      a thick creel of broken, withered sticks;
      you have pied black plumage, dear and flawless,
56 [and] an ungainly shape with raven's head,
      you are motley, fair in hue,
      your home is ugly, and raucous your voice,
      and every kind of speech of far-off tongues
60 you have learned, black-speckled wing.
      You, Magpie, black your head,
      help me, if you are [so] wise,
      and give me the best advice
64 that you may know for my sore sickness.'

      'I would impart to you sound advice
      before May comes, and do it, if you will.
      You have no right, poet, to the handsome girl:
68 there is for you but one advice
      [since you are] so deep in verses, become a hermit,
      alas, you foolish man! and love no more.'

      By my faith, God witness it,
72 if ever yet I see a Magpie's nest
      from this time on, she will not have
      God knows, either egg or fledgeling.

36   Henwr, wrthyd dy hunan.
Gwell yt, myn Mair air aren,
Garllaw tân, y gŵr llwyd hen,
Nog yma 'mhlith gwlith a glaw
40   Yn yr irlwyn ar oerlaw.'

'Taw â'th sôn, gad fi'n llonydd
Ennyd awr oni fo dydd.
Mawrserch ar ddiweirferch dda
44   A bair ym y berw yma.'

'Ofer i ti, gweini gwŷd,
Llwyd anfalch gleirch lled ynfyd,
Ys mul arwydd am swydd serch,
48   Ymleferydd am loywferch.'

'Dydi, bi, du yw dy big,
Uffernol edn tra ffyrnig,
Mae i tithau, gau gofwy,
52   Swydd faith a llafur sydd fwy—
Tau nyth megis twyn eithin,
Tew fydd, cryw o frwydwydd crin.
Mae't blu brithu, cu cyfan,
56   *Affan* o bryd, a phen brân,
Mwtlai wyd di, mae't liw tyg,
Mae't lys hagr, mae't lais hygryg.
A phob iaith bybyriaith bell
60   A ddysgud, freith-ddu asgell.
Dydi, bi, du yw dy ben,
Cymorth fi, od wyd cymen.
Dyro ym gyngor gorau
64   A wypych i'r mawrnych mau.'

'Gwyddwn yt gyngor gwiwdda,
Cyn dêl Mai, ac o gwnai, gwna.
Ni ddylyy, fardd, harddfun,
68   Nid oes yt gyngor ond un:
Dwys iawn fydr, dos yn feudwy,
Och ŵr mul! ac na châr mwy.'

Llyma 'nghred, gwylied Geli,
72   O gwelaf nyth byth i'r bi,
Na bydd iddi hi o hyn
Nac wy, dioer, nac ederyn.

26   The Owl

It is a pity that the handsome Owl
being sad and sick, will not be silent:
she does not let me chant my prayer,
4   she is not quiet while stars are visible.
I cannot get (alack the prohibition!)
any peaceful sleep at all.
Her back, [like to] a house of bats (?),
8   is hunched against the rain and snow;
each night, with small charm to me,
in my ears—pennies of memory—
when that I close—inevitable pain—
12   my eyes—chieftains [who demand] respect—
this wakes me—[and] I have not slept since—
the voice and screeching of the Owl,
her frequent outcry and her laugh,
16   and poetry's travesty from her tongue.

From then—such is the way I am—
till break of day, with wretched energy
she sings a wretched kind of song—
20   'Hw-ddy-hw'—a lively gasp—
with energy, by Anna's grandson,
she incites the hounds of night.
Dirty she is, with two raucous cries,
24   big-headed, with a hateful shout,
broad-browed, and berry-bellied,
old wide-eyed catcher of mice,
busy, vile, and colourless,
28   shrivelled her voice, her colour that of tin,
high is her screech within ten woodlands,
alas the cry! a roebuck's fetter in a wood (?)
and her face, like that of a gentle human being,
32   and her form, she-fiend of birds.
Each unclean bird of alien kind
will harass her; is it not strange she lives?

She is more garrulous on the hill-side
36   than is the nightingale from the wood;
nor will she by day—a firm belief—
withdraw her head from the great hollow tree.
Piercingly she shrieked: I recognise her form,
40   she is the bird of Gwyn ap Nudd.
Crazy Owl that sings to the robbers,
misfortune on her tongue and on her tune!

That I may scare the Owl away
44   from me, I have [this] song,
I will put, while enduring frost,
a bonfire in each ivied tree.

Y Dylluan (26)

Truan i'r dylluan deg
Oer ddistal na rydd osteg.
Ni ad ym ganu 'mhader,
4 Ni thau tra fo siamplau sêr.
Ni chaf (och o'r gwarafun)
Gysgu na heddychu hun.
Tŷ godrum, yr ystlumod,
8 Ei gefn rhag piglaw ac od.
Beunoeth, bychan rhaib ynof,
I'm clustiau, ceiniogau cof,
Pan gaewyf, poen ogyfarch,
12 Fy llygaid, penaethiaid parch,
Hyn a'm deffry, ni hunais,
Cân y dylluan a'i llais,
A'i chrochwaedd aml a'i chrechwen,
16 A'i ffals gywyddiaeth o'i phen.

O hynny, modd yr hanwyf,
Hyd wawrddydd, annedwydd nwyf,
Canu y bydd, annedwydd nad,
20 'Hw-ddy-hw,' hoyw ddyhead.
Ynni mawr, myn ŵyr Anna,
Annos cŵn y nos a wna.
Budrog yw, ddiwiw ddwywaedd,
24 Benfras, anghyweithas waedd;
Lydandal, griawal groth,
Lygodwraig hen lygadroth;
Ystig, ddielwig, ddiliw,
28 Westn ei llais, ystaen ei lliw.
Uchel ei ffrec mewn decoed,
Och o'r cân, iwrch aerwy coed,
A'i gwedd, wynepryd dyn gwâr,
32 A'i sud, ellylles adar.
Pob edn syfudr alltudryw
A'i baedd; pond rhyfedd ei byw?

Ffraethach yw hon mewn bronnallt
36 Y nos no'r eos o'r allt.
Ni thyn y dydd, crefydd craff,
Ei phen o geubren gobraff.
Udai'n ffraeth, adwaen ei ffriw;
40 Edn i Wyn fab Nudd ydyw.
Ŵyll ffladr a gân i'r lladron,
Anffawd i'w thafawd a'i thôn!

Er tarfu y dylluan
44 I wrthyf, mae gennyf gân,
Rhof tra fwyf yn aros rhew
Oddaith ymhob pren eiddew.

27   The Roebuck

You, Roebuck, antlered fugitive,
with the cloud's swiftness, in trousers of pale grey,
carry this letter with fine speed,
4   by God in Heaven, on your bare backside.
You are most fast, you have an armful's leap
—fair message-bearer with a song—
by God, Roebuck, I must ask
8   your help in carrying a word of love.

He grazes the tough grass of his heathery lair
above the crag, this wild-headed one,
asking a fair payment for a poet (?),
12   sharp-antlered, leaper of the height
—as a bare-rumped lamb he leaps—
to the hill-slope, fair his nose and face.
My fine lad, you will not be betrayed,
16   no hounds will slay you, tall and handsome baron.
A worthy feat must be your aim: allow no hound
after the heat to overtake you,
have no fear of sharpened arrow
20   nor hound pursuing you, if you can jump.
Look out for Pali, a brown-legged hound
and Iolydd, brown and skilful one.
The baying of the hunt is to be given heed
24   should they pursue you to the land of Tywyn.
Give good care lest you be seen—
run to the bracken-thicket across the hill.
Jump underneath the ancient gap
28   into the [open] field, and delay no more.

You are my generous-natured messenger
and my poet to Dyddgu, handsome, bountiful;
Trotting bravely, now proceed
32   upon this journey to her father's house.
Inspite of anger, go, avoid (?) all hindrances,
impelled by understanding Ovid's ways.
Come back at night beside the dyke,
36   and there beneath the forest trees
bring me a kiss—the straight girl will not fail me—
from fair-hued Dyddgu, [her hair] in a fine plait.
Excellent Roebuck, go now on your journey
40   [to that place] where I would wish and long to be.
Have joy and confidence, no hand shall flay you,
nor ever shall your coat wrap aged English churl,
nor, darling, ever shall false Jealous One obtain
44   your horns, your hooves, nor yet your body's flesh.

Y Carw (116)

Tydi'r caeriwrch ffwrch ffoawdr,
Rhediad wybren, lwydwen lawdr,
Dwg hyn o lythr talmythrgoeth
4   Er Duw nef ar dy din noeth.
Cyflymaf wyd cofl lemain,
Negesawl cywyddawl cain.
Rho Duw, iwrch, rhaid yw erchi
8   Peth o lateieth i ti.

    Grugwal goruwch y greigwen,
Gweirwellt a bawr gorwyllt ben.
Talofyn gwych teuluaidd,
12   Llamwr allt, llym yw ei raidd.
Llama megis bonllymoen
I'r rhiw, teg ei ffriw a'i ffroen.
Fy ngwas gwych, ni'th fradychir,
16   Ni'th ladd cŵn, hardd farwn hir.
Nod fawlgamp, n'ad i filgi
Yn ôl tes d'oddiwes di.
Nac ofna di saeth lifaid,
20   Na chi yn ôl o chai naid.
Gochel Bali, ci coesgoch,
Ac Iolydd, ci celfydd coch,
Adlais hued a gredir,
24   O dôn yn d'ôl Dywyn dir.
Ymochel rhag dy weled,
Dros fryn i lwyn rhedyn rhed.
Neidia goris hen adwy
28   I'r maes ac nac aro mwy.

    Fy llatai wyd anwydael,
A'm bardd at Ddyddgu hardd hael.
Dwg dithau, deg ei duthiad,
32   Y daith hon i dŷ ei thad.
Dos er llid, dewiswr lludd,
Deall afael dull Ofydd.
Dabre'r nos gerllaw'r ffosydd,
36   Dan frig y goedwig a'i gwŷdd,
Â chusan ym, ni'm sym seth,
Dyddgu liw gwynblu geinbleth.
Cyrch yno'r caeriwrch hynod;
40   Carwn, dymunwn fy mod.
Ni'th fling llaw; bydd iach lawen;
Nid â dy bais am Sais hen,
Na'th gyrn, f'annwyl, na'th garnau,
44   Na'th gig ni chaiff Eiddig au.

May God, wise guardian, preserve you
from treachery, with Cynfelyn's arm;
I too, if I shall have my way
48 will bless you, rose-hip coloured one.

28   The Fox

Yesterday with definite intent I was
loitering underneath the trees,
under Ovid's branches—woe to him who never sees her—
4 and waiting for the girl beneath the trees,
(she, in her mood, has made me weep).
When I looked out yonder I saw
a monkey's form there where I would not wish—
8 a red Fox (he does not love the voices of our hounds)
sitting like a domestic pet
upon his haunches, close beside his lair.

I aimed—[it lay] between my hands—
12 my yew-tree bow (a costly one) yonder [at him],
intending, as a well-armed man
on the hill's brow [to cause] a lively start,
—he like a weapon speeding on the open land—
16 to strike him with an arrow broad and long.
I drew, with [over] eager cast
[the bowstring] straight beyond [my] cheek
and—woe is me—a disastrous mishap,
20 into three fragments broke my bow.

I became [straightway] angered at the Fox
—vexatious animal—but not dismayed at that.
He is a lad who loves the hens,
24 and stupid fowl, and flesh of birds,
a lad who follows not the blast of horns;
his bark and his carol are harsh.
Ruddy he shows against the gravelly land,
28 an ape-like form amongst the fresh green trees.
Across the corners of the field he runs,
a dog's shape, craving for a goose,
a scare-crow, near to the hill's edge,
32 leaping the furrows, ember-hued.
Image of raven-target (?) and magpies at a fair,
like to the Dragon of the prophecies,
the summit of commotion (?), one who gnaws fat hens,

Duw i'th gadw, y doeth geidwad,
A braich Cynfelyn rhag brad.
Minnau wnaf, o byddaf ben,
48   Dy groesi, bryd egroesen.

Y Llwynog (22)

Doe yr oeddwn, dioer eddyl,
Dan y gwŷdd, gwae'r dyn nyw gwŷl,
Gorsefyll dan gyrs Ofydd,
4   Ac aros gwen goris gwŷdd;
Gwnaeth ar ei hwyl ym wylaw,
Gwelwn, pan edrychwn draw,
Llun gwrab lle ni garwn,
8   Llwynog coch, ni châr lle'n cŵn,
Yn eistedd fal dinastwrch,
Ger ei ffau ar gwr ei ffwrch.

Anelais rhwng fy nwylaw
12   Fwa yw, drud a fu, draw,
Ar fedr, fal gŵr arfodus,
Ar ael y rhiw, arial rhus,
Arf i redeg ar frodir,
16   Ei fwrw â saeth ofras hir.
Tynnais o argais ergyd
Heb y gern heibio i gyd.
Mau och, aeth fy mwa i
20   Yn drichnap, annawn drychni.

Llidiais, nid arswydais hyn,
Arth ofidus, wrth fadyn.
Gŵr yw ef a garai iâr,
24   A choeg edn, a chig adar.
Gŵr ni ddilid gyrn ddolef,
Garw ei lais a'i garol ef.
Gwridog yw ymlaen grodir,
28   Gwedd âb ymhlith y gwŷdd ir.
Deugwr talwrn y digwydd
Delw ci yn adolwg gŵydd.
Lluman brain gerllaw min bryn,
32   Llamwr erw, lliw marworyn.
Drych nod brain a phiod ffair,
Draig unwedd daroganair.
Cynnwr fryn, cnöwr iâr fras,

36   proverbial pelt, bloodthirsty flesh,
      a [piercing] auger of the fair earth's hollow belly
      a lantern in the corner of a window that is closed,
      a copper-coloured bow, with lissom tread—
40   like pincers, with a bloody snout.

      No easy thing for me to follow him
      since his dwelling is far down in Annwfn;
      red courser, he is too swift to be caught,
44   he would outstrip the troop of his pursuers
      with rapid onrush, leaping the gorse—
      a leopard with a dart in his back-side.

36   Cnu dihaereb, cnawd eirias.
     Taradr daeargadr dorgau,
     Tanllestr ar gwr ffenestr gau.
     Bwa latwm di-drwm draed,
40   Gefel unwedd gylfinwaed.

     Nid hawdd ymy ddilid hwn,
     A'i dŷ annedd hyd Annwn.
     Rhodiwr coch, rhydaer y'i caid,
44   Rhedai 'mlaen rhawd ymlyniaid.
     Llym ei ruthr, llamwr eithin,
     Llewpart â dart yn ei din.

Notes

20

Doubts as to the authenticity of this poem are dispelled by Dr Parry on grounds of craftsmanship, and inspite of the fact that the authenticity of Dafydd's other poem to the Thrush (no.21; GDG 123) rests on more assured grounds.

The key-word of this poem is *gloyw* 'bright, sparkling, polished, clear, loud, limpid', which is repeated singly and in compounds, in lines 2, 3, 10, 12.

6. *plethiad*. Lit, 'a plaiting, twisting', here used fig.

7. *plygain* or *plygaint* 'cockrow', from *pullicantio*. This was the first of the canonical hours, 4 a.m.

8. *ei gasul* 'chasuble', a robe worn by a priest over his alb when serving the Mass; later used generally for a cloak or mantle.

9-10. 'The loudest notes (of the Song Thrush) may be heard half a mile away on a still morning'—W.H.Hudson, *British Birds* (1902), 42.

12. *Pencerdd* 'Chief of the art (of poetry)'. The *pencerdd* was the highest grade of court poet under the native princes in the pre-Conquest social order. In the Law of Hywel Dda he is described as 'a bard who has won a chair' (presumably in a competition); he enjoyed an official status and certain legal privileges. See T.Gwynn Jones 'Bardism and Romance', THSC 1913-14, 207-13.

16. *organ* from Lat. *organon* E. *organe* means here the whole range of resources of musical instruments.

17. *cwlm*. A technical term for 'a particular kind of air in ancient music; song, tune, melody' (GPC). Its precise character is unknown. It is clear from a number of references (e.g. *Y Gainc* 'The Stave', GDG 142) that Dafydd was a harpist as well as a poet, and could accompany his own compositions on the harp. See Gwyn Thomas, *Y Traddodiad Barddol* (Cardiff, 1976), 153.

18. *Ymryson*. There is some evidence that Dafydd may have known of the contemporary cult of French poems dealing with bird-debates on matters of love, inset within the framework of a Vision or Dream: such knowledge may lie behind his choice of the word *ymryson* 'contention, debate' in the context of bird-life. For parallels in his poems to the French themes of bird-debates see *Tradn. and Innov.* 31-4.

19. *llywr llên*. The 'reader of literature' in a monastery was the one who read aloud and expounded *legenda*; usually some saint's Life.

21. *cerdd Ofydd*, and also *ofyddiaeth* are used by Dafydd as generic terms to denote love-poetry in general. On Dafydd's refs. to the poet Ovid, see n. to no.28, 1.3 below.

22. *Primas* i.e. 'Primate', the chief ecclesiastical authority in a district; but also used in the general sense of 'one who is first in rank or importance' (OED). Both Dafydd and Iolo Goch employ the term *primas* in their *marwnadau* to fellow poets (GDG 20, 1.22; IGE² 42, 1.17), though Iolo Goch also employs *primas* in its ecclesiastical sense in reference to the bishop of Llanelwy (IGE² 85,5). As used here of the Thrush, *primas* obviously retains both its ecclesiastical and its poetic connotations, being parallel to *pregethwr* and to *prydydd*. *Urddas*, denoting a religious order, completes the image.

29-30. *adar Paradwys*. Cf. no.21 (GDG 123), 1.48, (*P*)*rydydd serch o Baradwys*. Birds who sing enchantingly are a regular feature of the Otherworld scene in the Celtic literatures. The magical Birds of Rhiannon whose song 'awakes the dead and puts to sleep the living' figure in both *Culhwch and Olwen* and in *Branwen*, and they are closely paralleled in the magical birds who sing beside the magic fountain in *Owein* (ed. R.L.Thomson, 1.155-7; RM 168). The association of such birds with the Christian Paradise is a feature which is attested more clearly in Irish than in Welsh: it is an element in the pagan Celtic Otherworld scene which was borrowed at an early date into Christianized sources, as in the 8th century 'Voyage of Bran' where birds sing the canonical hours, or in the Life of St Brendan where there is an island Paradise of birds who sing the praises of their Creator.

21

I have called this poem 'The Mistle Thrush' since this identity is suggested by the emphasis which is placed in it on the bird's bold and authoritative demeanour, in contrast to the more muted character of the previous poem to the Thrush, where the emphasis falls on the bird's sweet singing. The song of the Mistle Thrush or 'Storm Cock' is more continuous and less varied than the music of the Song Thrush. 'Early in the year, when the weather is broken, the bird perches high on a tall tree; and in exultant and ringing tones defies the elements'—T.A. Coward, *The Birds of the British Isles and their Eggs* (1956), I, 213. The poem is found in only two MSS, which owing to their faded condition proved difficult to decipher: hence the *lacuna* in l.19, and perhaps elsewhere in the latter part of the poem. The bird's authoritative demeanour is clearly expressed in its Welsh name, *pen-y-llwyn* 'head of the grove'. Legal imagery is implicit throughout, but is particularly emphasized by the series of legal terms employed in the second half— *gwarant* 'warrant, authority', *rhol* '(parchment) role', *daered* 'legal due, reward', *dirwy* 'forfeit, fine', *cwyn* '(legal) complaint, indictment', *amod* 'contract, agreement', *ynad* 'judge'. These are preceded by a sequence of metaphors from administrative terms: the Thrush is in turn *sirif* 'Sheriff', *ustus* 'Justice', *ystiwart llys* 'Steward of the Court'.

3. *cantor.* A professional singer or musician, primarily in liturgical services. Used also of the Skylark, no.23 (GDG 114), l.27.

6. *drwy gyfraith a gân.* i.e. by singing he asserts his legal right to his individual territory—a customary procedure with some birds.

7. *pregethwr.* Used of the Thrush also in no.20 (GDG 28) l.19.

13. *fy nghyweithas;* i.e. the fellowship of birds.

19. The first words in both MSS are illegible. Some previous lines may also be missing, in which the poet gave more fully his instructions to the bird.
mwy(n) Creirwy cred. Creirwy is a traditional heroine of whom little is known, except that she was the object of love by a certain *Garwy Hir;* see TYP 311. The identical expletive is empoyed by Madog Benfras, DGG², LXVII, l.21.

29. *cydfaeth cant* 'a throng nurtured together'. The *sangiad* presumably refers to the birds who are the companions of the Thrush in the forest.

30. *ei lythr gwarant.* A *llatai* who carries the poet's message in written rather than in verbal form is exceptional (cf. however the Roebuck, in no.27 (GDG 116), 3 below), and recalls the feat of Branwen's starling in the *Mabinogi.*

39. *traserch merch.* Ambiguous, since it can mean either the poet's love for the girl, or the girl's love for him.

43. *gêl ei gofeg (f.)* can refer only to the girl, not to the bird-messenger, or to God.

43-50. The sentence with *sangiadau* interposed, is not finally completed until the last line, *Duw a wnêl . . . ei adael ef . . . yno y gweddai.*

46. *y gennad.* Here, probably, 'messenger' rather than 'message', but either is possible.

48. *o Baradwys.* Cf. no.20 (GDG 28), l.30 and n.

22

9. *Llythr unwaith*, i.e. as white as a sheet of paper (DGG² 192). Cf. *lliw papir* no.43 (GDG 137), 1.22, below, and n.

14. *Eigr*. See n. to no.16 (GDG 81), 1.20 above.

20. *Fwynwas coeth*. It is uncertain whether this applies to the poet himself, as proposed by Dr Parry, or is an address to the Seagull as *llatai*, as it is understood by Ifor Williams, DGG², 192 (reading *a bydd* for *Er budd*).

23-4. *Na Myrddin na Thaliesin*. Two of the *Cynfeirdd* or 'Early Bards' who are traditionally assigned to the sixth century; TYP 469-74; 509-11. These two names are continuously coupled together in poetry from an early period in the role of prophets foretelling future events. A group of early poems also assigns to Myrddin the role of a lover, but the *chwedl* or story which evolved round the name of Taliesin gives no evidence that he too was regarded in this light.

25. *Siprys dan giprys*. *Siprys* is probably to be explained as derived from *Kypris* meaning 'the Cyprian', a name for Aphrodite or Venus—following a suggestion made by A.Conran in *The Penguin Book of Welsh Verse* (1967), 279. The cult of Venus was very old in the island of Cyprus (H.J.Rose, *Handbook of Greek Mythology*, 122); the island was famous for its copper mines, and in the 'science' of alchemy, copper was associated with Venus. *Dan gopr* indicates that the girl had auburn hair; if Morfudd is intended, we may compare the description of her as *marworyn rhudd* 'a glowing coal' no.14 (GDG 79), 1.18 above. In any case the combination of 'copper' with 'Venus' can hardly be a coincidence, and strongly suggests that Dafydd had some knowledge of the association between the two. On the association between Venus, copper and the island of Cyprus see further notes by D.J.Bowen, *Ll.C.* VII, 247; VIII, 232 n.

23

1. *oriau*. Lit. 'canonical hours' and hence by extension 'prayers'. Both meanings may be implicit here.

2. *a dry fry*. The vb. *troi* is here used as the equivalent of *codi* employed intransitively, 'to rise, ascend'; D.J.Bowen, *Ll.C.* VII, 244. Cf. 1.61 below.

3. *berw* (as noun or adj.) in relation to poets and poetry means '(ferment of) inspiration; babbling, poetry'; cf. no.25 (GDG 63), 1.35 *mawr yw dy ferw*, and n. to 1.44.

5. *odlau*. Lit. 'rhymes', so by extension in this context I render 'harmonies'.

13. *iawn Gai angerdd*. According to *Culhwch and Olwen* one of the attributes of Arthur's warrior Cai was that of being 'as tall as the tallest tree in the forest whenever he might wish'; WM 471, 3-5. However, T.J.Morgan suggests (THSC 1946, 298) that *cai* may here denote 'musical key', in which case the meaning would be 'in the true key of passion'. For *angerdd* with the meaning of 'passion' cf. no.20 (GDG 28), 1.31 (of the Thrush) *o dro iawngof drwy angerdd* lit. 'by revolving memory with passion'.

23. *modd awdur serch*. The Skylark is the 'author' or 'source' of love, the intermediary by way of whose singing love is carried up to Heaven.

26. *(g)winau* 'reddish brown, chestnut'. The back and wings of the Skylark are in various shades of brown, the breast is yellowish-white tinged with brown, with a slight tuft—*copa llwyd* 1.30—on top of its head.

27. *Cantor*. See n. to no.21 (GDG 123), 1.3 (of the Thrush). In the present religious context it seems most appropriate to retain this technical term without translation.

32. *gwyndir* 'uncultivated, fallow land; fair or blessed country': here it denotes the wide and empty expanse of the sky; cf. l.57 below.

38. *mae iaith gennyd.* Cf. l.10 above *brig iaith.*

43. ff. This abrupt transition is disconcerting, almost shocking, by which the poet turns from contemplating the Skylark's song as an act of divine worship, to enrol the bird as a love-messenger, charged with evading the girl's jealous husband. But such conflation of the secular with the divine is not without parallel elsewhere in Dafydd's poetry: cf. the following poem, no.24 'The Woodland Mass' and the Prayer to St Dwynwen no.34. Nor is it rare in mediaeval poetry as a whole.

46. *lleuad Wynedd.* This may be Morfudd: it has been shown that she had connections with Meirionydd, *Ll.C.* VI, 107, and there is an eighteenth-century tradition that she was buried at Trawsfynydd. Alternatively, it may denote the mysterious 'fourth girl' of poem no.15.

47-8. A similar request is made of the Roebuck—to bring a kiss, or even seven; no.27 (GDG 116), l.37 below.

49. *Dyfri.* Ifor Williams interprets the compound as *dyfr* + *rhi* 'king of waters' (DGG² 194). Alternatively he notes that it could be a compound of *dy* + *bri* 'honour' (intensive).

53. *cyngherthladd.* Ifor Williams discusses the meaning of *cyngerth*, B.iii, 132, citing J. Davies's rendering 'perplexus, implicitus'. In relation to trees the word denotes branches twisted and interlocked together, making a thick mass. In this instance one may deduce that the word is used metaphorically with legal or semi-legal significance: just as the branches of trees twist and interlock together, so do the branches of family-relationships when the kindred (up to the ninth degree of cousinship) was required to pay *galanas* or compensation for homicide. In this case it is implied that the branches of relationship would embrace the whole of mankind. A secondary meaning of *cyngerth*, as adj. is 'sad'.

57. *sercl.* From E. 'circle'; here denoting the sky's expanse.

perclwyd, Ifor Williams explains as a compound of synonyms: E. 'perch' with *clwyd*, the whole meaning a bird-cage (DGG² 194-5).

61. *tro.* See n. to l.2.

uwch ei law. Lit. 'above his hand'.

62. *hobel* from Fr. 'hobel' or E. 'hobby', a falcon, used metaphorically for an arrow.

24

In this poem it is Morfudd herself who dispatches the Thrush as a *llatai* or love-messenger to the poet: the bird then celebrates Mass in the forest with the assistance of the Nightingale, essentially the bird of love. Far from being irreverent or blasphemous, Dafydd exalts the theme into a supreme expression of his vision of the birds giving their due homage of praise to their Creator. For a parallel in a French poem *La Messe des Oiseaux* by Jean de Condé (d. 1345) see Chotzen 187-8, *Trad. and Innov.* 34-5. Here too the Nightingale officiates, assisted by the other birds, but the theme is treated on a far less exalted level; in fact, as a deliberate parody. Some difficulties in the poem are discussed by R.G.Gruffydd, YB X, 181-9, see notes below.

5. *alathr.* According to W.O.Pughe 'polished, glossy, polite'; Richards 'polite'.

6. *Arwyddion: arwydd* has many meanings 'sign, miracle, portent, wonder, emblem, etc.', and as verb *arwyddaf* 'denote, signify'.

7. *pwyll ei annwyd.* There is possibly here an allusion to the hero of the *Mabinogi*, and we should read 'of (like) nature to Pwyll'. In favour of this Dr Gruffydd draws attention to the lack of analogy for the use of *pwyll* as an adj.

8. *ei siwrnai*. Dr Gruffydd suggests amending to vb. 3 sg. imperf. *siwrneiai* (following three MSS,) as indeed seems required by the syntax, and I translate accordingly.

9. *swydd goeth Gaer*. Ifor Williams and Dr Parry take this to be Carmarthenshire, described as *swydd* by Huw Dafi in the late 15th century. (Pen.MS.67,297). Dr Gruffydd prefers to take the ref. as being to Chester, pointing out that the place was evidently known to Dafydd, since the *englynion* in the Hendregadredd MS to the Cross at Chester are now accepted as belonging to the canon of his work (GDG², 556 n.). Another suggestion was made by W.J.Gruffydd (B.VIII, 306) who took *Caer* with *Geiriog* as one word (with tmesis), denoting Chirk—though this has received little acceptance.

11. *Geiriog*. I have taken this as an adj. from *gair*, and translated accordingly. Dr Gruffydd suggests that it is a place-name, and that we have here an instance of the old construction by which a destinaton after verbs of motion was expressed by lenition, without intervening preposition. *Ceirio* has been identified as a name for part of north Ceredigion, in the commote of Genau'r Glyn, close to Dafydd's home (*Ceirio* survives to this day as a tributary of the river *Clarach*). There are analogies for the development of 'g' at the end of place-names ending in *-io*.

12. *i Nentyrch*. Either an as yet unidentified place-name (YB X,184 n.); the older form of *Nannerch* in Clwyd (B.VIII, 306); or a corruption of *yn entyrch* (var. of *entrych*) as suggested by Ifor Williams, DGG² 197; if the latter 'to the upper part of the valley'.

15. *(c)asmai*; from Lat. *camisia* 'alb, mantle, ornament, decoration' (GPC). The 'alb' was a long vestment worn by a priest when serving the Mass; usually but not invariably it was white. Dr Gruffydd suggests that *camsai* was the original form, and interprets this as a var. of *camse* 'mantle, robe'. Since *casmai* is the reading of all the MSS this would imply that they all derive from a common archetype in which the misreading was already present.

17-18. *A'i gasul*. Cf. no.20 (GDG 28), 8 above, *plu yw ei gasul* (of the Thrush) 'feathers are his chasuble'. This favours taking *casul* together with *esgyll* 'wings'. If *gwyrdd fentyll* (cf. l.2) is also parallel with *esgyll* it must mean the leaves scattered or shaken by the wind.

debygesynt, from vb. *tebygu* 'think, suppose'; cf. no.49 (GDG 144), l.3 *dygesynt*.

25. *ynn* perhaps for *inni* 'For us' (Dr Parry's suggestion), since the consecrated wafer was lifted up high so that the congregation might see it. Alternatively, *ynn* may be the pl. of *onnen* 'an ash-tree mound'.

26. *Afrlladen*. See n. to no.30 (GDG 67), l.28 below.

27. *bangaw*; 'eloquent, fluent, skilful, melodious'. Used twice elsewhere by Dafydd of the Nightingale, no.3 (GDG 24), l.25; GDG 25, l.37. (See introduction p.xxiii, note on nightingale).

30. *clerwraig*. On the meaning of *clêr* see n. to no.43 (GDG 137), l.29.

34. *caregl* 'chalice, communion cup' (symbolizing the Passion of Christ).

25

This poem is a riotous reversal of the *llatai* theme: instead of sending a bird with a message of love to a girl, with characteristic self-mockery Dafydd places in the mouth of a Magpie (a mere *bird*) a gratuitous criticism of his chosen mode of life. A comparison between a love-sick poet's unproductive longing and the joyful nest-building activities of birds is a recurrent theme in mediaeval verse (for some parallels see *Trad. and Innov.* 37). But if Dafydd knew of any such models this would merely add to the quality of his burlesque: his treatment of the theme is so individual as almost to render irrelevant the possibility of any external influence. For him the Magpie's flaunted domesticity is a symbol of all the conventional social values on which Dafydd claims to have turned his back—hence the angry vituperative *dyfalu* of his answer to the bird's reproof. This reproof is in its implications not unlike the reproof of the Grey Friar (no.43). Dafydd shows intimate knowledge of the characteristics of magpies: the bird is noted for its excessive cunning (cf. 1.28 and n.); magpies pair for life and the male does in fact assist in building the nest (cf. 1.32). 'In disposition the magpie is restless, inquisitive, excitable, and loquacious . . . the usual sound emitted by the magpie is an excited chatter . . . but there is always a certain resemblance to the human voice in it (cf. ls.59-60), especially when the birds are alarmed, and converse with one another in subdued tones' (W.H.Hudson, *British Birds* (London, 1902), 162-3). There is much folklore connected with magpies, such as the good or ill fortune associated with seeing one or two of these birds together.

3. *pill* 'branch', then as here 'branch or stave of song'.

5. *A'r eos.* The nightingale is rarely heard before May, but the black cap, which is frequently mistaken for the nightingale, can be heard singing lustily in April.

12. *Cwcyllwyd. Cwcwll* is from Lat. *cucullus* 'cowl, hood, hat, bonnet'. The skylark's *copa llwyd* is mentioned again in no.23, 1.30 (see n.).

15. *edlaes* 'trailing, drooping, dangling', etc. Hence 'hovering'.

16. *Yn wysg ei gefn.* As K.Jackson points out in *A Celtic Miscellany* (Harmondsworth, 1971), 317, this may refer to the lark's fluttering and almost hesitating flight skywards.

22. *yn dwyn gwisg newydd.* Cf. no.3 (GDG 24), ls.13-16; GDG 9, 1.50, for a similar image.

23. *egin gwin.* The vine was quite frequently grown in Britain in the Middle Ages.

26. *drwynwyn* 'white-nosed', referring to the white flowers of the hawthorn.

28. *ffelaf*, from E. 'fell' in its earlier meaning of 'shrewd, cunning', etc. This e.g., with that in no.42, 1.43, are the earliest examples of the word recorded in Welsh. See EEW 116.

29. *brad brydferth. Brad* (here f., though more frequently m.) here probably means 'subtlety, stratagem, ruse, trick', rather than the more usual 'betrayal'.

31. *balch borth.* Lit. 'a proud support'; here denoting the Magpie's nest, ingeniously contrived out of somewhat unpromising materials.

34. *cwyn* here seems to be coloured by its legal meaning 'indictment' (rather than 'complaint'), anticipating the bird's coming abuse.

42. *dydd* may either be interpreted literally 'day', or as meaning 'lovers' meeting, tryst'.

44. *y berw. Berw* has the double meaning of 'ferment, fuss' and of 'poetic inspiration, poetry': the Magpie in 1.35 uses the word in the first sense; Dafydd here takes up her words, intending *berw* to have the second meaning.

45. *gweini gwŷd.* Lit. 'passion-serving'.

51. *gofwy* here appears to have its official sense of 'a visit of inspection', etc. (GPC). Hence I render it tentatively 'interference'.

56. *a phen brân.* According to E.A.Armstrong, *The Folklore of Birds* (London, 1958),72, beliefs about the magpie are frequently derived from and confused with beliefs about the raven, as a bird of ill-omen.

57. *mwtlai* 'motley'. This antedates the first appearance of the word in English, in Chaucer's *Prologue*, 1.271. Also *medlai*, no.15, 1.28.
tyg. According to DGG² 205 *tyg* is 'either an imaginary form for the masc. of *teg.* or derives from the root of *tycio, tygio* 'avails'.

49-60. Gwyn Thomas (*Ll.C.* X, 229) argues that there are two voices in this passage, and that Dafydd here uses extended *sangiad* as a means of alternating his (imagined) reactions of abuse to the bird—spoken under his breath—with his ostensibly polite rejoinder to it. I find it easier to take the whole passage as invective on the part of Dafydd, in which he contrasts the bird's fuss and commotion over her nest-building—*llafur sydd fwy* (l.52) with his own ferment (*berw*) over his *swydd serch* 'labour of love' (l.47). He means 'you have even greater labour than is mine'.

65-6. The couplet occurs in almost identical form in GDG 36, ls.9-10. *gwyddwn.* Lit. 'I would know'. The impf. is used conditionally, answering the subj. *a wypych* in the previous line.

69. *dos yn feudwy.* Cf. no.38 (GDG 48), ls.39-40 *Ys dir ym fyned fal gŵr/yn feudwy.*

74. *dioer* represents *Duw a ŵyr* 'God knows' (GMW 246).

26

The Owl, like the Magpie in the previous poem, is addressed by Dafydd only to be abused. Her appearance and her nocturnal habits, however, are closely observed: her cry, her fondness for eating mice (l.26), and for making her home in ivy-clad hollow trees (l.46). Dafydd also shows acquaintance with folklore concerning the Owl (ls.31-4). It seems likely, from his description, that the occasion for Dafydd's complaint here against the Owl's disturbance of the night is provided by a species no longer common in Great Britain, whose behaviour at certain times of the year is considerably more histrionic than the familiar gentle hooting of the brown owl. The long-eared owl, a variety which prospered in the dense woodlands of mediaeval Wales, is much greyer in appearance than the brown or tawny variety, its head is large and human-like and, according to *The Handbook of British Birds*, Vol II (Witherby etc), its 'Principal and most characterstic note is *song* (sic)—a long drawn-out "oo, oo, oo" a cooing rather than a hoot. The female has a higher-pitched variant "shoo-oogh" slurred downwards, repeated at much longer intervals, dying off softly like a heavy'sigh. When nesting place is invaded, call is sometimes prefaced by barking "woof-woof", and other notes include a short expiratory "Lagh" and a silvery chirruping like small silver coins shaken together . . . and squealing and caterwauling noises are evidently distinct.' In the light of this account perhaps, Dafydd may not have been exaggerating the Owl's invasion of his peace and devotions.

2. *oer.* Either 'cold' or 'sad'.

(*g*)*osteg.* Either i) 'a series of airs played to the harp, a song', or ii) 'silence, quiet'. In view of the allusion to the Owl's *ffals gywyddiaeth* in l.16, either interpretation seems possible here.

4. *siamplau*, lit. 'examples'.

7. *godrum.* See n. to no.52 (GDG 141), l.23.

9. *rhaib.* Lit. 'bewitching'.

10. *ceiniogau cof.* Unlike *fflwring* 'florin' (poem no.2) the *ceiniog* or 'penny' is an old word in Welsh, being attested in the 12th century legal codes, and in the Book of Taliesin, and recalling Hywel Dda's silver 'penny'. But it is an unexpected metaphor for the human ear.

21. *ŵyr Anna.* i.e. Christ; St Anna was the mother of the Virgin Mary.

22. *cŵn y nos.* the mythical and sinister hounds of Gwyn ap Nudd (l.40 below, see n.). Dafydd refers to the hounds again in no.36 (GDG 68), l.43, and in no.42 (GDG 129), l.32. Folklore collected in the last century told that 'their quarry consists in the souls of the departed, and their bark forebodes death, since they watch for the souls of men about

to die', J.Rhŷs, *Celtic Folklore* (Oxford, 1901), 216. On *Annw(f)n* see n. to no.4 (GDG 27), l.40 above.

25. *criawl* 'berry-bellied' (Dr Parry's interpretation). More specifically, *criafol, criawol* denotes the berries of the rowan or mountain ash, which are bright red. Perhaps the allusion is to the speckled belly of the (Long-eared) owl, or alternatively, it may imply a belief as to her food.

28. *(g)westn*; f. of *gwystn*, lit. 'withered, decayed, rotten', etc. *ystaen*. Cf. no.36 (GDG 68), 17 *rhidyll ystaen*. Dr Parry tells me that he would now favour the derivation of *ystaen* from Lat. *stagnum* 'tin' given by Davies (see Ifor Williams in *Y Traethodydd* 1955, 137-41), in preference to that from E. 'stain' (EEW 195). This would seem to correspond with the grey colouring of the Long-eared owl.

29. *decoed*. For *deg + coed* (?) The meaning is uncertain.

30. *cân*. Here (exceptionally) treated as m., though normally f. The allusion to 'a roebuck's fetter' is wholly obscure.

31. *dyn gwâr*. i.e. because the owl's eyes look forward from her face, like those of a human being; they are not placed on the two sides of her head like those of other birds. Lines 31-4 are a close echo of the story of the heroine Blodeuwedd who, according to *Mabinogi Math*, was transformed into an owl, and the judgment pronounced on her is . . . *bot gelynyaeth y rynghot a'r holl adar. A bot yn anyan udunt dy uaedu, a'th amherchi y lle i'th gaffant* (PKM 91, 11-13) 'there will be enmity between you and all birds, and it will be their nature to harass and molest you wherever they find you.' Even the somewhat rare word *baeddu* 'strike, harass, maltreat' is repeated here in the poem.

40. *Edn i Wyn fab Nudd*. Gwyn ap Nudd was known as a legendary figure in mediaeval literature: he plays a part in *Culhwch and Olwen* and in an early dialogue poem, in the Black Book of Carmarthen. In Welsh folklore he is the fairy huntsman, leader of the *cŵn Annw(f)n* or hellhounds (see above on l.22), Dafydd alludes to him a number of times (for refs. see E.Rowlands, *Ll.C.* V, 122-3), and always presents him in a sinister light; hence the Owl is 'his' bird; the bog-hole is 'his' fish-pond (GDG 127, l.29), the Mist a deception caused by him, no.36 (GDG 68; ls.32, 40).

41. *Wŷll ffladr*. *Wyll* (later *gwyll*) is cognate with E. 'owl' according to Ifor Williams, B.I, 234. In Thos. Wiliems's dictionary *(G)wyll = Aderyn y cyrph. Hudoles neu swynwraig a newidia wedd plant* 'bird of corpses: witch or enchantress who changes the form of children'. *Ffladr* from E. 'flatter' means 'simple, stupid, babbling,' etc. This is the earliest recorded e.g. in Welsh.

45. *yn aros rhew* 'while enduring frost', i.e. 'on a frosty night' (Dr Parry's interpretation); or perhaps with the more general implication 'when winter comes'.

27

Dafydd has three poems to animals—the Roebuck, the Fox (no.28) and the Hare (GDG 46). Each one of these three is a beast of the chase, and in each one of the three poems Dafydd lays stress on the animal's speed and ability to outdistance his or her pursuers. But the Roebuck is the only one of the three who is commissioned as a love-messenger—and it is to Dyddgu (l.30) that he carries his message.

3. *hyn o lythr*. Cf. the *llythr gwarant* or 'letter of warrant' carried by the Thrush, no.21, l.30 and n. *Llythr* is the older form of *llythyr*. *talmythrgoeth*. Cf. no.38 (GDG 48) l.35 and n. Dr Parry cites exx. of *talmithr* as a frequent variant, *talmythr* is however attested here by the *cynghanedd*. (The *m* is restored editorially). To the exx. of the word cited in his note, add Wm.Llŷn's Glossary: *talmithr, talmyrth = ebrwydd* (swift).

6. *cywyddawl: cywydd* + adj. ending 'song-bearing'; cf. no.23 (GDG 114) l.32 where it used of the Skylark.

11. *talofyn*. The word is unknown elsewhere. Conjecturally I have taken it as a compound of *tâl* 'payment' and *gofyn* 'ask'.

teuluaidd. The *bardd teulu* or 'household bard' had a fixed status and duties under mediaeval Welsh law; according to the Bardic Grammars these were subsequently inherited in part by the *teuluwr*. Since the Roebuck is called *bardd* in l.30, it seems likely that *teuluaidd* here has a bardic connotation.

21-2. *Pali* 'silk' and *Iolydd* 'desirable' (cf. CLIH.133) or 'suppliant' are the names of (perhaps real?) hounds.

24. *Dywyn dir*. An e.g. of the old construction by which the name of the destination is lenited after verbs of motion, without intervening preposition (see n. to no.24, l.11 above). Tywyn is Dyddgu's home, but it is uncertain which 'Tywyn' is intended: whether that north of the Dyfi estuary in Merionnydd, or the Tywyn in Y Ferwig in the southernmost corner of Ceredigion. The latter is advocated by Dr Parry, GDG xliv (GDG² xxv), but nevertheless there are arguments in favour of Tywyn, Meirionnydd; see below l.46 on *Cynfelyn*.

33. *dewiswr lludd*. Lit. 'chooser of hindrance'—implying that the Roebuck must pick his way, avoiding all obstacles.

34. *dull Ofydd*. On Dafydd's frequent appeals to the authority of the poet Ovid see n. to no.28, l.3 below.

38. *gwynblu*. Dyddgu's hair was dark (no.13, ls.28, 54), so that *gwynblu* 'white feathers' is unexpected unless *gwyn* merely denotes 'fair, handsome'.

46. *Cynfelyn*. The patron-saint of the church of Llangynfelyn, overlooking Corsfochno, on the south of the Dyfi estuary (LBS ii, 243). *Sarn Cynfelyn* is the name of a rocky causeway which stretches out to sea from Clarach, between Aberystwyth and Borth.

28

1. *dioer* (*Duw a ŵyr* 'God knows'), here used adjectivally 'certain, definite, true'.

2. *nyw gwŷl*. GMW 56 cites this as an e.g. of the old poetic construction by which the negative was combined with the 3 singular or plural of the infixed pronoun, which in this instance anticipates as its object *gwen* in l.4.

3. *dan gyrs Ofydd* 'under Ovid's branches' (Dr Parry's interpretation). *Cors*, plural *cyrs* can mean 'bog, swamp' as well as 'reeds, stalks, branches'. Here it is used fig. for the swamp of love. *Ofydd*, i.e. the poet Ovid, is the only foreign poet whom Dafydd ever names. His refs. to Ovid are fairly frequent, but imprecise. They indicate that for Dafydd as for many other mediaeval poets Ovid was the paramount authority on all matters relating to love, since he was in fact the ultimate source for the mediaeval European conventions of 'courtly love', of which Dafydd was well aware. Hence *ofyddiaeth*, *dull Ofydd*, and *cerdd Ofydd* were for him synonymous with love-poetry (cf. no.20, l.21; no.27, l.34 above). See *Tradn. and Innov.* 24-8.

7. *ni garwn*. Another old construction by which the negative in a relative clause is followed by lenition; GMW 61, n.

13. *ar fedr* 'intending to, for the purpose of'. On the constr. see B. l.25.

22. *Arth*, lit. 'bear' is here used fig. for the Fox.

25. *ni ddilid gyrn*. *Dilid* (as in l.41 below) is a var. of the verb-noun *dilyn* 'follow', but here it is used as the equivalent of 3 single pres. indic. Dr Parry interprets the line as meaning that the Fox is not startled by the cry of the hunt, but is always well ahead: i.e. he keeps well away from his pursuers.

26. *a'i garol.* This is the earliest recorded borrowing into Welsh of E. 'carol'.

27. *ymlaen grodir.* Alternatively 'before his sandy lair' (?), since *grodir* is employed fig. for 'grave'.

30. *yn adolwg.* Here the verbal root is used in place of the verb-noun *adolwyn* lit. 'desire'.

31. *lluman brain.* 'Scarecrow' is Dr Parry's suggestion.

33. The significance of these allusions is totally obscure.

34. *Draig unwedd daroganair.* The ref. is to *cerdd darogan*, the mediaeval cult of prophetic poetry, in which extensive use was made of animal symbolism, the red dragon typifying the Welsh nation, which it was foretold would eventually overcome the English.

35. *cynnwr fryn.* Dr Parry suggests that *bryn* here has an extended meaning, equivalent to 'height, prominence'; hence 'the summit of commotion'.

36. *cnu.* Lit. 'fleece'.
eirias. Lit. 'a glowing fire, a conflagration'. Here fig. 'glowing, fiery', hence in this instance, perhaps, 'passionate, violent, bloodthirsty'.

40. Dr Parry points out that this line has the fault of *camosodiad:* the consonants in the second half do not exactly reproduce those in the first half in the same order (CD 298-9).

41. On *dilid* as verb-noun see n. to l.25 above.

42. *Annwn.* On *Annw(f)n* see n. to no.4, l.40 above. The Fox's lair, like the Otherworld of pagan Celtic belief, is envisaged as down below the earth.

IV. OTHER MESSENGERS OF LOVE (29-34)

29   The Wind

      Sky Wind of impetuous course
    who travels yonder with your mighty shout,
    you are a strange being, with a blustering voice,
4   most reckless in the world, [though] without foot or wing.
    It is strange how marvellously you were sent
    lacking a foot, from out the store-house of the sky,
    and how swiftly it is you run
8   this moment now across the slope above.
    No need for a swift horse under you,
    nor bridge nor boat at river-mouth,
    you will not drown: you have been indeed forewarned,
12 you have no corners, [so] you will not get entangled.
    Though you might winnow leaves, seizing the nests,
    none will indict you, neither swift troop
    nor hand of magistrate will hold you back,
16 nor blue blade nor flood nor rain,
    neither officer nor retinue can hold you
    in your life-time, scatterer of the tree-tops' feathers;
    no mother's son can strike you ([it would be] wrong [even]
                                        to mention [it]),
20 no fire burns you, nor treachery restrains you.
    No eye can see you with your great barren wall,
    [but] a thousand hear you, nest of the great rain,
    swift-natured annotator of the clouds,
24 fair leaper across nine fallow lands.

      You are God's blessing over all the earth,
    with harsh roar shattering the tops of oaks:
    your nature dry, tenacious creature,
28 trampler of clouds, a mighty journey,
    shooter upon the snow-fields up above
    of futile noisy piles of chaff.
    Tell me, [my] devoted jewel,
32 your journey, North Wind of the valley?
    [When] bad weather agitates (?) the sea
    you are a reveller upon the shore.
    Eloquent author, you are an enchanter,
36 you are a sower, a pursuer of leaves,
    a privileged jester on the hill—you are a hurler
    of wild masts on the white-breasted sea.

      You fly the full length of the world,
40 the hill's limit (?): be above tonight,
    ah, man, and go to Uwch Aeron,
    [be] gentle and kind, with voice easily heard.
    Do not stop, do not hold back
44 nor fear, inspite of the Bwa Bach
    —that whining accuser, serving jealousy—

Y Gwynt (117)

Yr wybrwynt helynt hylaw
Agwrdd drwst a gerdda draw,
Gŵr eres wyd garw ei sain,
4 Drud byd heb droed heb adain.
Uthr yw mor aruthr y'th roed
O bantri wybr heb untroed,
A buaned y rhedy
8 Yr awron dros y fron fry.
Nid rhaid march buan danad,
Neu bont ar aber, na bad.
Ni boddy, neu'th rybuddiwyd,
12 Nid ai ynglŷn, diongl wyd.
Nythod ddwyn, cyd nithud ddail,
Ni'th dditia neb, ni'th etail
Na llu rhugl, na llaw rhaglaw,
16 Na llafn glas na llif na glaw.
Ni'th ddeil swyddog na theulu
I'th ddydd, nithydd blaenwydd blu.
Ni'th lladd mab mam, gam gymwyll,
20 Ni'th lysg tân, ni'th lesga twyll.
Ni'th wŷl drem, noethwal dramawr,
Neu'th glyw mil, nyth y glaw mawr;
Noter wybr natur ebrwydd,
24 Neitiwr gwiw dros nawtir gŵydd.

Rhad Duw wyd ar hyd daear,
Rhuad blin doriad blaen dâr.
Sych natur, creadur craff,
28 Seirniawg wybr, siwrnai gobraff.
Saethydd ar froydd eiry fry
Seithug eisingrug songry.
Dywed ym, diwyd emyn,
32 Dy hynt, di ogleddwynt glyn.
Drycin yn ymefin môr,
Drythyllfab ar draethellfor.
Huawdl awdr, hudol ydwyd,
36 Hëwr, dyludwr dail wyd.
Hyrddiwr, breiniol chwarddwr bryn,
Hwylbrenwyllt heli bronwyn.

Hydoedd y byd a hedy,
40 Hin y fron, bydd heno fry,
Och ŵr, a dos Uwch Aeron
Yn glaer deg, yn eglur dôn.
Nac aro di, nac eiriach,
44 Nac ofna er Bwa Bach
Cyhuddgwyn wenwyn weini;

that land which nourished her is closed to me.
Woe is me that I placed serious love
48 on Morfudd, on my golden girl—
a maiden who has made me exiled from the land—
run upwards [now] towards her father's house.

Beat on the door, make it be opened
52 before day [comes], to my messenger
and find a way to her, if it may be had,
and, with complaining, voice my sighs.
You come from the unchanging planets:
56 say this to my faithful generous [girl]:
however long I may be in the world
I shall remain her faithful follower.
Without her all my looks are sorrowful—
60 if it be true she is not faithless to me.
Go up, and you will see the fair girl:
go down, you darling of the sky,
go to the pale, fair, slender maid
64 and come back safely: you are the sky's treasure.

30 The Star

I am pining for a girl as pale as foam
—God understands the mind of every man—
If I am driven, through love of her,
4 my gentle dear, to travel to her land,
far be it from my thought to deputize
a costly messenger to [reach] her home,
or to commission some fierce grey-haired hag
8 officiously to be my messenger,
nor [will I] bear before me flaming lamps
or waxen torches, when it may be dark,
[preferring] rather that I sleep by day
12 and travel through the town by night.
Nobody sees me, no one recognizes me,
I am all innocence till it be day.

I shall, against mishap, tonight
16 find without any restraint
the candles of the Lord who rules the world
to guide me to my jewel of sprightly form.

A blessing on the Lord Creator's name,
20 who devised the craftsmanship of the Stars
in such a way that there is nothing brighter
than the small circle of a pure white star.

Caeth yw'r wlad a'i maeth i mi.
Gwae fi pan roddais i serch
48   Gobrudd ar Forfudd, f'eurferch;
Rhiain a'm gwnaeth yn gaethwlad,
Rhed fry rhod a thŷ ei thad.

Cur y ddôr, pâr egori
52   Cyn y dydd i'm cennad i.
A chais ffordd ati, o chaid,
A chŵyn lais fy uchenaid.
Deuy o'r sygnau diwael,
56   Dywed hyn i'm diwyd hael:
Er hyd yn y byd y bwyf,
Corodyn cywir ydwyf.
Ys gwae fy wyneb hebddi,
60   Os gwir nad anghywir hi.
Dos fry, ti a wely wen,
Dos obry, dewis wybren.
Dos at feinwen felenllwyd,
64   Debre'n iach, da wybren wyd.

Y Seren (67)

Digio 'dd wyf am liw ewyn,
Duw a ŵyr meddwl pob dyn.
O daw arnaf o'i chariad,
4   F'enaid glaer, fyned i'w gwlad,
Pell yw i'm bryd ddirprwyaw
Llatai drud i'w llety draw,
Na rhoi gwerth i wrach serth swydd
8   Orllwyd daer er llateirwydd;
Na dwyn o'm blaen danllestri,
Na thyrs cwyr, pan fo hwyr hi,
Dros gysgu y dydd gartref
12   A cherdded nos dros y dref.
Ni'm gwŷl neb, ni'm adnebydd,
Ynfyd wyf, yny fo dydd.

Mi a gaf heb warafun
16   Rhag didro heno fy hun
Canhwyllau'r Gŵr biau'r byd
I'm hebrwng at em hoywbryd.

Bendith ar enw'r Creawdrner
20   A wnaeth saeroniaeth y sêr,
Hyd nad oes dim oleuach
No'r seren gron burwen bach.

A radiant beacon from the Lord on high,
24   a candle of a clear nature is she,
a candle whose beauty will not fade,
and which cannot be stolen by deceit.
No wind on its autumnal course can quench her,
28   she is the consecrated wafer from the roof of Heaven.
The water of cowardly torrents will not extinguish her,
waiting-woman with the communal platter of the saints.
No thief's hand can reach towards her,
32   the bottom yonder of the Trinity's bowl.
It is useless from his dwelling [here below]
for any man to covet Mary's pearl.
She will shed brightness over every region,
36   a refined coin of yellow gold,
a true buckler of the light,
she is the image of the sky's brilliant Sun.

She reveals to me, proud golden jewel,
40   without concealment the place where Morfudd is.
Christ, from wherever she may be, will quench
and banish her—but that will not be soon
—form of a perfect white-flour loaf—
44   and send her into the shadow of a cloud to sleep.

31   A Dream

As I was once—I knew a hiding-place—
having a nap within my secret place,
I perceived, at very peep of day
4   a Dream upon the morning's brow.
It seemed to me that I was walking
my pack of greyhounds in my hand
and that I chanced, within a forest,
8   on a fair mansion—it was no wretched peasant's hovel.
Without delay I then unleashed
as I supposed, the hounds into the wood.
I heard baying, eager cries
12   of hounds pursuing, giving frequent tongue.

Beyond the clearing I perceived
a white doe—I enjoyed the hunt—
the pack of greyhoynds were in [hot] pursuit
16   following her—their excitement was just—
[she] sought the wooded hillside, across an entire ridge,
over two spurs and a ridge,
and back again across the mountain spurs:

Cannaid o'r uchel geli,
24 Cannwyll ehwybrbwyll yw hi.
Ni ddifflan pryd y gannwyll,
A'i dwyn ni ellir o dwyll.
Nis diffydd gwynt hynt hydref,
28 Afrlladen o nen y nef.
Nis bawdd dwfr llwfr llifeiriaint,
Disgwylwraig, dysgl saig y saint.
Nis cyrraidd lleidr o'i ddwylaw,
32 Gwaelod cawg y Drindod draw.
Nid gwiw i ddyn o'i gyfair
Ymlid maen mererid Mair.
Golau fydd ymhob ardal,
36 Goldyn o aur melyn mâl.
Gwir fwcled y goleuni,
Gwalabr haul gloyw wybr yw hi.

Hi a ddengys ym heb gudd,
40 Em eurfalch, lle y mae Morfudd.
Crist o'r lle y bo a'i diffydd
Ac a'i gyr, nid byr y bydd,
Gosgedd torth gan gyfan gu,
44 I gysgod wybr i gysgu.

Y Breuddwyd (39)

Fal yr oeddwn, gwyddwn gêl,
Yn dargwsg mewn lle dirgel.
Gwelais ar glais dichlais dydd
4 Breuddwyd yn ael boreddydd.
Gwelwn fy mod yn rhodiaw
A'm llu bytheiaid i'm llaw,
Ac i fforest yn gestwng,
8 Teg blas, nid tŷ taeog blwng.
Gollyngwn i yn ddioed,
Debygwn, y cŵn i'r coed.
Clywwn oriau, lleisiau llid,
12 Canu'n aml, cŵn yn ymlid.

Ewig wen uwch y llennyrch
A welwn, carwn y cyrch,
A rhawt fytheiaid ar hynt
16 Yn ei hôl, iawn eu helynt;
Cyrchu'r allt dros ddiwalltrum,
A thros ddwy esgair a thrum,
A thrachefn dros y cefnydd

20 [her] course of equal swiftness with a stag,
[but] having been tamed, she came
for my protection, distressed as I was.
[I felt] two naked nostrils: I awoke
24 a ravenous man—and in the hut I was.

I sought out an experienced old woman
when day came, joyfully enough,
and I confessed to her
28 the portent of the night, as it appeared to me:
'By God, wise woman, if you could
explain this magic in some way [for me]
(a hundred wounds I know)—not anyone
32 would I esteem as much as you: I have no hope.

'If you are a man, your dream
is a good portent, hopeless one:
the hounds—without concealment—that you saw
36 in your hand, if you knew persuasive speech (?)
[are] bringers of good luck upon your ardent quest,
they are your fearless *llateion*.
And the white doe, she is the lady
40 that you have loved, of like hue to the waves of [shimmering]
heat

This is the truth, that she will come [at last]
to your protection. May God guard you, so.

32   The Clock

With good intention and with happiness
I sing, because [my] world is good,
to the fair town by Rheon's slope
4 at the crag's corner, with its rounded fort.
A girl—her name was famed(?) in former times
Is there—she used to know me once.
Greetings here today [from me]
8 go to the dwelling of that worthy lass.
Nightly that wise and noble girl
hither [comes] to speak with me.

When that exhausted a man might fall asleep (?)
12 —it is a Dream, it hardly [need be] said—
with my head upon the pillow
yonder there comes before the day
into her (?) view, a semblance manifest(?)

20 Ar hynt un helynt â hydd,
   A dyfod wedy dofi,
   A minnau'n ddig, i'm nawdd i;
   Dwyffroen noeth, deffro wneuthum,
24 Ŵr glwth, yn y bwth y bûm.

   Cefais hynafwraig gyfiawn,
   Pan oedd ddydd, yn ddedwydd iawn.
   Addef a wneuthum iddi,
28 Goel nos, fal y gwelwn i:

   'Rho Duw, wraig gall, pei gallud
   Rhyw derfyn ar hyn o hud,
   Ni chyfflybwn, gwn ganclwyf,
32 Neb â thi. Anobaith wyf.'

   'Da o beth, diobeithiwr,
   Yw dy freuddwyd, od wyd ŵr.
   Y cŵn heb gêl a welud
36 I'th law, pei gwypud iaith lud,
   Da hwylwyr diau helynt,
   Dy lateion eon ŷnt.
   A'r ewig wen, unbennes
40 A garud di, hoen geirw tes,
   Diau yw hyn, y daw hi
   I'th nawdd, a Duw i'th noddi.'

Y Cloc (66)

   Cynnar fodd, cain arfeddyd,
   Canu 'dd wyf fi, can hawdd fyd,
   I'r dref wiw ger Rhiw Rheon
4 Ar gwr y graig, a'r gaer gron.
   Yno, gynt ei henw a gad,
   Y mae dyn a'm adwaeniad.
   Hawddamor heddiw yma
8 Hyd yn nhyddyn y ddyn dda.
   Beunoeth, foneddigddoeth ferch,
   Y mae honno i'm hannerch.

   Bryd cwsg dyn, a bradw y'i caid,
12 Breuddwyd yw, braidd y dywaid,
   A'm pen ar y gobennydd,
   Acw y daw cyn y dydd,
   Yng ngolwg eang eilun,

16   a little angel into the girl's bed.
     With my mundane (?) thought I had supposed
     that I was with my darling [as] of yore.
     [but] far from me, [my] memory seeking her
20   her face was when I came to wake.

     Alas the Clock beside the dyke
     black-countenanced, which awakened me;
     let its mouth and tongue be vain
24   with its two ropes and its wheel,
     the stupid balls which are its weights,
     with its four-square case (?) and hammer,
     with its ducks who think it day,
28   and its restless mill-wheels.
     Churlish Clock with foolish clatter
     like a drunken cobbler, its noise is mockery,
     with treacherous and lying entrails—
32   a hound's whelp gnawing at a bowl.
     With frequent clapper in the monks' cloister,
     an owl's mill, grinding in the night.
     Was ever saddler with a scabby crupper,
36   or yet a tiler, more unstable?
     A sad destruction on its crying,
     since out of Heaven it drew me here.

     I was enjoying, with comfortable trust,
40   sleep from Heaven at middle of the night,
     lapped in this girl's encircling arms,
     folded between the breasts of her of Deifr's form.
     Will the like vision—nourishment of grief—
44   be seen again, fair Eigr of the land?

     Run on your way to her again
     My Dream, for you it is no unpropitious course.
     Enquire of the golden-headed girl
48   if sleep will come to her tonight,
     so I may gaze, pure heart of gold,
     niece of the Sun, upon her face once more.

33 To the Wave on the River Dyfi

     Loud-voiced, rippling, crested Wave,
     do not prevent me—portent of success—
     from fording to the other side, whence comes my recompense:
4   do not delay me, do not hinder me.
     For God's sake, the Lord of succour,
     [you] watery tyrant, let me cross the Dyfi.
     Turn back, home of three hundred nets,
8   I am your poet: you are above the water.

16   Angel bach yng ngwely bun.
     Tybiaswn o'm tyb isod
     Gan fy mun gynnau fy mod.
     Pell oedd rhyngof, cof a'i cais,
20   A'i hwyneb pan ddihunais.

     Och i'r cloc yn ochr y clawdd
     Du ei ffriw a'm deffroawdd.
     Difwyn fo'i ben a'i dafod
24   A'i ddwy raff iddo a'i rod,
     A'i bwysau, pelennau pŵl,
     A'i fuarthau a'i fwrthwl,
     A'i hwyaid yn tybiaid dydd,
28   A'i felinau aflonydd.
     Cloc anfwyn mal clec ynfyd
     Cobler brwysg, cabler ei bryd.
     Coluddyn ffals celwyddawg,
32   Cenau ci yn cnöi cawg.
     Mynychglap, mewn mynachglos,
     Melin ŵyll yn malu nos.
     A fu sadler crwper crach
36   Neu deiler anwadalach?
     Oer ddilen ar ei ddolef
     Am fy nwyn yma o nef!

     Cael ydd oeddwn, coel ddiddos,
40   Hun o'r nef am hanner nos,
     Ym mhlygau hir freichiau hon,
     Ym mhleth Deifr ymhlith dwyfron.
     A welir mwy, alar maeth,
44   Wlad Eigr, ryw weledigaeth?

     Eto rhed ati ar hynt,
     Freuddwyd, ni'th ddwg afrwyddynt.
     Gofyn i'r dyn dan aur do
48   A ddaw hun iddi heno
     I roi golwg, aur galon,
     Nith yr haul, unwaith ar hon.

Y Don ar Afon Dyfi (71)

     Y don bengrychlon grochlais,
     Na ludd, goel budd, ym gael bais
     I'r tir draw, lle y daw ym dâl,
4   Nac oeta fi, nac atal.
     Gad, er Duw rad, ardwy ri,
     Drais y dwfr, fi dros Dyfi.
     Tro drachefn, trefn trychanrhwyd,
8   Dy fardd wyf, uwch dwfr ydd wyd.

Did any sing before by word of mouth
—sail's companion, gem of the waves—
such praise to your masterly roar
12 as I have, you crest of the sea?
There is no great wind, sent hither by the stars,
nor vehement swift attack between two banks,
nor lively contest, nor strong branch,
16 nor shoulder of a horse, nor yet of man
that I have not likened—well I know the anguish—
strong forceful Wave, to your own strength.
There was never harp nor organ
20 nor tongue of man with faultless praise
that I have not adjudged as strong,
grey flood, as is your splendid voice.
There will come no further word from me
24 about my love—Nia's beauty, by fortune betrayed (?)—
but praise of her bright loveliness,
and her fair form, as being like your flood.

Therefore, contrive you do not hinder me,
28 bright battling woman of the clear and sparkling flood,
from going yonder to Llanbadarn
through the birch-grove—my darling be my judge—
to that gentle girl who brought me back
32 —some kind of profit for my eloquence (?) —from death to
life.
I am in some perplexity,
my friend, horsewoman of the sea:
you are obstructing me from my homeland—
36 bridle the torrent now, with your [opposing] front.

Did you but know, grey-mantled Wave,
fair shining woman-*llatai* of the shoals of fish,
how great [will be] my reprimand for my delay!
40 you, like a mantle, [hide] the opposite shore.
Though it was for her I came, a second Indeg,
fair Wave, as far as to your breast,
no foeman's war it is will slay me
44 if you should hinder me from my girl's land,
but the seven score grades of love will kill me;
do not withhold me, then, from Morfudd, from my golden
girl.

A ganodd neb â genau
O fawl i'r twrf meistrawl tau,
Gymar hwyl, gem yr heli,
12 Gamen môr, gymain' â mi?
Ni bu brifwynt planetsygn,
Na rhuthr blawdd rhwng deuglawdd dygn,
Nac esgud frwydr, nac ysgwr,
16 Nac ysgwydd gorwydd na gŵr,
Nas cyfflybwn, gwn gyni,
Grefdaer don, i'th gryfder di.
Ni bu organ na thelyn,
20 Na thafawd difeiwawd dyn,
Nas barnwn yn un gyfref,
Fordwy glas, â'th fawrdeg lef.
Ni chair yr ail gair gennyf,
24 Am f'enaid, brad naid bryd Nyf,
Ond galw ei thegwch golau
A'i phryd teg yn lle'r ffrwd dau.

Am hynny gwna na'm lluddyych,
28 Ymwanwraig loyw dwfr croyw crych,
I fyned, f'annwyl a'm barn,
Drwy lwyn bedw draw Lanbadarn
At ferch a'm gwnaeth, ffraeth ffrwythryw,
32 Forwyn fwyn, o farw yn fyw.
Cyfyng gennyf fy nghyngor,
Cyfeilles, marchoges môr.
Ateg wyd rhof a'm cymwd;
36 Atal â'th drwyn ffrwyn y ffrwd.

Pei gwypud, don ffalinglwyd—
Pefr gain lateiwraig aig wyd—
Maint fy ngherydd am drigiaw!
40 Mantell wyd i'r draethell draw.
Cyd deuthum er ail Indeg
Hyd yn dy fron, y don deg,
Ni'm lladdo rhyfel gelyn,
44 O'm lluddyud i dud y dyn,
Neu'm lladd saith ugeinradd serch;
Na'm lludd at Forfudd, f'eurferch.

34 A Prayer to St Dwynwen

Dwynwen, your beauty like the hoar-frost's tears:
from your chancel with its blazing waxen candles
well does your golden image know
4   how to assuage the griefs of wretched men.
What man soever would keep vigil in your choir
(a holy, shining pilgrimage), [you with] Indeg's radiance,
there is no sickness nor heart's sorrow
8   which he would carry with him thence from Llanddwyn.

Your holy parish is your straggling flock:
[a man] sorrowful and worn with care I am;
because of longing for my mistress
12   my heart is swollen up with love,
deep pangs grounded in anxiety,
as I well know—this is my malady—
unless I can win Morfudd
16   if I remain alive, it is but life in vain.
Make me be healed, [you] most deserving of all praise,
from my infirmity and feebleness.
For one year be both messenger of love
20   as well as mediatrix of God's grace to man.
There is no need for you, unfailing golden image,
to be afraid of sin, the body's ever-present snare.
God does not undo what he has once done,
24   good is his peaceful disposition, you will not fall from
Heaven.
No coquette will observe you now this year
whispering with us in a narrow corner.
No angry Jealous One, cruel-minded,
28   will put a cudgel to [your back], chaste-minded one.

Come, of your kindness (?)—quiet, you will not be
suspected,
Virgin of enduring sympathy,
from Llanddwyn, a place of great resort,
32   to Cwm-y-gro, [you] gem of Christendom.
God has not withheld from you (easy to be reconciled),
the gift of ample speech, nor will man reject you.
Unquestionably to the work of prayer
36   God calls you (black your wimple).
May God, your host, restrain
the two hands of that man—may there be recalled
the violence of the person who would ravish her
40   when she would follow me through the leaves of May.
Dwynwen, if you would once cause
under May's trees, and in long summer days
her poet's reward—fair one, you would be good,

Galw ar Ddwynwen (94)

Dwynwen deigr arien degwch,
Da y gŵyr o gôr fflamgwyr fflwch
Dy ddelw aur diddoluriaw
4   Digion druain ddynion draw
Dyn a wylio gloywdro glân,
Yn dy gôr, Indeg eirian,
Nid oes glefyd na bryd brwyn
8   A êl ynddo o Landdwyn.

Dy laesblaid yw dy lwysblwyf,
Dolurus ofalus wyf;
Y fron hon o hoed gordderch
12   Y sydd yn unchwydd o serch;
Hirwayw o sail gofeiliaint,
Herwydd y gwn, hwn yw haint,
Oni chaf, o byddaf byw,
16   Forfudd, llyna oferfyw.
Gwna fi'n iach, weddusach wawd,
O'm anwychder a'm nychdawd.
Cymysg lateirwydd flwyddyn
20   Â rhadau Duw rhod a dyn.
Nid rhaid, ddelw euraid ddilyth,
Yt ofn pechawd, fethlgnawd fyth.
Nid adwna, da ei dangnef,
24   Duw a wnaeth, nid ei o nef.
Ni'th wŷl mursen eleni
Yn hustyng yn yng â ni.
Ni rydd Eiddig ddig ddygnbwyll
28   War ffon i ti, wyry ei phwyll.

Tyn, o'th obr, taw, ni thybir
Wrthyd, wyry gymhlegyd hir,
O Landdwyn, dir gynired,
32   I Gwm-y-gro, gem y Gred.
Duw ni'th omeddawdd, hawdd hedd,
Dawn iaith aml, dyn ni'th omedd.
Diamau weddïau waith,
36   Duw a'th eilw, du ei thalaith.
Delid Duw, dy letywr,
Dêl i gof, dwylaw y gŵr,
Traws oedd y neb a'i treisiai,
40   Tra ddêl i'm ôl trwy ddail Mai.
Dwynwen, pes parud unwaith
Dan wŷdd Mai a hirddydd maith,
Dawn ei bardd, da, wen, y bych;

44 for, Dwynwen, you were never base.
Prove, by your gifts of splendid grace
that you are no prim virgin, prudent Dwynwen.

Because of the penance that you did
48 through goodness, for the world, and its significance,
because of the devotions that you kept,
while you were alive, the faith of [all those] of religious kind,
because of the true dedication of a nun,
52 and the virginity of the fair captive flesh ·
for the soul's sake—if it be needful now—
of Brychan with the powerful strong arms—
implore, by the agony caused by your faith,
56 of the sweet Virgin to deliver me.

44 Dwynwen, nid oeddud anwych.
Dangos o'th radau dawngoeth
Nad wyd fursen, Ddwynwen ddoeth.

Er a wnaethost yn ddawnbwys
48 O benyd y byd a'i bwys;
Er y crefydd, ffydd ffyddryw,
A wnaethost tra fuost fyw;
Er yr eirian leianaeth
52 A gwyrfdawd y coethgnawd caeth;
Er enaid, os rhaid y rhawg,
Brychan Yrth breichiau nerthawg;
Eiriol, er dy greuol gred,
56 Ar em Wyry roi ymwared.

Notes

29

This poem and the following poem to the Star (no.30) are the outstanding expressions of Dafydd's wonder and awe at the mysteries of the cosmic forces; cf. also The Skylark, no.23 (GDG 114). But inspite of its cosmic freedom from all human restrictions, the Wind is finally tamed by the poet to act as his *llatai* to Morfudd, just as the Skylark is similarly dispatched. Dr Parry has made a close analysis of the poem's meaning and craftsmanship in YB IX, 48-56 (repr. from *Lleufer* XII (1956), 119-26), concluding 'A great poet here makes use of a traditional form—that of the *cywydd llatai*—but adapts and develops it in accordance with his own taste. He did not entirely abandon the tradition, but he gave it such a masterly twist that it could never be the same again.' It seems probable that Dafydd may have known of the old riddling poem to the Wind in the Book of Taliesin (BT 36-7), since certain of his lines come very close to it: in particular the Wind in the BT poem is personified as a *creadur cadarn* 'a powerful creature' without foot or head, flesh or bone; cf. *Gŵr eres . . . heb droed heb adain*, lines 3-4 below.

4. *Drud byd.* Lit. 'foolhardy one of the world'.

6. *O bantri.* The older meaning of 'pantry' was 'store-house' cf. no.7 (GDG 29) l.19 and n.

14. *Ni'th dditia neb.* Ditio from E. 'indict'; see OED *indict¹* 'to bring a charge against, to accuse (a person) of a crime, especially by legal process'. D.J.Bowen suggests (YB IX, 57-60; repr. from Ll.C. X, 113-5) that the significance of this lies in an implied comparison with the activities of the king's official messengers: it appears from a passage which he quotes from Langland's poem *Piers Plowman* (Text C. Pass. XIV, 33-59) that these were free to take short cuts across fields, even across a field of wheat, without paying the penalty exacted from other travellers. See on this J.J.Jusserand, *English Wayfaring Life in the Middle Ages; XIV Century* (London, 1891), 230.

15. *Rhaglaw:* the chief officer in a district, who issued summonses and collected rents.

18. *I'th ddydd. Dydd* has here the meaning of 'lifetime'; (the line is cited to exemplify this meaning in GPC).

19. *gam gymwyll. Cymwyll* 'reason, argument, mention, discourse' (GPC). Other instances of what appear to be variants of the same idiomatic phrase occur in no.12 (GDG 84), l.30 *cymwyll caeth*, and GDG 43, l.17 *oferedd gymwyll* 'argument of vanity'. It is perhaps the equivalent of 'no need to mention it' or 'spare the thought'. In contrast cf. GDG 136.8 *da gymwyll*, '(it is) good to mention'.

21. *Ni'th wŷl drem.* Cf. BT 37, 16 *kanys gwyl golwc* 'for no eye sees him'. An alternative meaning for *gwâl* is 'lair'.

23. *Noter wybr.* From E. *noter* 'a writer of the musical score in manuscripts' marker of a book, words, etc. with a musical score', OED. (The earliest instance in E. is by Lydgate, c.1440). The metaphor is complicated: Dr Parry suggests that the Wind disposes the clouds in the sky in the same way as the *noter* inscribes notes of music on parchment.

24. *naw tir gŵydd. Tir gŵydd* is uncultivated or fallow land. Cf. no.23 (GDG 114), 32 *gwyndir gŵydd*; GDG 93, 24 *talar gŵydd*; both with similar meaning.

31. *emyn.* GP 1391 cites this instance as diminutive of *gem* 'jewel'. The alternative *emyn* 'hymn' is not impossible, '(you with) assiduous chant', cf. IGE², 80, l.27 (of the plough) *aml y canai ei emyn*.

33. *ymefin.* Dr Parry notes only one other occurrence of this word, RBP 1281, 23, in which it may be either a noun or an adj. Here it is perhaps a verb-noun, but the translation given is purely conjectural.

34. *Drythyllfab. Drythyll (trythyll)* 'wanton, licentious', etc. is frequently used of horses, meaning 'lively'. It is used by Dafydd of the Blackbird, GDG 76, l.28.

40. *hin y fron.* Either 'weather of the hill' or cf. the *hin* in *hiniog* 'threshold'; hence 'limit'. The reading is supported by nearly all the MSS, though in the context its significance is not very clear.

41. *Uwch Aeron.* An e.g. of the old constr. by which destination after verbs of motion was expressed without intervening preposition. Uwch Aeron was the cantref lying north of the river Aeron which included Dafydd's birthplace at Brogynin, Aberystwyth, and Cwm-y-Glo, supposedly the site of Morfudd's paternal home; see n. to no.35 (GDG 83), l.40 below, and cf. no.34 (GDG 94), l.32. See map facing p.xiii.

46. *a'i maeth. Maeth* may be either a noun 'sustenance', or past passive of verb *maethu* 'to rear, foster, nourish'. This ambiguity is no doubt intentional.

49. *caethwlad* 'exiled'. GPC cites. T. Wiliems's dictionary as giving the only other recorded e.g. of the word.

55. *o'r sygnau. Sygn* 'sign (of the zodiac)' is from E. *segn*, Fr. *seigne*, or Lat. *signum* (EEW 43). It is used commonly by Dafydd and his contemporaries to denote the stars; cf. no.33 (GDG 71), l.13 *planetsygn;* no.36 (GDG 68), l.34 *teirsygn*, and introductory n. to the next poem.

57. *corodyn.* The word is derived from mediaeval E. *corrodie*, Lat. *corrodium* 'an allowance of provisions for lodging, board, etc. granted usually by a religious house to a guarantee as an annuity for the term of life; hence 'provision for maintenance, pension' (OED). It was frequenetly used of the allowance made by the king to retired minstrels. GDG 462 interprets the word as *peth bychan, teclyn, tegan*, and the corresponding 'treasure' seems to suit each of the three other instances in which Dafydd employs *corodyn*, though this meaning is hardly applicable here. Davies and T. Wiliems's dictionaries associate the word with W. *corr* 'dwarf', a popular etymology which may have influenced the meanings attributed to it.

62. *dewis wybren. Dewis* can be either a noun, an adj. or a verb. I take it here as a noun 'chosen person': this corresponds with its usage by Hywel ab Owain Gwynedd, *Fy newis i, rhiain firain feindeg* (OBWV no.23; RBP 1428, ls.3-4). *Wybr, wybren* can mean either 'sky' or 'cloud': either is equally valid here, as also in ls.1, 23, 64.

30

In this poem, even more than in the previous one (see introductory n.) the poet's conformity with the *llatai* convention appears most perfunctory, being almost confined to two lines (39-40). Dafydd's real subject is the splendour and magnificence of the stars by night: they are the supreme example of the perfect order of God's creation. The firm belief he held in common with his contemporaries in all countries in the decisive influence of the planets upon human affairs must inevitably have formed an element in his admiration.

1. *am liw ewyn.* Fondness for imagery of moving water in describing girls' beauty is a convention which Dafydd inherited from the Gogynfeirdd, and he employs it with varying degrees of sincerity and light irony; see *Tradn. and Innov.* 18-19.

5-6. *Pell yw i'm bryd ddirprwyaw.* Cf. the very similar wording in no.5 (GDG 121), ls.33-4 above.

7-8. *i wrach serth swydd.* Cf. GDG 80, l.13 where a *gwrach heinus ddolurus ddig* 'a wretched diseased hag' figures as one of the three gatekeepers of the Jealous Husband of the girl to whom the poet wishes to obtain access. Such a duenna is a commonplace in mediaeval literature, inherited from Ovid and from the Romance of the Rose.

15-16. In the interests of clarity my translation reverses the order of the lines in this couplet.

20. *saeroniaeth y sêr.* God's supreme artistry and craftsmanship as displayed in the stars is a concept which goes back to Boethius. It is widely celebrated in mediaeval literature; for instance, in the Romance of the Rose and in Chaucer.

23-38. These lines are a comparatively rare instance in which Dafydd uses the device of *dyfalu* for the purpose of praise rather than—as is far more frequent—for the purpose of satire or abuse. See note to no.33 below.

23. *cannaid* 'shining', as a noun denotes anything that shines or glistens, hence 'beacon'.

24. *ehwybrbwyll.* The rendering is conjectural: *ewybr* as adj. 'swift, clear, cloudless'; *pwyll* 'nature, disposition' (CLlH 85).

28. *Afrlladen.* The consecrated wafer symbolizing the body of Christ which in the service of the Mass is consecrated by the officiating priest. Cf. no.24 (GDG 122), l.26.

29-30. *Nis bawdd.* The syntax is slightly obscure, but the meaning is that the Star's brightness will not be 'drowned' or extinguished; the 'platter' will not be 'washed up'.

30.32. *dysgl saig; cawg.* Here again the imagery derives from the consecrated vessels holding bread and wine at the Mass.

36. *goldyn.* Dafydd has a particular fondness for imagery based upon currency: cf. his use of *fflwring* 'florin' for the leaves of May in no.2 (GDG 23) above (*Tradn. and Innov.* 43-4).

37. *Gwir fwcled. Bwcled* from E. 'buckler', a small round shield.

41. *o'r lle y bo.* The subject is the Star—not Morfudd.

43. *Gosgedd torth gan.* The image associates the Star with the consecrated bread of the Eucharist, this referring back to *afrlladen*, l.28.

31

This poem offers a unique parallel to the tale of the 'Dream of Maxen' in The Mabinogion, since in both a hunting-scene is the preliminary to a dream-vision in which the dreamer sees the girl that he loves. But Dafydd's dream has the form of an allegory which needs to be interpreted by a skilled interpreter, for the girl that he seeks appears as a white doe, and the hounds are explained as his *llateion* or love-messengers. This type of enigmatic or symbolic dream has a number of continental parallels, and it goes back ultimately to Ovid (*Amores III*, 5). It was regarded in the Middle Ages as highly meaningful and significant, and was the subject of learned commentary and analysis. (See *Tradn. and Innov.* 32-3).

1. *gwyddwn.* Dafydd uses the imperfect where we should expect the pres. *gwn;* similarly in no.25 (GDG 63), l.65; GDG 36, l.9.

3-4. *Gwelais . . . breuddwyd.* So also when Maxen fell asleep while hunting *y gwelai vreudwyt* 'he saw a dream'. The formula *gwelais* 'I saw' is often employed in the older poetry to introduce accounts of battle-scenes, but 'seeing' of this kind frequently implies the occult vision which in ancient society was the prerogative of the Celtic poet. (See I.Ll.Foster, YB V, 21-3).

11. *oriau* in this instance does not mean 'prayers' but 'barking, baying'; DGG[2] 198.

15. *rhawt* is from E. 'rout'; DGG[2] 199; EEW 208.

17-19. *esgair, drum,* and *cefn* 'mountain ridge' are really all synonymous, the variation between them being governed by metrical requirements. Dr Parry points out that by the time of Dafydd *drum* had become *trum* in speech, but that here as elsewhere the poet freely employed either contemporary or archaic forms as best suited the *cynghanedd*. For the vacillation between initial *dr-* and *tr-* see TC 460-1.

23. *Dwyffroen* 'two nostrils', i.e. the nose of the doe, whose touch awakened him.

24. *yn y bwth*. It seems unlikely that the *bwth* 'cottage' can be equated with the *teg blas* 'fair mansion' of l.8, but it is possible.

30. *rhyw derfyn*. Lit. '(if you could put) some end'.

31 *gwn ganclwyf*. This *sangiad*, which is little more than a line-filler, recurs GDG 90, l.3. It has other variants: *gwn gannoch* no.46 (GDG 17), l.3; *gwn gyni* no.33 (GDG 71), l.17; no.41 (GDG 89), l.35.

36. *pei gwypud iaith lud*. i.e. 'if you knew how to interpret them'.

40. *hoen geirw tes*. Lit. 'of vigour like to waves of heat'. This is an unusual variant of a very frequent conventional formula for a girl's beauty; cf. DGG² LXXXVIII (OBWV 77), 81 *hoen geirw afonydd*, RBP 1318 l.38 (Gr. ap Maredudd) *hoen geirw kreicneint* 'of vigour like the waves of rocky streams'. *Geirw* is 'waves, rippling water', but is not elsewhere recorded for waves of heat.

32

The *llatai* in this poem is not the Clock of the title, but the poet's Dream which was disturbed by it. It is necessary, as with the previous poem, to take account of the great significance which the mediaeval mind attached to dreams: in this case, the belief that in sleep the spirit actually leaves the human body and goes to the place of which a person dreams. (Here again, a comparison with the emperor's dream in 'The Dream of Maxen' is relevant.) Thus Dafydd's Dream was able to conduct his spirit to the presence of a girl whom he had loved at some former time (*cynnar fodd* l.1; *gynt* l.5; *gynnau* l.18), but his 'meeting' with her was shattered by the striking Clock. There is no record of any clock in Wales in the 14th century, though Dafydd makes several references to an *orlais, -oes* 'clock'; see no.10 (GDG 34), l.11 n. Late Latin *clocca* gave (via Fr. or E.) both *cloch* 'bell' as in no.41 (GDG 89), l.10; 24 (GDG 122), l.30, and *cloc* in Welsh; *cloc* and *orlais* (E. and Fr. *orloge*) seem to have been used interchangeably for a clock in both W. and E.; cf. Chaucer's description of Chantecleer 'Wel sikerer was his crowyng/than is a clokke or an abbey orloge'. The earliest clocks came into Britain in the third quarter of the 14th century and by the end of the century there were clocks at Salisbury, Wells, St Alban's, and other cathedral cities. Where Dafydd can have seen one remains quite uncertain, but his detailed references in ls.24-8 suggest first-hand knowledge of a clock on which the hours were mechanically struck, such as might have been possessed by some monastic institution (cf. l.33). His contemporary, Jean Froissart, composed before 1370 a love-poem called *Li Orloge Amoreus* in which the lover makes a detailed comparison of all parts of his anatomy with the mechanism of a clock—the case is his heart, the master-wheel with its weights and cords his desire, and other parts have appropriate allegorical meanings. But his analysis concentrates on the clock's mechanism rather than its sound: it therefore has very little in common with Dafydd's abusive *dyfalu* of the Clock for its disturbing noise. Dr I.C.Peate called attention to Froissart's poem (Ll.C. V,119-21; *Clock and Watch Makers in Wales* (1975), l.15), and speculated as to whether Dafydd could in any way have been influenced by it or by its author. But a comparison between the two poems is not really relevant, except as a curiosity: any similarity in their themes arises from the fact that the two 14th century poets were similarly fascinated by a recent scientific invention—and there is no lack of parallels in Dafydd's work for his introduction into his verse of metaphors based upon the very newest artefacts and inventions.

3-4. *I'r dref wiw . . . a'r gaer gron*. Dr Parry identified the *tref* with Brecon (GDG 498-9) on the basis of the place-names *Blaenrheon* and *Aberrheon* in the immediate neighbourhood, and in GDG² 557-8 he accepts Dr Peate's proposal that the 'rounded fort' is more likely to be Brecon's Norman castle than the Roman fort, as he had suggested earlier. Even if Brecon was the girl's home, however, this does not mean that the Clock which disturbed the poet was anywhere nearby: Dafydd may indeed have been many miles away.

6. *adwaeniad*. Archaic ending of 3 sg. imperf. (GMW 122).

15. *eang eilun*. Dr Peate *loc.cit.*, suggests that this is an allusion to the Cross at Brecon priory, formerly famous. I prefer to take it as parallel to *angel bach* in the following line: *eilun* means a semblance or reflection, not necessarily a concrete representation (as in GDG 4, 1.4). Moreover Dafydd uses *eilun* of himself elsewhere, *eilun prydydd* no.43. (GDG 137), 1.8; and of his shadow *rhyw eilun* no.52 (GDG 141), 1.5. *Eang* 'ample, spacious', etc., hence perhaps 'conspicuous, manifest'.

16. *Angel bach*. i.e. Dafydd's own *persona* or *spirit—his eilun*. Cf. *megis angel y'm gwely* no.50 (GDG 62), 1.31 below.

17. *o'm tyb isod*. Lit. 'with my thought below'.

26. *A'i buarthau*. GPC lists no other meaning for *buarth* than 'sheep-fold' enclosure, farmyard' and the like. In view of Dr Peate's specialized knowledge of clocks, I give here an approximation of his rendering of *buarthau* as 'yr ochrau petryalog' (Ll.C. V, 121); 'the rectangular sides' *Clock and Watch Makers in Wales* 14 'its yards'.

33. *mynachglos*. Saunders Lewis suggests (Ll.C. II, 206; *Meistri'r Can-rifoedd* 51) that this monastery may have been at Chester, or possibly Glastonbury, where there was a clock in 1335; cf. GDG² 558, and Geraint Gruffydd, YB X (1977),183. But either location—or indeed any other—must remain purely speculative.

34. *Melin ŵyll*. On the owl's sinister connotations see n. to no.26 (GDG 26) 41.

42. *Deifr*, more frequently *Dyfr*, listed in a triad as *Dyfyr Wallt Eureit* 'Golden-Haired D.', one of the maidens at Arthur's Court; TYP 215,335.

44. *Eigr*. See n. to no.16 (GDG 81), 20.

48. *A ddaw hun iddi heno*. Saunders Lewis, *Meistri'r Canrifoedd* 51-2, prefers the alternative reading *Ei hun a ddaw hi heno* 'will she herself come tonight?' for which he claims the support of a single MS, Llan-stephan 6. Although this appears more intelligible in the context, the emendation lacks adequate MS confirmation. The implication of the line as it stands in all the other MSS is that the girl must herself be sleeping in order that the poet may dream of her.

50. *Nith yr haul*. Cf. the similar—but derogatory—epithet *nith y gog* 'cuckoo's niece', no.18 (GDG 41), 1.38.

33

From this poem it might be inferred that for Dafydd the very essence of poetry consisted in the art of *dyfalu*, or imaginative flights of comparison: here he employs the device 'positively' to pay a tribute of slightly ironic praise to the river Dyfi and to his mistress. There exists a remarkable parallel in a poem in which Ovid remonstrates with a certain Italian river (not named) which, like the Dyfi, is in spate and prevents the poet from crossing to visit his lady (*Amores III*, 6; see *Tradn. and Innov.*, 26-7). A Celtic parallel which is also apposite tells how an Irish poet named Athirne satirized the river Mourne for refusing to provide him with a salmon; the river then rose in anger against him, but was pacified by the poet's tribute of a praise-poem, after which it returned to its normal course, leaving numerous stranded salmon on its banks. This is cited in an early Irish tract on the privileges of poets (*Ériu* XIII, 57) and in a 13th century bardic poem by Giolla Brighde Mac Con Midhe (ed, Nicholas Williams, *Irish Texts Society* vol. LI., no.XI). Other parallels might be cited for irascible rivers rising in vindictiveness against mortals, exx. *Iliad* XXI and in the Irish epic tale *The Cattle-Raid of Cooley*, but the two I have quoted have especial relevance, since on the one hand there is additional evidence which suggests that Dafydd may have had first-hand knowledge of the *Amores* (see nn. to nos.31 (GDG 39) and 37 (GDG 58); and on the other we have in the anecdote of Athirne an instance of another Celtic poet apostrophizing the river Mourne in praise-poetry (and satire) as Dafydd does the Dyfi.

1. *bengrychlon*. *Pengrych* means normally 'curly-headed' as in Dafydd's description of himself, no.51 (GDG 105),15; *llon* 'agitated, cheerful'. Personification is thus introduced at the outset; cf. *ymanwraig* 1.28, *marchoges mor* 1.34.

2. *goel budd*. The 'portent' is the poet's expected reward from the girl, presumably Morfudd. Cf. *coel nos* no.31 (GDG 39), 1.28 'portent of the night'.

6. *Drais y dwfr*. Lit. 'oppression (or tyranny) of water'.

7. *trefn trychanrhwyd*. Lit. 'by order (arrangement) of three hundred nets'.

12. *camen* 'turn, bend, loop'. Dr Parry suggests that the allusion is to the bend in the wave's crest just before it breaks. Tentatively I suggest 'inlet' as an alternative. The allusion is to the Dyfi where it enters its estuary.

13. *planetsygn*. Cf. no.29 (GDG 117), 1.55 n.

14. *deuglawdd*. It is difficult to dissociate the 'two banks' from the two opposing banks of the river, but the meaning is obscure.

24. *brad naid*. Lit. 'a leap of treachery' (?), though *naid* has also the secondary meaning 'fortune', as in no.51 (GDG 105), 1.17 below; (on this meaning see CLIH 124-5; IGE² 385). Perhaps this anticipates the poet's intention of turning all his praise of Morfudd into a comparison with the river (ls.25-6). With *brad* cf. *brad brydferth* no.25 (GDG 63), 29. On *Nyf* see n. to no.15, 56.

26. *yn lle*. In DGG² 203, Ifor Williams interprets *yn lle* as the equivalent of *fel* in this instance, rather than as having its usual meaning of 'instead of'. He compares *yn lle gwir* as the equivalent of *yn wir*. Henceforth Dafydd will praise Morudd's beauty as being like the river, since this is the highest praise he could give to it.

31. *ffraeth ffrwythryw*. Alternatively 'an eloquent kind of profit'. However translated, this *sangiad* relates to Dafydd's recurrent theme of the 'payment' he expects—and continually fails—to receive from girls for his tribute of praise-poetry.

33. *cyfyng . . . fy nghyngor*. *Cyfyng-gyngor* 'quandary, perplexity, embarrassement' (GPC).

35. *cymwd*. The 'commote' was the township or smallest territorial unit for administrative purposes.

36. *a'th drwyn*. Lit. 'with your nose'. The metaphor of the wave as 'horsewoman of the sea' is thus maintained.

41. *Indeg*. See n. to no.14 (GDG 89), 11.

34

It is clear from this poem that Dafydd knew of St Dwynwen (*Dwyn + gwen* 'holy') as the saint who had the interests of lovers particularly at heart: hence his impassioned plea, almost in a single breath, that she should go as his *llatai* to Morfudd, and that she should intercede for him with the Virgin. But how much more he may have known of any tradition concerning her remains quite uncertain. Dwynwen's own love-story is recounted for the first time in the *Iolo Manuscripts* (Llandovery, 1848), 84, 474. According to this she rejected her would-be ravisher, whom God then turned to stone; subsequently she became a nun, and obtained from God the boon that all true lovers who called on her would either win the object of their desire, or would cease for ever from wanting it. It is difficult to avoid the suspicion that the nucleus of this story is based on Iolo's own conjectural interpretation of ls.36-46 of the poem. However, Dafydd appears to have had first-hand knowledge of the church dedicated to Dwynwen on Llanddwyn island, off the west coast of Anglesey, whose ruins may still be seen. Here people flocked to pray to the saint for healing from all kinds of ailments, and Llanddwyn remained a very popular resort of pilgrimage throughout the Middle Ages (see Hartwell-Jones, *Y Cymmrodor* XXIII, 323; LBS ii, 387-92). A late 15th century *cywydd* by Sir David Trefor describes the site in graphic detail: the saint's statue (cf. l.3), the miracles wrought at her holy-well, and the crowds of young people who came there bearing candles and offerings, hoping for a cure for their various ailments (Hugh Owen, *Hanes Plwyf Niwbwrch* (Caernarfon, 1952), 62-3). In addition, Dafydd knew of an old tradition that Dwynwen was one of the daughters of Brychan Brycheiniog, that prolific progenitor of saints (l.54, see n.).

5. *dyn* is ambiguous as to sex, but *ynddo* in l.8 proves that a man is here intended; in lines 20, 34 it is generic for 'mankind'.

6. *Indeg*. See n. to no.14 (GDG 79), l.11 above.

19. *llateirwydd*. Lit. 'Mix the activity of a *llatai* for a year with God's graces (blessings) between you and man.'

23- 4. *Nid adwna*, etc. The proverb appears in Davies's collection, but at an earlier date in CLIH VI, 30c.

25. *mursen*. 'a coy person, a coquette, a flirt', as in no.38 (GDG 48), l.27. It derives from E. 'virgin', (EEW 130), but since *gwyry* (as in l.30) denoted this in Welsh, *mursen* developed in addition the secondary meanings given above, and it is by no means easy to be sure of the exact meaning in many instances: Gruffudd Gryg addresses the Moon as *mursen*, DGG[2] LXXIV, l.12, but Guto'r Glyn appears to use *mursen* in its literal sense of 'virgin', *Gwaith Guto'r Glyn*, XCIII, l.28.

26. *â ni*. Dafydd uses the pl., but evidently means himself.

28. *War ffon. Gwarffon* is 'a blow (with a stick) on the nape of the neck or back' (GPC).

29. *oth obr*. In legal usage *g(w)obr* meant 'maiden-fee', but developed wider meanings such as 'benefit, hire', etc. Hence my conjectural rendering.

31. *O Landdwyn*. See introductory n. above. On *cynired* see CLIH 105-6. The meaning of *tir gynired* is that Llanddwyn was a place 'frequented', i.e. a place of pilgrimage.

32. *I Gwm-y-gro*. This clearly denotes Morfudd's home, elsewhere *Nant-y-Glo* (no.35, l.40 below; see n.). this also is consistent with the ref. to her home as in *Uwch Aeron*, no.29 (GDG 117), l.41, and the description of her as *seren Nant-y-Seri*, no.15 (GDG 98), l.2. *Cwmseiri* and *Cwm-y-Glo* adjoin each other closely. Between the two lies a field called *Llety Gwilym* (B. VIII, 142).

34. *iaith aml* 'ample speech' here means 'ample means of expression, sufficient arguments'.

36. *du ei thalaith*. Dr Parry interprets *talaith* here as referring to the nun's head-dress, or wimple, worn by Dwynwen. A recurrent difficulty in the poem is the alternation between 2nd. and 3rd. person in address to Dwynwen; cf. l.28 above.

37. *dy letywr. Lletywr* means both 'lodger' and 'host'; cf. Salesbury's dictionary 'an hoste'. This last is evidently the meaning here.

38-40. *y gŵr . . . y neb a'i treisiai.* These lines are obscure: they may possibly refer to Morfudd's husband. The subject of *tra ddêl* (l.40) is equally ambiguous as to whether it should be rendered 'she' or 'he'.

47. *dawnbwys. Dawn da* means 'blessing, virtue, quality (of character)' (GPC); *pwys* 'importance', hence 'significance'.

49. *y crefydd.* i.e. the religious observances, ordinances, or sacraments.

54. *Brychan Yrth.* 'Powerful B.' The father of Dwynwen, according to the 11th century tract *De Situ Brecheniauc.* This attributes to Brychan a family of ten sons and twenty-four daughters, most of whom became saints; see EWGT 14-16; TYP 288.

55. *er dy greuol gred.* Lit. 'because of your bloody faith'. In rendering this as 'the agony (caused by) your faith' I am influenced by Bleddyn Fardd's reference to the *croes greuol* (H.29a, 52) 'the agony of the Cross'. Perhaps the allusion here is to Dwynwen's matyrdom: an early 18th century MS (pre-Iolo), *Cardiff 26* tells us in a memorandum dated 1710 that some people report that Dwynwen was martyred beside her well on Llanddwyn island 'and that many superstitious people go there to find out their fortune, or their lovers, whether they will get them or not', Rep. ii,215.

V. LOVE'S FRUSTRATIONS (35-43)

35   Journeying for Love

Did ever anybody, tyrannized by love,
travel as I have done, for a girl's sake,
through frost and snow—what an enormity—
4   through rain and wind for her of dazzling form?
Nothing but exhaustion did I get from it,
for never in my life did my two feet endure
greater unease in going to Cellïau'r Meirch,
8   compelled by her attraction for [my] gain (?), across Eleirch,
a wilderness, direct by night and day,
and I no nearer my reward.

O God, I shouted out
12   aloud in Celli Fleddyn,
giving voice [only] for her sake,
to make profession of my love for her.
Bysaleg, with low raucous noise,
16   a hollow boiling flood, a short and narrow river,
extremely often, for her sake,
I waded every day through it.
[Then] I would go, proud and free
20   yet in my deep dejection, to the Pass of Dafydd's Sons;
then away over to the Camallt,
and to the hillside for the girl with lovely hair.
Swiftly I would make my way
24   to the forked gap of Gyfylfaen,
to cast my eye along the pleasant valley
for the maiden dressed in fur.
She will not wander either here or there,
28   passing beyond me stealthily.
I was assiduous and without rest
going along Pant Cwcwll in the summer,
and around Castell Gwgawn
32   —pouncing like a goose-chick where he might get a stalk.
I ran past Heilin's dwelling
with course like to a husky, tired hound.

I stood below the court of Ifor
36   like a monk in hidden corner of the choir,
attempting, with no promise of gain,
to get a meeting with sweet Morfudd.
There is no hillock nor deep hollow
40   on either side the valley of Nant-y-Glo
whose twists and turns my passion does not know
by heart, a sprightly-minded Ovid.
Easy for me, by calling through my fist
44   with true intention of possessing, [at] Gwern-y-Talwrn,
where I had a glimpse, a cherished favour
of the slender girl beneath her sober mantle;

Taith i Garu (83)

A gerddodd neb er gordderch
A gerddais i, gorddwy serch?
Rhew ac eiry, y rhyw garedd,
4 Glaw a gwynt er gloyw ei gwedd.
Ni chefais eithr nych ofwy,
Ni chafas deudroed hoed hwy
Ermoed i Gellïau'r Meirch,
8 Eurdrais elw, ar draws Eleirch,
Yn anial dir yn uniawn
Nos a dydd, ac nid nes dawn.

O Dduw, ys uchel o ddyn
12 Ei floedd yng Nghelli Fleddyn,
Ymadrodd er ei mwyn hi,
Ymarddelw o serch bûm erddi.
Bysaleg, iselgreg sôn,
16 Berwgau lif, bergul afon,
Mynych iawn, er ei mwyn hi,
Y treiddiwn beunydd trwyddi.
I Fwlch yr awn, yn falch rydd,
20 Mau boen dwfn, Meibion Dafydd.
Ac ymaith draw i'r Gamallt,
Ac i'r rhiw er gwiw ei gwallt.
Ebrwydd y cyrchwn o'r blaen
24 Gafaelfwlch y Gyfylfaen,
I fwrw am forwyn wisgra
Dremyn ar y dyffryn da.
Ni thry nac yma na thraw
28 Hebof yn lledrad heibiaw.
Ystig fûm ac anaraf
Ar hyd Pant Cwcwll yr haf,
Ac ogylch Castell Gwgawn,
32 Gogwydd cyw gŵydd lle câi gawn.
Rhedais heb Adail Heilin,
Rhediad bloesg fytheiad blin.

Sefais goris llys Ifor
36 Fal mynach mewn cilfach côr,
I geisio, heb addo budd,
Gyfarfod â gwiw Forfudd.
Nid oes dwyn na dwys dyno
40 Yn neutu glyn Nant-y-glo
Nas medrwyf o'm nwyf a'm nydd
Heb y llyfr, hoywbwyll Ofydd.
Hawdd ym wrth leisio i'm dwrn,
44 Gwir nod helw, Gwern-y-Talwrn,
Lle y cefais weled, ged gu,
Llerwddyn dan fantell orddu,

where will for evermore be seen
48   without growth of grass or springing trees
our bed's shape beneath fine saplings,
a place of trodden leaves, like Adam's path.

Woe to the soul that is without reward,
52   if that for very weariness and without pay
it wanders in precisely the same way
the miserable body went.

36   The Mist

Yesterday, Thursday, [being] a day for drinking,
a gift I got, and glad I was to get it—
a portent of learning (?)—I am lean with faithful love
4   for her—and I obtained an interlude
under the shining branches of the forest's green
with a girl: she grants to me this tryst.

No one, under God our genial Father
8   could have known—and she was well-endowed—
when Thursday came, at early dawn,
how replete I was with joy
as I went to see her fair form,
12   to the place where was the slender maid.
But there came Mist, resembling night,
across the expanse of the moor,
a parchment-roll, making a back-cloth for the rain,
16   coming in grey ranks to impede me
like a tin sieve that was rusting,
a snare for birds on the black earth,
a murky barrier on a narrow path,
20   an endless coverlet to the sky,
a grey cowl discolouring the ground,
placing in hiding every hollow valley,
a scaffolding that can be seen on high,
24   an enormous bruise over the hill, a vapour on the land,
a thick and pale-grey, weakly-trailing fleece,
like smoke, a hooded cowl upon the plain,
a hedge of rain to hinder my good fortune,
28   coat-armour of the oppressive shower.
Of aspect dark, deceiving men,
a shaggy mantle on the land.
Troublesome high towers belonging
32   to the family of Gwyn, the province of the wind.
His two harsh cheeks conceal the land
torches seeking the three stars (?)
thick and ugly (?) darkness as of night

Lle y gwelir yn dragywydd,
48 Heb dwf gwellt, heb dyfu gwŷdd,
Llun ein gwâl dan wial da,
Lle briwddail fal llwybr Adda.

Gwae ef yr enaid heb sâl,
52 Rhag blinder heb gwbl undal,
O thry yr unffordd achlân
Y tröes y corff truan.

Y Niwl (68)

Doe Ddifiau, dydd i yfed,
Da fu ym gael, dyfu ym ged,
Coel fawrddysg, cul wyf erddi,
4 Cyfa serch, y cefais i
Gwrs glwysgainc goris glasgoed
Gyda merch, gedy ym oed.

Nid oedd, o dan hoywdduw Dad,
8 Dawn iddi, dyn a wyddiad,
Or bydd Difiau, dechrau dydd,
Lawned fûm o lawenydd,
Yn myned, gweled gwiwlun,
12 I'r tir ydd oedd feinir fun,
Pan ddoeth yn wir ar hirros
Niwl yn gynhebyg i nos;
Rhol fawr a fu'n glawr i'r glaw,
16 Rhestri gleision i'm rhwystraw;
Rhidyll ystaen yn rhydu,
Rhwyd adar y ddaear ddu;
Cae anghlaer mewn cyfynglwybr,
20 Carthen anniben yn wybr.
Cwfl llwyd yn cyfliwio llawr,
Cwfert ar bob cwm ceufawr.
Clwydau uchel a welir,
24 Clais mawr uwch garth, tarth y tir.
Cnu tewlwyd gwynllwyd gwanllaes
Cyfliw â mwg, cwfl y maes.
Coetgae glaw er lluddiaw lles,
28 Codarmur cawad ormes.
Twyllai wŷr, tywyll o wedd,
Toron gwrddonig tiredd.
Tyrau uchel eu helynt,
32 Tylwyth Gwyn, talaith y gwynt.
Tir a gudd ei ddeurudd ddygn,
Torsedd yn cyrchu'r teirsygn.
Tywyllwg, un tew allardd,

36 blinding the world, to cheat the poet.
A broad web of valuable cambric
has been spread abroad like rope
[or] like a spider's web—the produce of French shops—
40 the heathy headland of the family of Gwyn.
It is often speckled smoke:
the rising vapour which surrounds the woods of May.
Unsightly fog wherein the dogs are barking,
44 ointment of the witches of Annwfn.
In sinister-wise it wets like dew,
the heavy, sodden mail-coat of the earth.

Easier to journey on the moors
48 by night, than in a day-time Mist;
the stars shine from the sky
like the flames of waxen candles,
but there comes—pain of frustrated promise—
52 neither God's stars nor moon in Mist.
Churlishly did the Mist imprison me,
for ever captive in the dark—it was gloomy—
it kept me from my path under the sky;
56 a dark-grey sheet impedes love's envoy,
and hinders me from going,
and reaching quickly to my girl of slender brows.

37   To Love a Poet or a Soldier?

'Sweet slender maiden, hesitating (?) girl,
dark-browed, and wearing gold and precious stones,
Think, Eigr, with your store of augrim [stones],
4 is there, beneath fresh leaves, some payment due to me'
—a clear reproach, voiced obviously—
'for what I sang, [you] jewel of beauty,
in brilliant copious speech, to your fair hue,
8 and lovely image, bright as gossamer?'

'I can for long renounce you, Dafydd,
love has been dulled—it is reproach to you—
for being—recognizing [all] impediments—
12 too cowardly, to give it a right name.
None, with God's help, shall ever win me, but
the one who is the bravest, you preposterous man.'

'[Girl] crowned with fine-spun hair like gossamer
16 you wrong me, most discerning one.
Though I, a genial cultured youth
be cowardly in battle, with undefended breast,

134

36 Delli byd i dwyllo bardd.
   Llydanwe gombr gostombraff,
   Ar lled y'i rhodded fal rhaff.
   Gwe adrgop, Ffrengigsiop ffrwyth,
40 Gwaun dalar Gwyn a'i dylwyth.
   Mwg brych yn fynych a fydd,
   Mygedorth cylch Mai goedydd.
   Anardd darth lle y cyfarth cŵn,
44 Ennaint gwrachïod Annwn.
   Gochwith megis gwlith y gwlych,
   Habrsiwn tir anehwybrsych.

   Haws cerdded nos ar rosydd
48 I daith nog ar niwl y dydd;
   Y sêr a ddaw o'r awyr
   Fal fflamau canhwyllau cwyr,
   Ac ni ddaw, poen addaw pŵl,
52 Lloer na sêr Nêr ar nïwl.
   Gwladaidd y'm gwnaeth yn gaeth-ddu
   Y niwl fyth, anolau fu;
   Lluddiodd ym lwybr dan wybren,
56 Llatai a ludd llwytu len,
   A lluddias ym, gyflym gael,
   Fyned ar fy nyn feinael.

Merch yn Edliw ei Lyfrdra (58)

   'Yr edlaesferch wawr dlosfain
   Wrm ael, a wisg aur a main,
   Ystyr, Eigr ystôr awgrym,
 4 Is dail ir, a oes dâl ym,
   Ymliw glân o amlwg lais,
   Em o bryd, am a brydais
   I'th loywliw, iaith oleulawn,
 8 A'th lun gwych, wythloywne gwawn.'

   'Hir y'th faddeuaf, Ddafydd,
   Hurtiwyd serch, hort iti sydd,
   O'th fod, rhyw gydnabod rhus,
12 Yn rhylwfr, enw rhywolus.
   Ni'm caiff innau, noddiau Naf,
   Uthr wyd, ŵr, eithr y dewraf.'

   'Cwfl manwallt, cyfliw manwawn,
16 Cam a wnai, ddyn cymen iawn.
   Cyd bwyf was cyweithas coeth
   Llwfr yn nhrin, llawfron rhynoeth,

yet am I not, where there be fresh green trees,
20 a coward in the work of Ovid's book.

'Think also, Eigr's peer in beauty,
that payment is obligatory [and should be]
a foremost (?) care; nor is it good to love
24 a hero (it has been [a cause of] grievous trouble)
lest—it is not a pleasant thought—
[being] a soldier [he should be] too harsh.
Too boorish will he be, his nature wild,
28 he will love war, and all accursedness.
If he should hear—a fierce, perverse compulsion—
of battle in the land of France, or Scotland,
to seek adventure, yonder on his way,
32 a man enlisted, he will run off there.
If it by chance befall that he escape
from there, with skill curbing the French
he'll be all scarred, a bowman will have shot him,
36 and brutal [too], my splendid dazzling girl.
He prefers yonder his heavy lance
and his sword—woe who puts faith in him—
his corselet of steel and stupid shield
40 and his war-horse, to a sweet girl.
He won't protect you when there comes a cry of pain:
only by violence will he fetch you from your home.

'But I, endowed with sprightly speech,
44 were I to win you, bright hue of shining gossamer,
well do I know—I would weave expert praise,
come, girl—how I would ever cherish you.
Were I to win with certain grasp
48 two kingdoms—lass with Deifr's charm,
and twice the brightness of the sun—not [even] for those
would I depart
eight times the splendour of the day, forth from your
shining home.'

38 The Girls of Llanbadarn

I am distraught with passion:
a plague on all the parish girls!
because I never—violation of trysts—
4 was able to win even one of them,
no maiden—a gentle request—
nor little maid, nor hag, nor wife.

What bashfulness is this, what mischief?
8 How have I failed, that they'll have none of me?
What harm, to lass with slender brows,

136

Nid gwas, lle bo gwyrddlas gwŷdd,
20 Llwfr wyf ar waith llyfr Ofydd.

'A hefyd, Eigr gyhafal,
Ystyr di, ys diwyr dâl,
Neitio cur, nad da caru
24 Gwas dewr fyth, a gwst oer fu,
Rhag bod, nid cydnabod cain,
Rhyfelwr yn rhy filain.
Rhinwyllt fydd a rhy anwar,
28 Rhyfel ac oerfel a gâr.
O chlyw fod, taer orfod tyn,
Brwydr yng ngwlad Ffrainc neu Brydyn,
Antur gwrdd, hwnt ar gerdded
32 Yn ŵr rhif yno y rhed.
O daw, pei rhôn, a dianc,
Oddyno, medr ffrwyno Ffranc,
Creithiog fydd, saethydd a'i sathr,
36 A chreulon, ddyn wych rylathr.
Mwy y câr ei drymbar draw
A'i gledd, gwae a goel iddaw,
A mael dur a mul darian
40 A march o lu no merch lân.
Ni'th gêl pan ddêl poen ddolef,
Ni'th gais eithr i drais o dref.

'Minnau â'r geiriau goroyw,
44 Pei'th gawn, liw eglurwawn gloyw,
Da y gwn, trwsiwn wawd trasyth,
Degle, ferch, dy gelu fyth.
Pei rhôn ym gael, gafael gaeth,
48 Deifr un hoen, dwy frenhiniaeth,
Deune'r haul, nid awn er hyn,
Wythliw dydd, o'th loyw dyddyn.'

Merched Llanbadarn (48)

Plygu rhag llid yr ydwyf,
Pla ar holl ferched y plwyf!
Am na chefais, drais drawsoed,
4 Onaddun' yr un erioed
Na morwyn fwyn ofynaig,
Na merch fach, na gwrach, na gwraig.

Py rusiant, py ddireidi,
8 Py fethiant, na fynnant fi?
Py ddrwg i riain feinael

to meet me in the forest's thick-set dark?
No cause of shame it were to her
12   to see me in my leafy lair.

    There never was a time I did not love—
(nor ever was there such persistent charm as this,
[even] beyond the passion of men like to Garwy)
16   —one or two of them in a single day;
and yet I never any closer came
to winning one of them, than if she'd been my foe.
No Sunday ever was there in Llanbadarn
20   that I would not be—and others will condemn it—
facing [some such] lovely girl
with my nape to God's true loveliness.
And when I have long surveyed
24   across my feathers, the people of my parish,
one sweet tender lass will say
to her companion, lively, famous, wise:

    'That grey-faced flirt of a boy
28   wearing on his head his sister's hair,
lascivious is the look he has,
he has a side-long glance; he must know mischief well.'

    'Is that how it is with him?'
32   the other by her side replies,
'He'll get no answer while the world endures,
to the devil with him, stupid thing!'

    Shocking (?) to me was the bright girl's curse,
36   a trifling payment for distracting love.
Needs must that I contrive to cease
this habit, with its tantalizing dreams.
It is imperative that I become
40   a hermit—job for a dejected man.
Because of ever looking—awful lesson—
over my shoulder, an image of distress,
it has befallen me, [though] poetry's friend,
44   to go wry-headed, without any mate.

Yng nghoed tywylldew fy nghael?
Nid oedd gywilydd iddi
12   Yng ngwâl dail fy ngweled i.

   Ni bu amser na charwn,
Ni bu mor lud hud â hwn—
Anad gwŷr annwyd Garwy—
16   Yn y dydd ai un ai dwy.
Ac er hynny nid oedd nes
Ym gael un no'm gelynes.
Ni bu Sul yn Llanbadarn
20   Na bewn, ac eraill a'i barn,
Â'm wyneb at y ferch goeth
A'm gwegil at Dduw gwiwgoeth.
A gwedy'r hir edrychwyf
24   Dros fy mhlu ar draws fy mhlwyf,
Y dywaid un fun fygrgroyw
Wrth y llall hylwyddgall hoyw:

   'Y mab llwyd wyneb mursen
28   A gwallt ei chwaer ar ei ben,
Godinabus fydd golwg
Gŵyr ei ddrem; da y gŵyr ddrwg.'

   'Ai'n rhith hynny yw ganthaw?'
32   Yw gair y llall gar ei llaw;
'Ateb ni chaiff tra fo fyd;
Wtied i ddiawl, beth ynfyd!'

   Talmithr ym reg y loywferch,
36   Tâl bychan am syfrdan serch.
Rhaid oedd ym fedru peidiaw
Â'r foes hon, breuddwydion braw.
Ys dir ym fyned fal gŵr
40   Yn feudwy, swydd anfadwr.
O dra disgwyl, dysgiad certh,
Drach 'y nghefn, drych anghyfnerth,
Neur dderyw ym, gerddrym gâr,
44   Bengamu heb un gymar.

39   The Goose-Shed

As I [came] once, upon a certain night
—alas my expedition, but the girl was worth it—
after having wandered [far] astray, in coming
4   to the place where lived a wise accomplished lass
[She]: 'Has it seemed long you have been [seeking me]?
A long-enduring lover you must be.'
[He]: 'My love, you know that it has been too long,
8   Why should it have been otherwise than so?'

All at once I heard a savage man
throw a stag's leap, with look as of a lion,
and make a lightning-rush to pursue me,
12   ferocious and replete with wrath
and anger for his dazzling wife;
by God and [all the] relics, he was strong and brave!
I had the sense to take to flight from him—
16   the pale youth knew it was a dream of terror.

[The Man]: 'Not likely you have a steel spur:
wait for me by myself tonight;
bad weapons wherewithal to fight
20   are the *cywyddau* that you have.'

I fled to a deceptive haven, a shed,
all adorned for the geese it was.
I said [to myself] from my shed
24   'Never was there better hiding-place from care.'
An old hollow-nostrilled mother-goose got up—
her feathers were a shelter to her young.
She spread her cape around my sides—
28   a very vengeance of a nurse she was.
And the stubborn grey goose harassed me
and to destroy me threw me under her.
Badly was I treated by this sister
32   of her dear heron, [with] a broad grey wing.

My sweetheart said to me next day,
fair maiden, with her prudent speech,
that she thought seven times worse than our predicament,
36   us two, and than her husband's words
[it was] to see that ancient feathered mother-goose
with evil twisted neck molesting me.
If the lordship of Chester's men,
40   with their obstructing tricks, were to allow,
I would to that mother-goose, in an offensive way,
cause disgrace to her body, nine years old,
whoever might dare warn me [not to do so]:
44   for her exploit the goose will weep!

Y Cwt Gwyddau (126)

Fal yr oeddwn gynt noswaith,
Gwiw fu'r dyn, gwae fi o'r daith,
Gwedy dyfod yn grwydrball
4 Yn lle'dd oedd gwen gymen gall,

'Ai hir gennyd yr ydwyd?
Dyn goddefgar serchog wyd.'

'Fy aur, gwyddost mai rhyir;
8 Am baham oedd na bai hir?'

Nycha y clywwn ŵr traglew
Yn bwrw carwnaid, llygaid llew,
Yn dwyn lluchynt i'm ymlid
12 Yn greulawn ac yn llawn llid,
O ddig am ei wraig ddisglair,
Un dewr cryf, myn Duw a'r crair!
Gwybuum encil rhagddaw,
16 Gwybu'r gwas llwyd breuddwyd braw.

'Hwyr yt felan ysbardun,
Aro fi heno fy hun.
Arfau drwg i ddigoni
20 Yw'r cywyddau sydd dau di.'

Ciliais i ystafell, gell gau,
Ac addurn oedd i'r gwyddau.
Meddwn i o'm ystafell,
24 'Ni bu rhag gofal wâl well.'
Codes hen famwydd drwynbant,
A'i phlu oedd gysgod i'w phlant.
Datod mantell i'm deutu,
28 Dialaeth o famaeth fu.
A'm dylud o'r ŵydd lud lai,
A'm dinistr a'm bwrw danai.
Cares, drwg y'm cyweiriwyd,
32 Cu aran, balf lydan lwyd.

Meddai fy chwaer ym drannoeth,
Meinir deg a'i mwynair doeth,
Seithwaeth genthi no'n cyflwr
36 Ni'n dau, ac no geiriau'r gŵr,
Gweled hen famwydd blwydd blu
Gogam wddw goeg i'm maeddu.
Pei gatai arglwyddïaeth
40 Gwŷr Caer a'u gwaraeau caeth,
Gwnawn i'r famwydd, dramgwydd dro,
Rhybuddied rhai a'i beiddio,
Amarch i'w chorpws nawmlwydd;
44 Am ei hwyl yr ŵyl yr ŵydd.

40 Trouble at an Inn

I came to a choice city
with my fine young servant after me,
a place of lavish entertainment, liberal meals:
4   I was proud from childhood, so I took
a public lodging, dignified enough,
and I took some wine.

I perceived a slim and lovely girl
8   in that house, my pretty darling:
I set my heart entirely on my blessed slender dear
who had an aspect like the rising sun.
It was not [just] to show off that I bought a roast
12   and costly wine [for] me and for that girl.
Young men love sport, and so I called the girl
(a modest creature) to [join me] at the bench.
Truth to say, I whispered to her
16   two words of magic—I was bold and pressing
nor was love [with her] idle—and I made
agreement to come to the sprightly lass
when all the company should have gone off
20   to sleep: she was a black-browed girl.

When everyone was sleeping but myself
and her—it was a desperate journey—
I summoned all my skill to reach
24   the maiden's bed: disastrous was [the attempt],
I made a noise and got a wretched fall—
nought prospered for me [there]:
easier it was—foolhardy mischief—
28   to get up clumsily than expeditiously.
Not jumping without hurt, I struck
my shin—woe to my leg—above my ankle
against the side—some ostler's negligence—
32   of a stupid noisy stool.
Getting up, it was a sorry tale,
Welshmen love me!
I struck—for too much eagerness is bad—
36   my brow against the table's edge
where there was placed for me—I could not jump safe—
a frequent snare—stupidity to hit it—
a basin standing loose
40   and a clattering brass bowl.
The table fell—it was a mighty piece of gear—
with its two trestles and all the furniture,
the brass bowl cried out after me
44   —it could be heard far off—
I was an idiot, with the basin screaming,
and the dogs barking after me.

Trafferth mewn Tafarn (124)

Deuthum i ddinas dethol,
A'm hardd wreangyn i'm hôl.
Cain hoywdraul, lle cwyn hydrum,
4 Cymryd, balch o febyd fûm,
Llety urddedig ddigawn
Cyffredin, a gwin a gawn.

Canfod rhiain addfeindeg
8 Yn y tŷ, *mau* enaid teg.
Bwrw yn llwyr, liw haul dwyrain,
Fy mryd ar wyn fy myd main.
Prynu rhost, nid er bostiaw,
12 A gwin drud, mi a gwen draw.
Gwarwy a gâr gwŷr ieuainc—
Galw ar fun, ddyn gŵyl, i'r fainc.
Hustyng, bûm ŵr hy astud,
16 Dioer yw hyn, deuair o hud;
Gwneuthur, ni bu segur serch,
Amod dyfod at hoywferch
Pan elai y minteioedd
20 I gysgu; bun aelddu oedd.

Wedi cysgu, tru tremyn,
O bawb eithr myfi a bun,
Profais yn hyfedr fedru
24 Ar wely'r ferch; alar fu.
Cefais, pan soniais yna,
Gwymp dig, nid oedd gampau da;
Haws codi, drygioni drud,
28 Yn drwsgl nog yn dra esgud.
Trewais, ni neidiais yn iach,
Y grimog, a gwae'r omach,
Wrth ystlys, ar waith ostler,
32 Ystôl groch ffôl, goruwch ffêr.
Dyfod, bu chwedl edifar,
I fyny, Cymry a'm câr,
Trewais, drwg fydd tra awydd,
36 Lle y'm rhoed, heb un llam rhwydd,
Mynych dwyll amwyll ymwrdd,
Fy nhalcen wrth ben y bwrdd,
Lle 'dd oedd gawg yrhawg yn rhydd
40 A llafar badell efydd.
Syrthio o'r bwrdd, dragwrdd drefn,
A'r ddeudrestl a'r holl ddodrefn;
Rhoi diasbad o'r badell
44 I'm hôl, fo'i clywid ymhell;
Gweiddi, gŵr gorwag oeddwn,
O'r cawg, a'm cyfarth o'r cŵn.

Nearby, beside high walls, there were
48   three English [tinkers] in a smelly bed,
fretting, [each one], for their three packs—
[their names were] Hickyn, Jenkyn, and Jack.
With beery lips, one of them whispered
52   to the other two this angry speech:

'It is a Welshman makes this uproar to deceive,
he prowls around here bent on treachery,
he is a robber, if we suffer it,
56   look out! and guard yourselves from him!'

The ostler roused up all the folk
together, it was a dreadful tale.
They were threatening all around me
60   while seeking everywhere to find me,
and I, in angry ugly rage
kept silence in the darkness.
I prayed, and that was in no fearless way,
64   being in hiding, as a man in terror:
and by the strength of true and loving prayer,
and by the grace of faithful Jesus
I yet was able, though I got no pay,
68   [and was] fettered by sleeplessness, to reach my own bed.
[So] I escaped—well that the saints are near—
and my forgiveness [now] I ask of God.

41   Under the Eaves: A Serenade

The door of the house has been locked:
listen to me, my love, for I am sick;
come that you may be seen, my lovely one,
4   for generous God's sake, come and show yourself.
Why should a lying girl prevail?
By Mary, such a fault causes madness.

Impelled by maddening cold, I struck
8   three knocks: the latch, securely fastened, broke,
was it not audible [to all]?
Did you not hear it? It was like a bell.
Morfudd, my love with chaste intent,
12   mistress of the enticement of deceit,
my couch is the far side of the wall from you,
I have to *shout* [for you to hear me], girl.
Have mercy on my fevered sleeplessness,

Yr oedd gerllaw muroedd mawr
48 Drisais mewn gwely drewsawr,
Yn trafferth am eu triphac—
Hicin a Siencin a Siac.
Syganai'r gwas soeg enau,
52 Araith oedd ddig, wrth y ddau:

'Mae Cymro, taer gyffro twyll,
Yn rhodio yma'n rhydwyll;
Lleidr yw ef, os goddefwn,
56 'Mogelwch, cedwch rhag hwn.'

Codi o'r ostler niferoedd
I gyd, a chwedl dybryd oedd.
Gygus oeddynt i'm gogylch
60 Yn chwilio i'm ceisio i'm cylch;
A minnau, hagr wyniau hyll,
Yn tewi yn y tywyll.
Gweddïais, nid gwedd eofn,
64 Dan gêl, megis dyn ag ofn;
Ac o nerth gweddi gerth gu,
Ac o ras y gwir Iesu,
Cael i minnau, cwlm anun,
68 Heb sâl, fy henwal fy hun.
Dihengais i, da wng saint,
I Dduw'r archaf faddeuaint.

Dan y Bargod (89)

Clo a roed ar ddrws y tŷ,
Claf wyf, fy chwaer, clyw fyfy.
Dyred i'th weled, wiwlun,
4 Er Duw hael dangos dy hun.
Geirffug ferch pam y gorffai?
Gorffwyll, myn Mair, a bair bai.

Taro trwy annwyd dyrys
8 Tair ysbonc, torres y bys
Cloedig; pand clau ydoedd?
Ai clywewch chwi? Sain cloch oedd.
Morfudd, fy nghrair diweirbwyll,
12 Mamaeth tywysogaeth twyll,
Mau wâl am y wialen
 thi, rhaid ym weiddi, wen.
Tosturia wrth anhunglwyf,

16   the night is dark, a swindler of our joy.
Look at the sorry nature of my plight,
woe for such weather from the heavens tonight!
So many torrents falling from the eaves
20   on my [poor] flesh, [my] passion's instrument.
Not greater is the rain than is the snow
that falls on me; a wretched state is mine.
This shivering gives no comfort to me—
24   never was greater pain to mortal flesh
than I have suffered by my watchfulness.
By Him who made me, never was worse couch:
nor in Caernarfon castle ever was
28   a dungeon worse than is in this street.

     I would not stay without doors through the night,
nor would I groan, for anyone but you,
assuredly I would not suffer
32   did I not love you, nightly pain for you,
nor would I endure, under rain and snow
one single moment, except for your sake.
I would not have relinquished—well do I know anguish—
36   the whole world, were it not for you.

     I am out here in the cold:
yours is the [good] fortune, [for] you are indoors.
My pure soul is there within,
40   my phantom only is out here.
Anyone who could hear would marvel,
my dear one, that I should be here alive.
My thoughts will not go hence away,
44   my madness it is that has kept me here.

     A contract you have made with me:
here am I to fulfil it—where are *you?*

42   Parting at Dawn

     I sighed deeply [at the thought of it]:
so long a night the night that was before the last;
that night, my modest brilliant love,
4   a single night, my darling, was a week;
and yet, a judge would say, a maid
shortens the night, who utters no word of denial.

     Last night, I was in strange perplexity:
8   with fair Nia, with heaven's candle.
insisting on repayment for my sleeplessness,
with complete respect at the girl's side.
When my grip was at its strongest,

146

16 Tywyll yw'r nos, twyllwr nwyf.
    Adnebydd flined fy nhro;
    Wb o'r hin o'r wybr heno!
    Aml yw rhëydr o'r bargawd,
20 Ermyg nwyf, ar y mau gnawd.
    Nid mwy y glaw, neud mau glwyf,
    No'r ôd, dano yr ydwyf.
    Nid esmwyth hyn o dysmwy,
24 Ni bu boen ar farwgroen fwy
    Nog a gefais drwy ofal,
    Ym Gŵr a'm gwnaeth, nid gwaeth gwâl.
    Ni bu'n y Gaer yn Arfon
28 Geol waeth no'r heol hon.

       Ni byddwn allan hyd nos,
    Ni thuchwn ond o'th achos.
    Ni ddown i oddef, od gwn,
32 Beunoeth gur, bei na'th garwn.
    Ni byddwn dan law ac ôd
    Ennyd awr onid erod.
    Ni faddeuwn, gwn gyni,
36 Y byd oll oni bai di.

       Yma ydd wyf drwy annwyd,
    Tau ddawn, yn y tŷ ydd wyd.
    Yna y mae f'enaid glân,
40 A'm ellyll yma allan.
    Amau fydd gan a'm hirglyw
    Yma, fy aur, ymy fyw.
    Ymaith fy meddwl nid â,
44 Amwyll a'm peris yma.

       Amod â mi a wneddwyd;
    Yma ydd wyf, a mae 'dd wyd?

Y Wawr (129)

    Uchel y bûm yn ochi,
    Echnos y bu hirnos hi.
    Echnos, dyn goleudlos gŵyl,
4   Wythnos fu unnos, f'annwyl;
    A bernos, medd y beirniad,
    A bair gwen heb ungair gwad.

       Neithiwyr y bûm mewn uthr bwyll,
8   Nyf gain, gyda nef gannwyll,
    Yn mynnu tâl am anun,
    Yn aml barch yn ymyl bun.
    Pan oedd ffyrfaf fy ngafael,

12 my mettle at its best—she had dark brows—
the coverlet above [us], and my zest most eager—
alas! good God, behold the dawn of day.

'Get up,' the maid said, in her brightly-coloured robe,
16 'hide this; see there the lively sign—
your love brings grievous weeping;
be off with you to the devil—see, it is now day.'

[He]: 'Good maiden, tall and stately, slender, perfect
beauty,
20 that is not true: better [interpret] thus,
it is the moon which the Lord God has given,
and stars there are surrounding her.
If indisputably I lay this down,
24 [only] imagination is it that it's dawn.'

[She]: 'Assuredly, if that were true
why is the raven croaking up above?'

[He]: 'Vermin are attempting there
28 to kill her—keeping her from sleep.'

[She]: 'Hounds are baying in the hamlet yonder,
and others too are fighting with each other.'

[He]: 'Believe me, my denial [comes] near [the mark],
32 it is the Hounds of Night cause this distress.'

[She]: 'Cease your excuses, lad of poetry,
a shallow mind puts pain afar,
it is now high time for you to start
36 [and] to set forth on some adventurous raid today.
For Christ's sake, get up quietly,
and open yonder heavy door.
Take very large strides with both your feet,
40 the hounds are most importunate; run off to the wood.'

[He]: 'Alas, the thicket is not far,
and I run quicker than a hound;
unless a sly one sees me, I shall not be caught,
44 if God allows it so, on that [short] space of ground.'

[She]: 'Tell me, good devoted poet,
for God's sake, shall you come here [again]?'

[He]: 'I am your nightingale, and I shall come
48 assuredly, my dear, when the night comes.'

12 A gorau 'mhwynt, gwrm ei hael,
   Uchaf len, awch aflonydd,
   Och wir Dduw, nachaf wawr ddydd.

   'Cyfod,' eb gwen len liwloyw,
16 'Cêl hyn; weldyna'r coel hoyw.
   Deigr anial dy garennydd,
   Dos i ddiawl; weldiso ddydd.'

   'Hirfun dda hwyr gain ddiell,
20 Hyn nid gwir; hynny neud gwell.
   Lleuad a roes Duw Llywydd,
   A sêr yn ei chylch y sydd.
   Hyn o dodaf henw didyb,
24 Honno y sydd dydd o dyb.'

   'Gair honnaid, pei gwir hynny,
   Paham y cân y frân fry?'

   'Pryfed y sydd yn profi,
28 Lluddio ei hun, ei lladd hi.'

   'Mae cŵn dan lef ny dref draw
   Ag eraill yn ymguraw.'

   'Coelia fy nâg yn agos,
32 Cyni a wna cŵn y nos.'

   'Paid â'th esgusawd wawdwas;
   Pell boen a fynaig pwyll bas,
   Wrth gael taith, anrhaith unrhyw,
36 Antur i'th ddydd, anterth yw.
   Er Crist, cyfod yn ddistaw,
   Ac agor y dromddor draw.
   Rhyfras camau y ddeudroed,
40 Rhydaer yw'r cŵn, rhed i'r coed.'

   'Ochan! Nid pell y gelli,
   A chynt wyf finnau no chi.
   Oni'm gwŷl ffel ni'm delir,
44 O rhan Duw, ar hyn o dir.'

   'Dywed di, fardd diwyd da,
   Er Duw ym, o doi yma.'

   'Deuaf, mi yw dy eos,
48 Diau, 'y nyn, o daw nos.'

43 The Poet and the Grey Friar

Woe is me that the much-vaunted maid
whose court is in the forest, does not know
my conversation with the mouse-hued Friar
4 I had concerning her today.

I went to the Friar
in order to confess my sin:
I confessed to him, with truth,
8 that I was a poet of a sort,
and that I had loved ever constantly
a dark-browed, pale-faced maid,
yet from my murderer I did not get
12 any profit or advantage as to my lady,
but only loving her long and constantly,
and languishing for love of her,
and carrying her praise throughout [all] Wales
16 —yet lacking her inspite of all—
and longing [only] that I might feel her
in my bed between me and the wall.

The Friar then replied to me:
20 'I would give you good advice,
if you have loved [a girl of] foam-like hue
paper-white, for long till now,
abate the penance that will come,
24 cease, for the welfare of your soul,
and be silent with your songs
and be busy with your prayers:
not for the sake of *cywydd* nor *englyn*
28 did God redeem the soul of man.
In your songs, you wandering poets,
there is nought but vain and idle words,
and inciting men and women
32 to falsehood and to sin.
Praise of the body is not good,
it will but bring the soul to Hell.'

I made answer to the Friar
36 concerning every word he said:
'God is not so cruel
as old people tell.
God will not condemn a good man's soul
40 for loving a wife or a girl.
Three things are loved throughout the world:
Woman, health, and smiling weather.
A maiden is the fairest flower

Y Bardd a'r Brawd Llwyd (137)

Gwae fi na ŵyr y forwyn
Glodfrys, â'i llys yn y llwyn,
Ymddiddan y brawd llygliw
4 Amdani y dydd heddiw.

   Mi a euthum at y Brawd
I gyffesu fy mhechawd;
Iddo 'dd addefais, od gwn,
8 Mai eilun prydydd oeddwn;
A'm bod erioed yn caru
Rhiain wynebwen aelddu;
Ac na bu ym o'm llofrudd
12 Les am unbennes na budd;
Ond ei charu'n hir wastad,
A churio'n fawr o'i chariad,
A dwyn ei chlod drwy Gymry,
16 A bod hebddi er hynny,
A dymuno ei chlywed
I'm gwely rhof a'r pared.

   Ebr y Brawd wrthyf yna,
20 'Mi a rown yt gyngor da:
O cheraist eiliw ewyn,
Lliw papir, oed hir hyd hyn,
Llaesa boen y dydd a ddaw;
24 Lles yw i'th enaid beidiaw,
A thewi â'r cywyddau
Ac arfer o'th baderau.
Nid er cywydd nac englyn
28 Y prynodd Duw enaid dyn.
Nid oes o'ch cerdd chwi, y glêr,
Ond truth a lleisiau ofer,
Ac annog gwŷr a gwragedd
32 I bechod ac anwiredd.
Nid da'r moliant corfforawl
A ddyco'r enaid i ddiawl.'

   Minnau atebais i'r Brawd
36 Am bob gair ar a ddywawd:
'Nid ydyw Duw mor greulon
Ag y dywaid hen ddynion.
Ni chyll Duw enaid gŵr mwyn
40 Er caru gwraig na morwyn.
Tripheth a gerir drwy'r byd:
Gwraig a hinon ac iechyd.
'Merch sydd decaf blodeuyn

44   in Heaven, but for God himself;
from woman every man was born
in all nations, but for three.
And therefore it is no surprise
48   that girls and women should be loved
[since] from Heaven every joy was got
and from Hell all sorrows [came].

'Songs cause to be happier
52   both old and young, both sick and well.
Poetry is as much my need
as it is your need to preach,
and a poet's circuit is as right for me
56   as it is for you to beg.
Are not hymns and sequences
no other than *englynion* and odes?
and the psalms of the prophet David
60   are but *cywyddau* to holy God.

'Not by a single kind of food and relish
does God provide man's sustenance.
A time was bestowed [on us] for food
64   and a time for [our] devotions:
a time for preaching
and a time for merriment.
Songs are sung at every feast
68   to entertain the girls,
and prayers in the church
to seek the land of Paradise.

'It was true what Ystudfach [once] said,
72   carousing together with his poets:
"A happy face makes a full house,
to a sad face misfortune clings."
Though some may love holiness
76   others [too] love merriment.
Rare is the man who knows a sweet *cywydd*,
but all men know their prayers.
And therefore, punctilious Friar,
80   it is not verse that is the greatest sin.
When everyone shall be as pleased
to listen to a prayer [sung to] the harp
as are the girls of Gwynedd
84   to hear a song of ribaldry—
then, by my hand, I'll [swear to] sing
my paternoster without cease.
But till then, shame be on Dafydd
88   if he sing a prayer, but rather a *cywydd*.'

44   Yn y nef ond Duw ei hun.
      O wraig y ganed pob dyn
      O'r holl bobloedd ond tridyn.
      Ac am hynny nid rhyfedd
48   Caru merched a gwragedd.
      O'r nef y cad digrifwch
      Ac o uffern bob tristwch.

      'Cerdd a bair yn llawenach
52   Hen ac ieuanc, claf ac iach.
      Cyn rheitied i mi brydu
      Ag i tithau bregethu,
      A chyn iawned ym glera
56   Ag i tithau gardota.
      Pand englynion ac odlau
      Yw'r hymnau a'r segwensiau?
      A chywyddau i Dduw lwyd
60   Yw sallwyr Dafydd Broffwyd.

      'Nid ar un bwyd ac enllyn
      Y mae Duw yn porthi dyn.
      Amser a rodded i fwyd
64   Ac amser i olochwyd,
      Ac amser i bregethu,
      Ac amser i gyfanheddu.
      Cerdd a genir ymhob gwledd
68   I ddiddanu rhianedd,
      A phader yn yr eglwys
      I geisio tir Paradwys.

      'Gwir a ddywad Ystudfach
72   Gyda'i feirdd yn cyfeddach:
      ''Wyneb llawen llawn ei dŷ,
      Wyneb trist drwg a ery.''
      Cyd caro rhai santeiddrwydd,
76   Eraill a gâr gyfanheddrwydd.
      Anaml a ŵyr gywydd pêr
      A phawb a ŵyr ei bader,
      Ac am hynny'r deddfol Frawd,
80   Nid cerdd sydd fwyaf pechawd.

      'Pan fo cystal gan bob dyn
      Glywed pader gan delyn
      Â chan forynion Gwynedd
84   Glywed cywydd o faswedd,
      Mi a ganaf, myn fy llaw,
      Y pader fyth heb beidiaw.
      Hyd hynny mefl i Ddafydd
88   O chân bader, ond cywydd.'

Notes

35

A number of the place-names in this poem have been identified with varying degrees of assurance as lying within a closely circumscribed area: the triangle of country between Aberystwyth, Tal-y-bont, and Ponterwyd. These are places in the immediate neighbourhood of Dafydd's early home at Brogynin and—presumably—that of Morfudd (see n. to Nant-y-Glo, l.40) The principle identifications were first pointed out by David Jenkins, B.viii, (1937), 140-5, with some further suggestions in *Y Traethodydd* CXXXIII (1978), 83-8. Others were made by R.J.Thomas, *Y Llenor* XXI (1942), 34-6, and B.xx (1964), 255. See also GDG xxxiv-viii; GDG² xvi-xviii. See map p.xii.

5. *nych ofwy*. Lit. 'a visitation of weakness'.

7. *Cellïau'r Meirch*. A mile from Brogynin there was, until the last century, a *tyddyn* called *Llety'r Meirch:* this could well denote the site. (*Llety* is not uncommon in farm-names in the area.)

8. *eurdrais elw*. Lit. 'profit of fine (golden) oppression'. Being highly condensed, the meaning of the *sangiad* can only be suggested by periphrasis.
Eleirch. Today the village of Elerch, just over a mile from Brogynin.

12. *Celli Fleddyn*. The *Ministers' Account* for Cardigan, 1277-80 (THSC 1897,129-30) lists *terra filii Blethin* as lying within the commote of Genau'r Glyn (the northernmost commote in the cantref of Uwch Aeron).

13. *Ymadrodd*. Lit. 'speaking for her sake'.

14. *Ymarddelw* 'avow, assert, profess, acknowledge', etc.

15. *Bysaleg*. David Jenkins points out that *Massalek fluvius* is the name given on the maps of Saxton (1578) and Speed (1610) to the river Stewi, by a ford on which Brogynin stands. In 1910 an eighty-year old woman informed T.Gwynn Jones that the river Stewy was known as *Saleg* when she was a girl, and that a house or houses on its bank were known as Maesaleg. But another small river, the S(e)ilo, also flows through Penrhyn-coch to meet with the Stewy, and on Saxton's map this is called *Salek fluvius*. Evidently there has been confusion between the names of the two rivers. The evidence suggests that about the end of the 18th century 'Stewy' began to displace *Maesaleg* as the name of the first.

19-20. *Bwlch Meibion D*. In 1937 *Pen Bwlch Meibion Dafydd* was still remembered by old people as the name of a track leading from Brogynin to Elerch.

21. *i'r Gamallt*. This place is as yet unidentified, 'curved (wooded) slopes' being a common enough feature in the neighbourhood.

24. *Gafaelfwlch y Gyfylfaen*. In B.xx (1964), 255 R.J.Thomas identified this as *Bwlch y Maen*, a name marked on the large-scale Ordnance Survey maps, and still remembered locally as denoting a place about two miles east of Elerch. The simple name was elaborated by Dafydd for the purposes of *cynghanedd*. *Bwlch y Maen* is the meeting-place of a number of paths where small valleys come together: *cyfyl* 'border, end' may have originally signified that the *maen* was an important boundary-stone. *Gafael* was a term for a unit of land-tenure.
Pant Cwcwll. Not precisely identified, but *Tal pont Cuculh* is listed in the *Calendar of Charter Rolls* in respect to a gift of land made to the monastery of Ystrad Fflur in 1336. The likelihood is that this place lay within *Tir y Mynach*, part of the extensive lands belonging to Ystrad Fflur which lay to the north of the river Stewy. *Pant* 'valley' and *pont* 'bridge' are probable enough in adjoining place-names, if indeed the one

is not a corruption of the other: David Jenkins has suggested that the modern Tal-y-bont may be the place intended.

30. *Castell Gwgawn*. The *Calendar of Charter Rolls* lists *Castelh Gugaun* among gifts made to the monastery, and it presumably lay within the same area, between Llanfihangel Genau'r Glyn and Llanbadarn Fawr. The original owner of the *castell* was perhaps *Gwgawn Gleddyfrudd*, a traditional hero of Ceredigion; TYP 389-90.

32. *cawn* 'reeds, stalks, stubble', fig. 'something valueless'.

33. *Adail Heilin*. Again not precisely identified, but presumably in the same area; perhaps *Tyddyn Bron Heilyn* in the commote of Genau'r Glyn. The *Ministers' Account* for Cardigan, 1277-80 lists *terra Heylin filii Howeli* as lying within the parish of Llanfihangel Genau'r Glyn.

34. *bloesg*. Lit. 'indistinct, inarticulate, husky'; *dywedyd yn floesg* 'to speak indistinctly or lispingly'.

35. *llys Ifor*. This place is unknown, and the similarity with the name of Ifor Hael is only too likely to mislead. But 'Ifor' is such a common name that its occurrence here must be regarded as a coincidence, which has no connection with Ifor ap Llywelyn of Morgannwg (see GDG xxxvii).

40. *Nant-y-Glo*. *Cwm-y-Glo* is the name of a *tyddyn* or small farmstead half a mile from Brogynin. Cf. no.34 (GDG 94), 1.32 where *Cwm-y-Gro* is clearly designated as the home of Morfudd.

42. *Ofydd*. See n. to no.28 (GDG 22), 1.3 above.

44. *Gwern-y-Talwrn*. This may be *Pen-y-Talwrn* near Ponterwyd, about five miles from Brogynin. But allowance must be made for the fact that *talwrn* 'field' is a very common place-name element.

45. *Lle y cefais weled*. Lit. 'where I could see'.

50. *llwybr Adda*. Two of Dafydd's contemporaries, Gruffudd ab Adda and Iolo Goch, make similar references to the devastated land which Adam and Eve left behind them as they fled from Eden; see DGG² LXV, ls.39-42 (OBWV 91), and IGE² 77, ls.21-6. Possibly there is a recollection of *Genesis* 3,17, where God cursed the ground because of Adam's transgression. Gwern-y-Talwrn—wherever it was—was the most favoured meeting-place of Dafydd with Morfudd, hence the path to it was well-trodden.

51-4. These last lines link the poem with the mediaeval *genre* of dialogues between the Soul and the Body. Iolo Goch turns the inherited convention of such poems into an account of a *taith clera* or bardic circuit between the homes of his patrons (IGE² XXVI), see n. to no.52 below. Since it is this very poem which contains the ref. cited above to Adam's flight from Paradise, it is not impossible that Dafydd here intends a veiled allusion to Iolo's poem, though this is of course impossible to substantiate owing to the lack of evidence as to the relative dating of the two poems. The cynicism of these lines is in marked contrast to the near-lyricism of the preceding ones.

36

8. *a wyddiad*. Old ending of the 3 sg. imperfect; GMW §132(2).

9. *Or bydd*. Lit. 'if it is' (o 'if' with perfective *ry*; GMW §272) and pres. indic., though obviously referring to a past event.

15-16. *Rhol fawr*. From E. *rolle* (EEW 183), a roll of parchment, often of considerable length, such as was used for legal documents. This is one of the numerous borrowings of administrative terms which Dafydd employs in a figurative sense. The rain is then envisaged as lines (*rhestri*) of writing upon the long scroll. For a similar image cf. no.29 (GDG 117), 23 (see n.).

27. *er lluddiaw lles*. Dafydd uses *lles* elsewhere to signify his expected 'profit' or reward from the girl he is addressing; cf. no.43 (GDG 137), 12.

28. *Codarmur.* An obvious E. borrowing (EEW 171), meaning a coat of mail. This is one of the many instances of words denoting foreign imports which Dafydd employs in a figurative sense (cf. *rhol.* 1.15); see *Tradn. and Innov.* 42-3. This is the earliest recorded occurence of the word in Welsh.

30. *gwrddonig.* A variant of *gwyrddonig,* listed in GPC as meaning 'coarse, rough, shaggy, hairy', following the interpretation *blewog* 'hairy, shaggy' proposed by Thomas Jones, *Y Llenor* XXVII (1948), 152; cf. D.E.Evans, SC I (1966), 27-31. This again is the earliest recorded instance.

32,40. *Tylwyth Gwyn.* For Gwyn ap Nudd, leader of the fairy-host, see no.26 (GDG 26), 1.40 and n. Cf. 1.43 below.

34. *teirsygn. Sygn* is used by Dafydd elsewhere as a general term for the stars, eg. no.29 (GDG 117), 55 (see n.); but I know of no explanation for 'three'. Some MSS read *cuddio* for *cyrchu,* but 'concealing the 3 stars' offers no improvement in intelligibility.

35. *allardd* 'ugly, hideous, formidable', GPC. This meaning is based on Dr Parry's conjecture; no other instance of the word has been recorded.

37. *(c)ombr gostombraff. Combr* 'cambric', see n. to no.17 (GDG 139), 1.18. *Costom* in *costombraff* has the meaning of E. 'custom(s)'. Dr Parry quotes the OED's definition as 'toll levied by the lord or local authority upon commodities on their way to market'. Hence 'valuable'. There was a heavy tax upon such foreign luxuries as cambric (cf. D.J.Bowen, YB X (1977), 207).

43. *y cyfarth cŵn.* i.e. the sinister hounds of Gwyn ap Nudd; see n. to no.26 (GDG 26), 1.22.

44. *Annwn.* See n. to no.4 (GDG 27), 1.40 above.

46. *Habrsiwn.* From E. *habergeon* 'a sleeveless coat-of-mail' (EEW 74). Cf. n. to *codarmur,* 1.28 above.

50. *canhwyllau cwyr.* With the image of the stars as God's candles, cf. no.30 (GDG 67), ls.24-5.

37

The debate as to whether a 'clerk' or a soldier made the more desirable lover for a woman was a popular theme in French poetry throughout the 13th century. Frequently it was set within the framework of a dream, and was presented as the subject of elaborate discussion by bird-protagonists (for refs. see Chotzen, 228-9; *Tradn. and Innov.* 31-2). An ultimate origin may be found in Ovid's *Amores* iii, 8; a poem in which the poet remonstrates with a girl for preferring a soldier to him—a poet—as a lover. Dafydd may have derived his inspiration from Ovid, especially since others of his poems find parallels in the *Amores* (see notes to nos.31, 33 above), or he may have encountered the theme, directly or indirectly, in one of its numerous French or mediaeval Latin intermediaries, see DGG², lx. But even if the idea came to him from some external source, Dafydd gives to it, as always, an inimitably individual character in the elaborate irony in which he frames his rhetorical address to the girl.

1. *Yr edlaesferch.* Since *diedlaes* means 'unhesitating, sure' I suggest 'hesitating, vacillating, undecided' as the meaning of *edlaes* in this instance, rather than 'trailing, drooping' as in no.25 (GDG 63), 1.15 *edlaes edling* 'a hovering prince' (of the Skylark, see n.) or 'mournful, sad' (GPC).

3. *Eigr.* See n. to no.16 (GDG 84), 1.20; and cf. 1.21 below. Here the name of a traditional heroine—Arthur's mother—is used as a form of address to the girl.

awgrym. From Ml.E. *augrim(e),* etc., EEW 128. The meaning I have given is that suggested by Ifor Williams, DGG² 182, who cited the E. word as being derived from the name of the Arabic inventor of algebra, used by extension to denote the Arabic system of numerals, and hence 'arithmetic'. 'Augrim stones' were used for counting; hence Dafydd asks the girl to reckon what she owes him, presumably for his poems to her. But the alternative meaning of *awgrym* 'nod, sign, hint' would also fit well in the context—'your store of nods'.

8. *wythloywne gwawn*. Lit. 'eight times the shining hue of gossamer'. This was a stock comparison for a girl's beauty, particularly of her hair as in 1.15 below, which Dafydd inherited from the Gogynfeirdd. See *Tradn. and Innov.* 18; and, for exx. from an earlier date, T. Gwynn Jones, *Rhieingerddi'r Gogynfeirdd* 28.

9. *y'th faddeuaf*. For *maddau* in this older meaning 'let go, dispense with, absolve' see n. to no.41 (GDG 89), 35.

15. *Cwfl*. Lit. 'head-dress, cowl' as in no.36, ls.21, 26.

17. *cyweithas coeth*. The same phrase is used of the apostle Thomas, GDG 4, 1.32.

20. *ar waith llyfr Ofydd*. i.e. in the affairs of love. Cf. no.35 (GDG 83), 1.42 *llyfr hoywbwyll Ofydd*. On Ovid see n. to no.28 (GDG 22), 1.3.

22. *diwyr* 'regular, constant, correct', etc Hence 'obligatory'.

23. *neitio cur*. Lit. '(over)leaping care'.

29. *Brwydr*, etc. The battle of Crécy was fought in 1346, and in the same year the Scots were defeated in the battle of Nevill's Cross. See below on 1.48.

32. *Yn ŵr rhif*. *Rhifo* 'count, enumerate, make a list' (PKM 138). Hence 'enlist'.

39. *mul*. Alternatively 'sober'. Ifor Williams suggests 'dark-coloured', DGG² 183, but in B.vi, 321 n. it is shown that *mul* can sometimes have the extended meaning of *ffôl* 'foolish' as in nos.25, ls.47, 70; 45, 1.16.

41. *poen ddolef*. Perhaps referring to the pains of child-birth.

42. *i drais*, 'by force'. An idiomatic phrase in which *i* (from older *ddi*) retains its earlier meaning 'from', corresponding to Lat. *de*. See B.xiii, 3 which cites this e.g. among other examples; DGG² 183; TYP 50.

48. *Deifr un hoen*. On *Deifr* or *Dyfr* see n. to no.32 (GDG 66), 1.42. *dwy frenhiniaeth*. In THSC 1913-4, 99-100 Ifor Williams interpreted this allusion as referring to Edward III's supposedly inordinate ambition, after the victories of 1346, to win for himself the crown of France as an addition to that of his own kingdom. Another poem which may refer to the events of 1346 is GDG 75, in which Dafydd tells of the departure of certain of his friends and relations to the French wars, while GDG 140 has been interpreted as referring to the siege of Calais lifted in the following year. Although too vague to allow of certainty, the evidence suggests that the French campaigns of the 40's and 50's form the background to these three poems.

38

The church of Llanbadarn Fawr, Aberystwyth, would have been Dafydd's parish church for as long as he lived at Brogynin. References in other poems corroborate the nearness of Llanbadarn to his home: no.18 (GDG 41), 1.21; 33 (GDG 71), 1.30; and cf. the ref. to *Uwch Aeron*, the northernmost *cantref* of Ceredigion, in which Llanbadarn lay, as the poet's home, no.29 (GDG 117), 1.41. The present church dates from *circa* 1200. See map p.xii.

7. *Py rusiant*. Lit. 'what hesitation?'

14. *mor lud* 'so diligent'. Dafydd was in the grip of an enchantment which meant that he could not cease from loving some girl or other, whatever the consequences. This compulsion was even greater than that which he attributes to 'men like Garwy'.

15. *Garwy*. The name of *Garwy Hir* was known to poets as that of the father of *Indeg* (see n. to no.14, 1.11) and as a celebrated lover, being enamoured of *Creirwy* (see n. to no.21, 1.19). For a collection of refs. see TYP 354-5.

21-2. *coeth/gwiwgoeth*. The same epithet as is applied to the girl, 'lovely' is enhanced in the compound, where it is applied to God 'really, truly lovely'. This meaning can only be translated by turning the compound adj. into a noun.

24. *Dros fy mhlu* 'over my feathers'. Presumably there were feathers in the hat which Dafydd had removed in church, and then held to conceal his face while he looked from out behind it.

fy mhlwyf. *Plwyf* can mean not only 'parish' but also 'people of the parish'.

27. *mursen*. See n. to no.34 (GDG 94), 1.25 above.

30. There is here a play upon the two meanings of *gŵyr:* as verb 3 sg. 'knows' and as adj. 'slanting, oblique'; Dr Parry interprets the first as the adj. and the second as the verb, which gives good sense to the line.

35. *Talmithr*. Cf. *talmythrgoeth* no.27 (GDG 116), 1.3 and n. as to the variant forms. Davies's dictionary: *improviso, subito*; Thos. Wiliems', *improvise*. Both are inappropriate here; DGG² 180 suggests *creulon, gerwin* 'cruel, severe'; hence *rhyfeddol, syfrdanol* 'wonderful, startling'.

40. *yn feudwy*. This is also the advice attributed to the Magpie, no.25 (GDG 63), ls.69-70—that Dafydd should give up love and become a hermit.

39

A group of poems recounts disasters which befell Dafydd in the pursuit of his love-intrigues with various un-named girls. They are somewhat in the style of the international *fabliaux:* short, episodic poems generally of a ribald character (like Chaucer's Miller's and Merchant's Tales). But Dafydd's treatment of such anecdotes is unique in that he tells them in the first person, and is invariably an actor in his *fabliaux:* they are ironic and self-deprecatory, and the laugh lies in his own discomforture. This poem and the following one are the outstanding examples: this poem has the three stock *fabliau* characters of the girl, her 'Jealous Husband' and her clerk-lover—the latter role being invariably the role which Dafydd assigns to himself. No.14 above describes a similar escape by the poet from the husband of Morfudd. (Cf. also GDG nos.127, 128).

1. *Fal yr oeddwn*. A stock opening-formula for Dafydd's anecdotes; cf. nos.18, 31 above (GDG nos.39, 40, 41, 125).

2. *Gwiw*. Lit. 'worthy'.

3. *yn grwydrball*. *Crwydr* 'wandering' and *pall* 'failure'.

14. *crair*. i.e. a holy relic.

15. *Gwybuum encil*. Lit. 'I knew (how to take) flight'.

17. *(m)elan*. 'Steel of Milan' (EEW 62). The form is confirmed by Guto'r Glyn's ref. to *dur Melan, Gwaith Guto'r Glyn* XXIX, 2; (see n.). The *a* is here editorially restored from MSS which read *felen, felain* (see GDG 536).

25. *drwynbant*. From *trwyn* 'nose' and *pant* 'valley, dent'.

29. *(g)lud* 'stubborn', or 'diligent, persistent', as in no.38, 1.14 above. *(l)lai* 'pale grey'; cf. B.xiii, 196-7; PKM² 97.

31-2. *Cares . . . Cu aran*. An ironic description of the mother-goose. *Garan* 'heron', being a bird with a long neck like a goose, is not entirely inappropriate as a 'relative' of the goose, and *cares* 'sister, sweetheart, female friend' can be used figuratively. *Palf*, normally 'palm, paw' is here obviously for 'wing'.

33. *chwaer* 'sister' is here used fig. for 'sweetheart'.

40-2. *Gwŷr Caer.* The reference is obscure, and I am indebted to Dr
Parry for my rendering of the lines. There is some evidence that Dafydd
may have known Chester, since it is now accepted that the *englynion* to
the Cross at Chester (H.356-8) are his work; see GDG² 556; YB X
(1977), 183.

<h2 style="text-align:center">40</h2>

A number of allusions evince Dafydd's familiarity with tavern life
(*tafarn*, pl. *tefyrn*) and with the liquors which were provided in these.
For the most part it is to be expected that such taverns would have been
found in the English boroughs, with their mainly English population,
which enjoyed commercial privileges: Robin Nordd in no.15 (GDG 98)
was evidently a wealthy burgess in Aberystwyth. Even if such places
were in some respects alien territory to the poet, there is no indication
that he felt any the less hesitation in frequenting them. But there was at
least one borough which was well-known to Dafydd and well-loved by
him: Rhosyr in Anglesey (where Newborough was founded in 1305), a
place where the burgesses were mainly, if not exclusively Welsh, and to
which he composed a *cywydd* of praise, GDG 134. This is the scene of
the incident recalled in GDG 128, in which a girl repulsed his advances
by throwing his gift of wine at his messenger's head; it is also a place
which would have lain on the poet's direct route to Llanddwyn; cf.
no.34 (GDG 94). It has also been suggested that Rhosyr was the place at
which occurred the riotous escapade, either real or imaginary, which is
celebrated here. (On the international *fabliaux*, to which the poem bears
a certain resemblance, see introductory note to no.39). This poem is
rich in innuendo, and admits of interpretation on more than one level.

2. *(g)wreangyn.* From *gŵr* + *ieuanc* 'youth, page, squire'.

4-5. *Llety . . . cyffredin.* A 'common' or public lodging (house), i.e. an
inn.

8. *mau* is an editorial emendation; the MSS give a number of variants,
fy/un/yn enaid.

9-17. *lliw haul dwyrain.* This is one of the not infrequent instances in
which Dafydd employs an inherited traditional formula for a girl's
beauty with obvious ironic intent; similarly *dyn gŵyl* in l.14. I interpret
ni bu segur serch in l.17 with equal irony, as meaning that the girl was
sufficiently forthcoming in her response.

21-46. The abrupt and excited jerky movement of this passage with its
frequent *sangiadau* expressing a series of rapidly consecutive events,
makes it impossible to translate couplet-by-couplet, so that interjected
phrases often have to be postponed to the end of the sentence—the lines
being 'sentence-structured' rather than 'couplet-structured'.

26. *nid oedd campau da.* Lit. 'they were not good (lucky) feats'.

27-8. *Haws codi,* etc. Evidently a proverbial expression, or saying.

34. *Cymry a'm câr.* No parallel has as yet been found for this
expletive. It must be either a colloquialism, or perhaps a skit on some
such phrase as *Duw a'm câr* 'God loves me'. Until the 16th century
Cymry and *Cymru* were merely orthographical variants, and no dis-
tinction was made between the name for the people and for the country.
Either meaning is possible in the present instance, and I have opted for
the first. The verb may be taken as either pres. or fut., though one might
well have expected a subjunctive.

41. *dragwrdd drefn.* *Trefn* 'room, house' here appears to stand for
dodrefn 'gear, furniture', etc. Ifor Williams in B.ii, 310-11 discusses the
meanings of *trefn* and shows that they include this meaning.

50. *Hicin,* etc. These names are all diminutives: *Hicin* for Richard,
Siencyn for Jenkyn, and *Siac* for Jack or John. Dafydd is inventing token-

names for the tinkers, implying that these were the kind of names by which he would expect to hear such men called.

68. *Heb sâl.* A repetition of Dafydd's recurrent complaint that he rarely, if ever, received the 'payment' or reward which was due to him in the form of favours from the girl whom he celebrated in song or (in this case) had plied with food and drink.

41

This poem has unquestionable affinities with the *sérénade*, as this poetic genre developed during the 13th century in the literatures of Italy and Portugal—countries in which more genial weather-conditions than those of Wales could have better favoured a lover's nightly voicing of his complaints beneath his mistress's window! In French poetry *sérénades* are barely instanced before the 15th century (Jeanroy, *Les Origines de la Poésie Lyrique en France*, 146, 197 and *passim*), and they are almost unknown in English, though there is evidence that in both countries such poems persisted 'underground' in a sub-literary tradition. Chotzen (284-5) therefore regarded the present poem and two others, GDG 64 and 91, as among the earliest examples of the genre to come from western Europe. This could be explained as due to the influence of unrecorded *sérénades* in French (and perhaps also in English) popular poetry of the 13th and 14th centuries. Recently a fragment of an English serenade has come to light which offers a strikingly sympathetic parallel to Dafydd's uncomfortable wooing in the rain and snow (it dates from *circa* 1300): *So long ic have, lavedi* (lady)/*yhoved* (lingered) *at thi gate,/that mi fot is ifrore* (foot is frozen), *faire lavedi,/for thi luve faste to the stake!* (P.Dronke, *The Mediaeval Lyric* (London, 1968), 147). For a comparison of Dafydd's poems with the *sérénade* see also DGG² xl, THSC 1913-14, 119).

5. *y gorffai. 3 sg. imper.* gorfod, lit. 'overcome'.

10. *cloch.* See introductory n. to no.32 above.

11. *fy nghrair.* Lit. 'my (holy) relic', but fig. 'my darling'.

12. *Mamaeth tywysogaeth twyll.* A closely similar phrase occurs in the poem in which Morfudd is compared with the Sun, no.8 (GDG 42), l.22, *Mamaeth tywysogaeth tes.*

13. *Mau wâl. Gwâl* here, as in l.26 below, means the poet's uneasy stance beneath Morfudd's window; elsewhere the same word designates Dafydd's 'lair' or hide-out in the forest, no.35 (GDG 83), l.49.

22. *dano.* Lit. 'that I am under'.

26. *Ym* 'by' is used in oaths as the equivalent of *myn*; GMW 245.

27. *Ni bu'n y Gaer yn Arfon.* Caernarfon Castle, which dominates the seaward entrance to the Menai Straits. The site was a royal residence under the two Llywelyns, but the present castle was built by Edward I, and reached approximately its present form by *circa* 1330. Dafydd's allusion reminds us of the overwhelming impression which this immense edifice must have made upon the local inhabitants. It is possible, also, that there is an irrecoverable topical allusion here, and that some well-known prisoner in the Castle may be intended by it.

35. *Ni faddeuwn. Maddau* has here the meaning 'let go, dispense with, absolve' cf. GDG 481.

gwn gyni. The same *sangiad* is employed in no.33 (GDG 71), l.17.

40. *ellyll* 'phantom, spirit, demon', etc. Used by Dafydd of the Moon, *Haul yr ellyllon yw hi* GDG 70, l.32; and of his Shadow, no.50 (GDG 141), l.22. For other occurrences of the word see TYP nos.63, 64 and notes.

42

The parting of lovers at dawn is an ancient poetic theme in many literatures, but from the 12th century the *alba* (Fr. *aube, aubade*) which originated in Provence, developed certain common characteristics which are to be found widespread through western Europe. Most frequently these poems are in dialogue form: one or other of the pair of lovers expresses fear of discovery (sometimes by *le Jaloux*—the Jealous Husband) if their parting is delayed, and points out to the other the signs of approaching day—the rising sun, the singing of birds, and the crowing of cocks. These signs are promptly denied by the other partner: it is the moon and not the sun that affords the light, and it is the nightingale who sings and not the lark. (The classic example in English is of course the *aubade* in the play of *Romeo and Juliet*). The present poem is one of two examples in Welsh, both of which have been translated by Melville Richards in A.T.Hatto's compendium *Eos: An Enquiry into the Theme of Lovers' Meetings and Partings at Dawn in Poetry* (The Hague, 1965), 568-74. (In places my rendering differs widely from M.R's). On linguistic grounds Dr Parry decisively rejected the companion piece (BDG XCVII) and expressed some doubts also as to the authenticity of this one, though it finally received the benefit of the doubt and was included in GDG. There are two points of interest about the poem: firstly, it bears unmistakable evidence of the poet's cognisance of foreign models in its form and allusions, and secondly, it is no less certain that it is a parody of the foreign model. For comparable instances of indirect external influence see notes to the previous poem and to no.18 above; poems which show certain resemblances to the *serenade* and the *pastourelle* repectively. (On the three poems see *Tradn. and Innov.* 49, n.). The idiomatic colloquial dialogue in this poem is especially lively.

5. *beirniad.* Lit. 'a judge says'. But 'judge' is not used in a legal sense, but in that of 'critic, knowledgeable person', as in no.13 (GDG 45) ls.55, 56 where Dafydd appeals to the judgement of his listeners, addressing them as *beirniaid*, 'critics'.

8. *Nyf.* On this pseudonym for the girl addressed see n. to no.15, l.56 above. The modern equivalent is 'Nia'.

9. *Yn mynnu tâl.* This is ambiguous, since it could be the girl who wished for 'payment' for herself. But it is more likely to be a re-iteration of Dafydd's frequetly-voiced complaint that he receives no reward of any kind for his devotion, and for the poems of praise he has addressed to the girl of his choice.

16. *coel hoyw.* The 'lively sign'—later to be denied by the poet—is presumably the sun.

18. *weldiso.* For *a wely di isod* 'do you see down there?'

25. *Gair honnaid. Gair* can mean 'pledge', as in no.3, l.30 *gair hyfaidd* 'a daring pledge'; *honnaid* 'evident, famous'; for *gair honnaid* cf. IGE², 117, 21 'assertion, assurance' (?).

27. *pryfed y sydd yn profi. Profi* lit. 'to test, taste' as in IGE² LXXXV, 21-2, *A thrychant, meddant i mi/O bryfed yn ei brofi.*

31. *fy nag yn agos,* 'my denial is near (the mark), i.e. 'stands firm'.

32. *cŵn y nos.* An unmistakable reference to the *cŵn Annwn,* the sinister pack of the mythical Gwyn ap Nudd, see n. to no.26, ls.22, 40.

33. *gwawdwas. Gwawd* has here its older meaning of 'praise-poetry', rather than its later one of 'satire', though Dafydd employs both; see n. to no.8 (GDG 42), l.57 above.

36. *anterth yw.* From lat. *ante tertiam* 'before the third (hour)' by the old monastic reckoning, i.e. 9 a.m. Here fig. 'it is high time'.

39. *rhyfras.* Lit. 'very great'.

41. *Ochan* 'alas' hardly seems appropriate: two MSS read *o chaf* 'if I can'.

43. *ffel* from E. 'fell' in its older meaning of 'crafty, cunning, sly'; cf. no.25, l.28 (of the Magpie) *ffelaf edn o'r byd* 'most cunning bird in the world'.

43

This poem is composed in the metre known as *traethodl*, a simple verse-form in seven-lined rhyming couplets, out of which the *cywydd* evolved (see Dr Parry's discussion, THSC 1939, 210-2; *Hanes Llen-yddiaeth* 108-9; CD 312). The asymmetrical rhyme of the *cywydd* occurs from time to time, but is not obligatory; rhyme between unaccented syllables is found frequently (e.g. lines 3-4); *cynghanedd* is an occasional ornament but is not essential, the style is light-hearted and conversational, even mocking. In *Ll.C.* X, 116-8 D.G.Bowen points out that the friars were notorious for composing both Latin and vernacular verse to secular tunes: these are in fact the earliest carols (an example is OBWV no.34, a Christmas 'carol' by the Franciscan(?) friar Madog ap Gwallter). He suggests that by using the *traethodl* as the metre for this poem Dafydd was adopting a measure employed characteristically by the friars in Wales for religious purposes. It is a measure which is to be found amongst the earliest examples of the *canu rhydd* or free-metre poetry (e.g. OBWV no.102): from this it may legitimately be deduced that in the 14th century it was one which characterized productions of the lower orders of poets. Criticism of friars was widespread in the vernacular literatures in the 14th and 15th centuries; examples are to be found in Chaucer and Langland, cf. also Iolo Goch, IGE[2] XXII. Dafydd treats the same theme in no.17 above, and in GDG nos.136,138.

7. *od gwn*, 'if I know it', 'assuredly' (PKM 118-9).

8. *eilun prydydd*. See n. to no.32, l.15 on *eilun*.

11. *o'm llofrudd* 'from my murderer'. Cf. the use of *gelynes* 'enemy', no.38.18.

15. *Mi a rown yt*. With the use of the imperf. here in conditional sense, cf. no.25, l.65 *gwyddwn yt*.

21. *eiliw ewyn* 'colour of foam'. For the ironic use of such traditional epithets see n. to no.40, 9-17.

22. *lliw papir* 'hue of paper'. In B.xxxviii, 404 Gwyn Thomas suggests that behind this rather unusual comparison lies the friar's wish to emphasize to the poet the fragile character of all earthly beauty, as being like a scrap of paper. Cf. however DGG[2] XXV, 31 where a nun's beauty is compared to *memrwn* 'parchment' also the comparison of the Seagull as *llythyr unwaith* no.22, 9 'as white as a sheet of paper' (DGG[2] 129 n.), (oddly enough, the following line describes the bird as *lleian* 'a nun'). These comparisons remind us that a pallid complexion was considered beautiful in the Middle Ages.

27. *cywydd nac englyn*. These metrical terms are discussed in the introduction.

29. *cerdd*. The primary meaning is 'art, craft' as in the cognate Old Irish *cerd(d)*; traces of this meaning survive in older Welsh literature, see GPC 465.

y glêr. A term which is used in Welsh as the equivalent of *clerici vagantes*, the 'wandering scholars' or *joculatores* of other countries. Dr Parry shows (GDG 439-41) that the word may be employed (as in Irish) as a comprehensive and entirely non-committal term for poets in general. It appears to have been an early borrowing from Irish *cleir* (which has this latter meaning) and was later influenced semantically by French *clers*, which gave it a pejorative colouring. It is occasionally confusing that

Dafydd may use *clêr* and *clerwr* in either sense: positively, when he speaks of himself as one of a body of honourable practitioners of the art of poetry, as (indirectly) in nos.13, 1.11; 44. 1.14, and negatively and disparagingly when he contrasts himself with the *clêr ofer* or 'vain versifiers' (such as the unfortunate Rhys Meigen whom he satirized, GDG 21, ls.52, 74)—poets who lacked his own high qualifications.

34. *i ddiawl.* Lit. 'to the devil'.

41-2. *Tripheth,* etc. A free-metre poem, OBWV no.108, gives a very suggestive series of triads relating to the affairs of love, indicating a likely source for this triad in some similar popular and sub-literary composition.

43. *Merch sydd deca blodeuyn,* etc. Chotzen shows (235-6) that the defence of women on theological grounds played a prominent part in the contemporary controversy between the poets or *clerici vagantes,* and the friars.

46. *ond tridyn.* Ifor Williams suggested, (DGG² 212) that this means Adam, Eve, and Melchisedec (according to *Hebrews* vii, 3 the latter was born 'without father nor mother nor any genealogy').

55. *clera.* i.e. to go on a bardic circuit, visiting a succession of patrons.

58. *segwensiau.* Latin hymns sung immediately before the Gospel in the service of the Mass. Famous examples are the *Stabat Mater* and *Dies Irae,* but many more existed in former times than those which have survived (DGG² 212).

63-4. *Amser i fwyd amser i olochwyd* is included in Davies's collection of proverbs at the end of his dictionary.

66. *i gyfanheddu.* The Red Book text of the Bardic Grammar lists *kyuanhedu* 'to entertain' among the requirements of the *teuluwr,* one of the lesser grades of poet; GP 17. (The version in Ll.3 substitutes *digrifwch,* GP 37).

71. *Ystudfach.* According to tradition an early poet to whom *cynghore* or 'precepts' are attributed in the 16th century MS Cardiff 6; see *Rep.II,* 109, 110 (which gives examples). W. Salesbury also refers to him in the preface to his book of proverbs; see Saunders Lewis, *Meistri'r Canrifoedd,* 135 for the passage.

73-4. The proverb is given in the Red Book collection, col.964-74, *Rep.II* 7, and also in *Englynion y Clyweit,* B.III, 13, no.49.

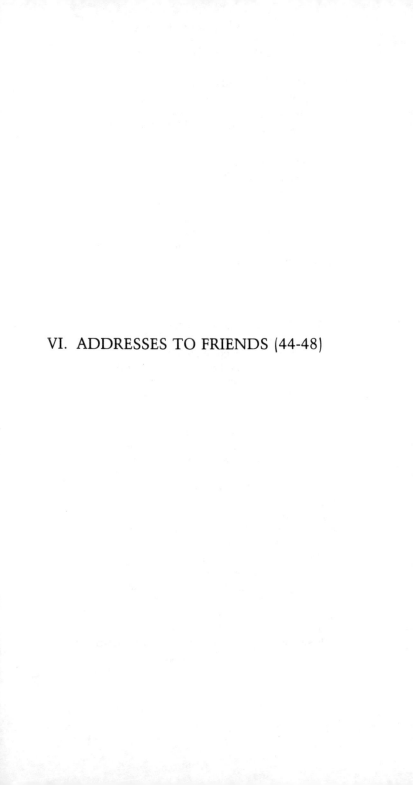

VI. ADDRESSES TO FRIENDS (44-48)

44   Ifor the Generous

A splendid stewardship is mine,
Ifor, [with you], a pleasant nurturing,
for I am steward of your wealth,
4   greatly-gifted, eloquent, and powerful lord.

Brave and considerate you are,
a good man, bountiful to me:
I paid you praise in vibrant words,
8   dark shining bragget you paid back to me.
You gave me treasure, as a pledge of love,
I give you [in return] Rhydderch's great name.
An armed warrior whom weapons do not smite,
12   friend and servitor of bards,
a mighty hero, of a noble warrior stock,
subservient to poets, a wealthy lord.

Most brave and valiant of men you are
16   to follow, not a weakling.
Your lineage has been of good repute:
[by] God who rules, twice more subservient
you are to your poet than one hand to the other,
20   ruler of hosts, wise and above reproach.

I carry from my land your fame,
a lordly growth, and return [to you], Ifor.
From my words there has been framed
24   [for you] an epithet not mean, [for it is] true.
From my lips, great lord of hosts,
Eight score myriad words shall praise you.
As far as man may travel furthest,
28   as far as the bold summer sun turns on its course,
as far as wheat is sown,
and as far as fair dew-fall moistens,
as far as the unclouded eye may see
32   —strong he is—and far as ear may hear,
as far as the Welsh tongue is known,
and as far as fair crops grow,
splendid Ifor, of sprightly ways
36   —long your sword—your praise will be sown.

Cywydd i Ifor Hael (7)

Ifor, aur o faerwriaeth
Deg yw'r fau, diagr o faeth;
Myfi yw, ffraethlyw ffrwythlawn,
4 Maer dy dda, mawr yw dy ddawn.

    Ys dewr, ystyriol ydwyd,
Ystôr ym, ys da ŵr wyd.
Telais yt wawd tafawd hoyw,
8 Telaist ym fragod duloyw.
Rhoist ym swllt, rhyw ystum serch,
Rhoddaf yt brifenw Rhydderch.
Cyfarf arf, eirf ni'th weheirdd,
12 Cyfaillt a mab aillt y beirdd.
Cadarn wawr, cedyrn wiwryw
Caeth y glêr, cywaethog lyw.

    Dewraf wyd a gwrddaf gŵr
16 Dy ddilyn, dieiddilwr.
Da oedd a syberw dy ach;
Duw a fedd, dau ufuddach
Wyd i'th fardd, pellgardd pwyllgall,
20 Llywiwr llu, no'r llaw i'r llall.

    Myned o'm gwlad, dyfiad iôr,
Â'th glod, a dyfod, Ifor.
O'm iaith y rhylunieithir,
24 Air nid gwael, arnad y gwir.
O'm pen fy hun, pen-cun cyrdd,
Y'th genmyl wyth ugeinmyrdd.
Hyd yr ymdaith dyn eithaf,
28 Hyd y try hwyl hy haul haf,
Hyd yr hëir y gwenith,
A hyd y gwlych hoywdeg wlith,
Hyd y gwŷl golwg digust,
32 Hydr yw, a hyd y clyw clust,
Hyd y mae iaith Gymräeg,
A hyd y tyf hadau teg,
Hardd Ifor hoywryw ddefod,
36 Hir dy gledd, hëir dy glod.

45 Basaleg

Go lad, (he loves choice green,
fine his condition) over green birches, fair,
carry my greetings from Morgannwg
4   to Gwynedd, a path [bestrewn with] choicest mead,
(I am a favourite, with the world's ebullient force):
Take greetings with you to the land of Môn.

Say, from my country I have not been allowed
8   —you bear no guilt [for it], God knows—
[but that] I have now been a while (the psalm of
                                        Solomon)
courting a being near to Cardiff [here].
No fortune ugly or perverse is mine,
12   no love for slender, smooth-lipped (?) girl,
but I am overwhelmed with love for Ifor,
more than the love for any girl it is.
I have celebrated Ifor's love
16   which is not like the love of stupid Saxon churl;
nor will I go, most perfect lord,
for Ifor's love, if he should ask—
one single day to wicked towns,
20   or pass one night [away] from Morgannwg.

He is descended from a race of heroes,
a noble band, gold-helmed and generous.
Honoured, wealthy, hawk [of men],
24   sturdy his limbs upon his horse;
swift to accomplish overthrow in battle,
a falcon excellently wise in argument,
a stag who does not die, who does not brook the Deirans,
28   [all] men will find him true.
His discourse is humble and wise
compared with fair Ifor [other] men have little worth.

Great is the honour which I have received:
32   for while I live, I am allowed
to hunt with hounds—there is no more generous lord—
and drink with Ifor,
and shoot a straight course at the stags,
36   and cast hawks to the wind and sky,
and [enjoy] sweet songs by word of mouth
and entertainment [here] at Basaleg.
Is it not pleasant before hosts,
40   the aim of poets, to shoot the mark?
to play at backgammon and chess
on equal status with the mighty lord?
By mutual consent, if either one should win

Basaleg (8)

Cerdda, was, câr ddewiswyrdd,
Ceinfyd gwymp, uwch ceinfedw gwyrdd;
O Forgannwg dwg dydd da
4   I Wynedd, heilfedd hwylfa,
Ac annwyl wyf, befrnwyf byd,
Ac annerch wlad Fôn gennyd.

    Dywed, o'm gwlad ni'm gadwyd,
8   Duw a'i gŵyr, dieuog wyd,
Fy mod es talm, salm Selyf,
Yn caru dyn uwch Caerdyf.
Nid salw na cham fy namwain,
12 Nid serch ar finrhasgl ferch fain.
Mawrserch Ifor a'm goryw,
Mwy no serch ar ordderch yw.
Serch Ifor a glodforais,
16 Nid fal serch anwydful Sais,
Ac nid af, berffeithiaf bôr,
Os eirch ef, o serch Ifor,
Nac undydd i drefydd drwg,
20 Nac unnos o Forgannwg.

    Gŵr yw o hil goreuwawr,
Gwiw blaid, helm euraid, hael mawr.
Goludog hebog hybarch,
24 Gŵr ffyrf iawn ei gorff ar farch.
Cwympwr aer cyflymdaer coeth,
Cwmpasddadl walch campusddoeth.
Carw difarw, Deifr ni oddef,
28 Cywir iawn y câi wŷr ef.
Ufudd a da ei ofeg;
Ofer dyn ond Ifor deg.

    Mawr anrhydedd a'm deddyw:
32 Mi a gaf, o byddaf byw,
Hely â chŵn, nid haelach iôr,
Ac yfed gydag Ifor,
A saethu rhygeirw sythynt,
36 A bwrw gweilch i wybr a gwynt,
A cherddau tafodau teg,
A solas ym Masaleg.
Pand digrif yng ngŵydd nifer,
40 Pennod, saethu claernod, clêr,
Gwarae ffristiol a tholbwrdd
Yn un gyflwr â'r gŵr gwrdd?
O châi neb, cytundeb coeth,

44   excellent precedence above the other
      (with verse I freely him endow)
      [in this] I win the precedence from Ifor.

      For generosity his like cannot be found,
48   nor for his valour; is he not a prince?
      I will not leave his court, the all-confident lord,
      no one is humble except Ifor.

46 Elegy for Rhydderch
(on behalf of Llywelyn Fychan of Glyn Aeron)

      Yesterday, on a high slope
      I heard three cries, and sought retreat;
      I know groans well, and yet I never thought
4   that man could ever utter such a cry.
      In my land—free gift—there never was
      outpouring of lament, nor huntsman's voice,
      nor piercing (?) horn [heard] over wooded slope,
8   nor bell louder than that cry.

      What noise is this, [what] sigh of woe?
      keen pang, who was it gave that cry?
      Llywelyn Fychan, from the abode of love,
12   gave this cry because of Rhydderch,
      near to his beautiful court.
      He was to Rhydderch a sworn brother (swift his end);
      [like] Amlyn's cry from his afflicted home
16   for Emig, like a foster-mother's grief;
      a cry of bitter grief from one
      who passionately loved his friend,
      a third cry, like the Valley's bell,
20   was the one uttered by Llywelyn.

      When Rhydderch's lips, wine-giver, were interred,
      love was seven times buried deep;
      perished is now the lord of fair Deheubarth,
24   well do I know I am undone (?)
      perished the lavish custom of [dispensing] mead,
      valour is perished and committed to the ground.
      [Like] a white swan imprisoned in a pound
28   he lies in his grave of stone.
      Nature's affliction—not longer is the grave
      than seven feet—dear proud one, once erect.

      What a strange lesson that there should be subdued
32   beneath so small a compass of dark turf
      all knowledge, all the aptitudes of love,

44 Rhagor rhag y llall rhygoeth,
    Rhugl â cherdd y'i anrhegaf,
    Rhagor rhag Ifor a gaf.

    Nid hael wrth gael ei gyfryw,
48 Nid dewr neb; pand tëyrn yw?
    Nid af o'i lys, diful iôr,
    Nid ufudd neb ond Ifor.

Marwnad Rhydderch (17)
(dros Llywelyn Fychan o Lyn Aeron)

    Doe clywais, mi geisiais gêl,
    Dair och ar lethrdir uchel.
    Ni meddyliwn, gwn gannoch,
4   Y rhôi ŵr fyth y rhyw och.
    Ni bu i'm gwlad, rhoddiad rhydd,
    Na llif cwyn, na llef cynydd,
    Na meingorn uwch llethr mangoed,
8   Na chloch uwch no'r och a roed.

    Pa'r dwrw yw hwn, pryderoch?
    Pefr loes, pwy a roes yr och?
    Llywelyn, o'r syddyn serch,
12 A roddes hon am Rydderch,
    Fychan garllaw ei lân lys,
    Ffyddfrawd Rhydderch ddiffoddfrys.
    Och Amlyn o'i dyddyn dig,
16 Alaeth mamaeth, am Emig;
    Och gŵr a fai'n awch garu
    Ei gâr, o fawr alar fu;
    A'r drydedd och, gloch y Glyn,
20 Ail yw, a rôi Lywelyn.

    Pan gaewyd, saith guddiwyd serch,
    Gwin roddiad, genau Rydderch,
    Darfu, gwn y'm dierfir,
24 Ben Deheubarth wen yn wir.
    Darfu'r foes dirfawr o fedd,
    Darfu daearu dewredd.
    Gorwyn alarch yng ngwarchae,
28 Gorwedd mewn maenfedd y mae.
    Natur boen, nid hwy yw'r bedd,
    Syth drudfalch, no saith droedfedd.

    Pregethu ryfedd oedd weddu
32 Dan hyn o dywerchyn du
    Gwybodau, synhwyrau serch,

the all-embracing, splendid gifts of Rhydderch
and his wise, unfailing worthiness;
36 his strong white body, merry and astute,
his virtues—tale of natural endowments,
his brilliant learning and his shining gifts,
his charm—a genial conversationalist—
40 his fame—alas the coming of his day!

Tumultuous (?) was the cold sorrow of his burial,
he was a merciful knight.
May mercy, through sincerity of love
44   be given by God to Rhydderch.

47   Elegy for Gruffudd ab Adda

When, near to a lime-washed wall
[enclosing] a proud group of orchard trees
by night and day a nightingale has called
4   from underneath the apple-trees,
pure, clear-voiced bird, with long-drawn, plaintive song,
from her enclosing nest, like Heaven's child,
with voice of golden song upon the pleasant slopes,
8   [like] a sweet bell upon the glistening branch—
how great the difference, if there should come
(keen edifice of song) a wildly-leaping sharp-shooter
intent by grievous treachery to destroy
12   with birch-wood arrow, barbed four-square:
even though the trees may be replete
with comely load of fruit, a gift of joy,
poetry will be bereft, with intense grief,
16   of the sweet treasure of the flowering trees.

Powys, a fruitful land of shining eloquence,
endowed with sweet drinking-horns in gleaming taverns,
was such an orchard, [once] inhabited,
20   before [that] gifted lad was slain with a blue sword;
henceforth this land of heroes will not have
—woeful bereavement—any nightingale of song.
[Land of] dejected poets, their *awdlau* unesteemed
24   is this [land], most hateful of all hated things.
If for three months there has been heavy grief,
alas! there never was grief but was less [than this]
because of the impact—cry of mighty rage—
28   of a keen weapon where it was not loved.

Gruffudd, sweetest singing-bird,
son of Addaf, most innocent of men;
every man of worth used to call him

172

Gwmpas rodd gampus Rydderch,
A'i wiwdawd digolltawd gall,
36 A'i gryfgorff gwyn digrifgall,
A'i gampau, chwedl doniau dawn,
A'i loywddysg a'i oleuddawn,
A'i ras, gyweithas ieithydd,
40 A'i glod, och ddyfod ei ddydd!

    Trwst oedd oer trist ddaearu,
Trugarog o farchog fu.
Trugaredd trwy symlwedd serch
44 A roddo Duw i Rydderch.

Marwnad Gruffudd ab Adda (18)

Rhagawr mawr ger mur gwyngalch,
Lle y bo perllanwydd, llu balch,
Bod yn galw is afalwydd
4 Eos yn nos ac yn nydd;
Cathlolaes edn coeth loywlef,
Cau nyth, megis cyw o nef;
Eurwawd lef ar weddeiddfainc,
8 Orlais goeth ar irlwys gainc.
Gwedy dêl, gwawd adeilym,
Gwyllt saethydd, llamhidydd llym,
O ddwystraul brad i ddistryw,
12 Â bollt bedryollt bedw ryw,
Cyd bai llawn, dawn dywenydd,
O berffrwyth, gweddeiddlwyth gwŷdd,
Y bydd cerdd fydr, o hydr hoed,
16 Heb loyw degan blodeugoed.

    Powys, gwlad ffraethlwys ffrwythlawn,
Pêr heilgyrn pefr defyrn dawn,
A oedd berllan gyfannedd
20 Cyn lladd doethwas â glas gledd.
Bellach y mae, gwae gwedd-dawd,
Beues gweilch, heb eos gwawd.
Adlaw beirdd, awdl heb urddas,
24 Ydyw hon, caseion cas.
Osid trymoch es trimis,
Och! ni bu och na bai is,
Am gyhwrdd, lef agwrdd lid,
28 Awch arf yn lle ni cherid.

    Gruffudd, gerddber aderyn,
Fab Addaf, difeiaf dyn,
Pob dyn disalw a'i galwai

32 prince of the lovely twigs of trees in May,
    a merry organ, penetrating far,
    beloved golden nightingale,
    the ever-ready bee of poetry,
36 spring-time of wisdom in Gwenwynwyn's land.

    It was villainous for his friend to smite him
    in reckless anger, with steel blade in hand.
    A weapon gave—a fearful disposition—
40 to my brother, a deep sword-wound.
    through the short hair of [this] hawk of proud descent—
    alas, how sharp his weapon's edge!
    by his sharp sword (was it not sad?)
44 he gave just such a cut as with a saw
    through the good brave man's yellow hair—
    an ugly cleft [made] through his merry pate,
    just such a cleft in twain as if it were a goose,
48 I am enraged; was it not barbarous?

    Two cheeks the colour of a golden angel,
    turret of gold—[and yet] the man is dead.

48   Elegy for Madog Benfras

    This life, deceptive [as it is]
    is throughout like a broken sieve:
    the lad who is replete with joy tonight,
4   and happy though his life may be,
    a terrible and swift harsh dream
    will turn upon the morrow to his death.

    Why should swift inspiration trouble me
8   (a bright impression, bravely shining path)
    concerning Madog Benfras, poetry's twin?
    there never has been better servitor of song.
    He was both brave and bold, and there will be henceforth
12 no man like Madog—conqueror of verse—
    for skill in fashioning the lines—
    for a good poem—it was a miracle—
    for serious and for learned song,
16 for generous merriment and sociability,
    for love surpassing anyone,
    for wise repute, for wisdom's self.

    Harsh was my outcry this year
20 for stealing away Madog, my blessing he was.
    Terrible the pang for this teacher of men,
    [no] poet's disciple but will utter it,
    illustrious [his repute] afar, discretion's chief,

32 Pendefig mireinfrig Mai,
    Ac organ dra diddan draidd,
    Ac aur eos garuaidd,
    Gwenynen gwawd barawdwir,
36 Gwanwyn doeth Gwenwynwyn dir.

    Diriaid i'w gâr ei daraw,
    Dewr o lid, â dur i'w law.
    Arf a roes, eirioes orofn,
40 Ar fy mrawd gleddyfawd ddofn,
    Trwy fanwallt gwalch o falchlin,
    Och fi, ddäed awch ei fin!
    Triawch y cledd (pand truan?)
44 Trwy felynflew dyn glew glân.
    Trawiad un lladdiad â llif,
    Toriad hagr trwy iad digrif,
    Dig wyf, un doriad â gŵydd,
48 Deuddryll, pond oedd wladeiddrwydd?

    Deurudd liw angel melyn,
    Dwred aur, deryw y dyn.

Marwnad Madog Benfras (19)

    Rhidyll hudolaidd rhydwn,
    Rhyw fyd ar ei hyd yw hwn.
    Y macwy llawen heno
4   Hyfryd ei fywyd a fo,
    Breuddwyd aruthr ebrwyddarw,
    A dry yfory yn farw.

    Pam y'm cên awen ewybr,
8   Pefr orgraff, oleubraff lwybr?
    Am Fadog, farddlef efell,
    Benfras, ni bu wawdwas well.
    Bu ddewr hy, ni bydd y rhawg,
12 Ormail mydr ŵr mal Madawg
    O fedru talm o fydroedd,
    O gerdd dda, ac arwydd oedd,
    O ddwysgwbl gerdd, o ddysgaid,
16 O ddigrifwch fflwch a phlaid,
    O gariad yn anad neb,
    O ddoeth enw, o ddoethineb.

    Dengyn ym mlwyddyn fy mloedd,
20 Dwyn Madog, dawn ym ydoedd.
    Uthr yw gwayw am athro gwŷr,
    Disgybl o'r beirdd nid esgyr.
    Pell eglur, penadur pwyll,

24 peacock of splendid converse, was he not free from guile?
    in contest [an incisive] auger, with a gentle heart,
    one who smoothed out the sense and sound
    in poetry's craft; he was the peer of Myrddin,
28 yoke of protection, eyes like wine,
    bell of [free] choosing in the month of May,
    the trumpet and the horn of song,
    chorus of affection and of love,
32 burnisher of song and contest's rivalry,
    bright organ, faultless instrument,
    chieftain of the poetry of poets.

    Dejected [are the] poets, whose land is sad,
36 and without *cywydd* will the world remain;
    rarely did he not deserve fine gold—
    destitute will be the tender leaves of May,
    with no song of the small sweet nightingale,
40 a welling access of subdued(?) tears;
    birch-trees, not knowing him, will lack honour in song,
    and without hope the ash-grove: he was good.

    A strong and prompt support, chapel of poetry,
44 each one a copper coin to him, [each] girl deprived:
    It were boorish—he has left the lands—
    if there be life, that he were not alive.
    Woe to the host of bards—he had a splendid voice—
48 [now] in God's keeping he is left.

24 Paun da ddadl, pand oedd ddidwyll?
Cad daradr, ceudod tirion,
Canwyr y synnwyr a'r sôn.
Cwplws caniatgerdd Ferddin,
28 Cwpl porthloedd, golygoedd gwin,
A thampr o ddewis mis Mai,
A thrwmpls y gerdd a'i thrimplai,
A chôr y serch a chariad,
32 A choprs cerdd a chiprys cad,
Pefr organ, degan digeirdd,
Pennaeth barddonïaeth beirdd.

Dihoywfro beirdd dihyfryd,
36 Digywydd y bydd y byd.
Diaml aur mâl nis talai,
Diarail fydd manddail Mai.
Digerdd eos befrdlos bach,
40 Dwf acses, deigr difocsach.
Dibarch fydd bedw nis edwyn;
Da beth oedd; diobaith ynn.

Cwpl ewybr, capel awen,
44 Copr pawb wrthaw, gwaglaw gwen.
Gwladaidd oedd, gwledydd eddyw,
O bai fyd, na bai ef fyw.
Gwae feirddlu, gwiw ei farddlef,
48 Gyda Duw y gadwyd ef.

Notes

44

Four *cywyddau* were addressed by Dafydd to his friend and patron Ifor ap Llywelyn, and of these the present poem is the most famous. Ifor appears to have been a close contemporary of the poet, and to have been in his prime *circa* 1340-60. His home was at Gwernyclepa in Gwent, about a mile from the present village of Basaleg (see the following poem), between Cardiff and Newport. At what period of his life Dafydd addressed these poems to Ifor can only be a matter of speculation. Their language is relatively unadorned and simple, and as D.J.Bowen has cogently demonstrated (*Ll.C.*V,164-73) their style is relaxed and personal, and employs nature-imagery of a kind which is strikingly similar to the imagery employed by Dafydd elsewhere in his poems of love and nature (cf. ls.28-34 below). At the same time these four *cywyddau* embody certain concepts which have come down in direct descent from the praise-poetry of the Gogynfeirdd: Dafydd stresses the mutual dependence of poet and patron (ls.7-10), and alludes in these poems more frequently than elsewhere to the traditional heroes of the 'Old North', envisaging himself as another Taliesin in his relation to his patron.

1. *aur o faerwriaeth.* *Aur* as a prefix is used as frequently figuratively 'splendid, excellent' as literally; for exx. see G.496-7, TYP 176-8. Dr Parry interprets *maerwriaeth*, a form unattested elsewhere, as the equivalent of *maeroni(aeth)* 'stewardship'.

6. *ystôr*, from E. 'store', EEW 184.

10. *(p)rifenw Rhydderch.* Rhydderch Hael was one of the legendary *Tri Hael* or 'Three Generous Men' among the sixth century Britons of the 'Old North', according to an early triad frequently alluded to by the poets; see TYP 5-6, 504-5. In bestowing the epithet *hael* upon his friend, Dafydd effectively added Ifor to the triad, as an equally illustrious benefactor. And the epithet became indissolubly linked with his name, as is plain from a series of allusions by subsequent poets to 'Ifor Hael', the earliest of which is by Madog Dwygraig, a near contemporary who addressed poems to Ifor's half-brother (DGG² 212-3, G.J.Williams, *Traddodiad Llenyddol Morgannwg*, 12).

11. *Cyfarf arf.* *Arf* is apparently used figuratively for Ifor, but *cyfarf* 'well-armed' can also be employed as a noun 'warrior'. The compound *cyfarf arf* is also used by Gruffudd ap Maredudd, RBP 1315, 7.

12. *Cyfaillt a mab aillt.* *Mab* in such terms as this means simply a male person; cf. *mabsant* 'patron saint'. On *mab aillt* see D.Jenkins, *Llyfr Colan*, (Cardiff, 1963), 48; TYP 179-80. *Aillt* 'subject, yeoman, vassal' and *cyfaill(t)* both contain an element cognate with Irish *alt* 'joint'; hence *cyfaill(t)* 'bound together (in the bond of friendship)'. Dafydd appears to recognise the relation of the words to each other, and to mean that Ifor as his friend was at the same time essentially someone who served him (Iolo Goch employs the same collocation of his patron, IGE² 54, ls.27-8). In the Law of Hywel, *mab aillt* originally denoted an unfree landholder, as opposed to the *caeth* (cf. 1.14), the bondsman captive to the soil. But the word declined in status, being by the 13th century the equivalent of *taeog* 'villein, churl'. Though there is nothing derogatory in its use in the present instance, the same cannot be said of GDG 119, 1.12, *nid neithior arf barf mab aillt*, where it is obviously derogatory.

14. *Caeth y glêr.* On the two senses in which Dafydd employs the word *clêr* see n. to no.43,29: here it is plainly employed for poets in general, and in no depreciatory sense. *Caeth* must be rendered as 'subservient' rather than literally 'captive'.

18. *Duw a fedd*. For the asseveration *myn Duw a fedd* 'by God who rules' see B.I.28.

dau ufuddach. Dafydd applies the adj. *ufudd* 'humble' to Ifor in two other poems, GDG 6, l.13, and no.45 (GDG 8), l.50, below; 'subservient' again seems the nearest English equivalent.

24. *Air nid gwael*, 'an epithet not mean', i.e. the epithet *hael* 'the Generous'.

25. *cyrdd*. Here, probably, this is the pl. of *cordd* 'host, company' rather than of *cerdd* 'song', but the ambiguity may be intentional.

31. *digust*. This is the only recorded instance of the word; GPC renders it as 'clear, open, unobscured'; the element *cust* being cognate with Lat. *obscurus* (see B. XI,83).

36. *hëir dy glod*. Elsewhere Dafydd describes himself as 'sowing' his praise of Morfudd by circulating his poems, e.g. no.10 (GDG 34), ls.13-16; alternatively, it is the seeds of love which are sown, as in no.6 (GDG 87) and no.54 (GDG 102), ls.5-6.

45

See introductory note to the preceding poem. In this poem Dafydd celebrates the delights of Ifor's home at Gwernyclepa, called Basaleg (l.38; cf. GDG 9, l.54) after the name of the adjoining village. The somewhat excessive terms in which the poet speaks of his love for Ifor (ls.9-20) may partly reflect a recognised literary convention; since as D.J.Bowen points out (THSC 1969, 285) such a convention is to be found in Irish bardic poetry, where there are instances in which a poet's relation to his patron is actually envisaged in the terms of a marriage. The same passage (ls.9-20) expresses overtly a reaction on Dafydd's part against composing love-poetry.

5. *annwyl* 'favourite' as well as 'beloved'.

befrnwyf byd. Lit. 'the forceful energy of the world'. The whole line stands in parenthesis, and with l.6 is omitted from a large number of MSS.

7. *o'm gwlad*. By 'my country' in the present context Dafydd clearly means Morgannwg (*pace* Saunders Lewis, *Meistri'r Canrifoedd*, 44, who would amend the reading to *i'm gwlad*, understanding 'my country' to be Anglesey).

8. *dieuog wyd*. The line must be interpreted as meaning 'whatever my excuse for having stayed away—it's not *your* fault'.

9. *salm Selyf*. This unexpected allusion to the Song of Solomon is interesting as showing that in the 14th century men could recognise in one of the books of the Bible a precedent for secular love-poetry. Gilbert Ruddock points out (YB X, 231-2) that imagery based on this book becomes increasingly prominent in the *cywyddau* of the following century.

10. *dyn* is here significantly ambiguous, since it can mean either man or woman, though it is used most frequently by Dafydd for a girl.

uwch Caerdyf 'above Cardiff'. This early form of the name is based upon an old oblique case of the name for the river *Taf*, later it became *Caerdydd* through confusion of *-f* and *-dd* (Ifor Williams *Enwau Lleoedd*, 51).

12. *ar finrhasgl ferch*. The literal meaning of *minrhasgl* is 'rasping lips', but Ifor Williams interprets this epithet when applied to Taliesin (IGE² 42, 21, see glossary) as meaning 'smooth-lipped, i.e. a fine singer': in this latter instance it is obviously complimentary.

16. *anwydful* 'foolish-natured'. According to H. Lewis, B.VI, 321 n. the meaning of *mul* was originally 'modest', but later it deteriorated to mean 'foolish'.

18. *os eirch ef*. I take this as meaning 'if he ask me to stay'.

21-2. The allusion to the patron's noble descent is a convention inherited from antecedent praise-poetry; so also is the obviously incongruous epithet 'gold-helmed' as applied to Ifor. Cf. no.13 (GDG 45), ls.1-2 and n.

26-7. *(g)walch; carw*. Names for animals and for birds of prey are used figuratively for warriors in Welsh poetry from the earliest times; for some analogies cf. TYP 94.

27. *Deifr ni oddef* 'who does not suffer the [men of] Deira'. This figure also goes back to the earliest Welsh poetry, and is a petrified image, whose meaning lies in its associations. The men of *Deur* (Deira, in south-east Yorkshire) and *Brynaich* (Bernicia, in Northumbria) were the English enemies who opposed the Britons in Aneirin's poem the *Gododdin*. Dafydd alludes to the Deirans several times in his praise-poetry to his uncle Llywelyn and to Ifor Hael.

29. *Ufudd*. See n. to no.44,18 above, and cf. l.50 below. Here the meaning of *ufudd* is 'humble' or perhaps 'discreet', rather than 'subservient'.

30. *Ofer dyn*. Cf. GDG 6, where in a sequence of *englynion* Dafydd ascribes to Ifor a list of qualities in the possession of which all other men are *ofer* or 'vain' in comparison with his hero. Dafydd describes himself as *oferfardd* 'vain' or 'idle poet' in no.8 (GDG 42), l.11; see n.

31. *deddyw*. 3 sg. perfect of *dyfod*; GMW 134.

38. *solas* from E. 'solace' has here its older meaning of 'entertainment, recreation, amusement' (as it has in Chaucer).
ym Masaleg. *Basaleg* is derived from Lat. *basilica*; on the derivation see B.VII, 277.

43-6. Dr Parry interprets these lines as meaning that if anyone can beat Ifor in anything, he (Dafydd) can beat him at chess and backgammon—*ffristiol a tholbwrdd*—l.45 being in parenthesis. On these games see F.R.Lewis 'Gwerin Ffristial a Thawlbwrdd', THSC 1941, 185-205; TYP 246.

49. *diful*. Lit. 'bold, confident, outspoken' rather than 'immodest' as in GDG 56, ls.27-8, where *mul* 'modest' and *dilful* 'immodest' are contrasted.

46

According to the superscription found in a number of MSS (GDG lxv), the subject of this poem is Rhydderch ab Ieuan Llwyd of Glyn Aeron in Ceredigion, a member of a family renowned during the 14th century for their patronage of poets, and himself an authority on the law, an administrator, and many other things—a man whose name has come down to posterity, in particular, as the owner of the famous 'White Book of Rhydderch'. It appears from an *awdl* addressed to the pair by Llywelyn Goch ap Meurig Hen (RBP 1308-9) that Rhydderch and Llywelyn Fychan (ap Llywelyn Gaplan?) were a pair of close friends who both came from Glyn Aeron: this would help to explain the note which claims that Dafydd's 'elegy' for Rhydderch was composed primarily on behalf of Llywelyn Fychan. It is, however, impossible that the poem can be a 'genuine' elegy, since Rhydderch is known to have been still alive in 1391, more than a decade after Dafydd's own career appears to have terminated. It is indeed by now generally accepted that it is a *marwnad ffug* or 'fictitious' elegy: a graceful compliment paid by the poet—ostensibly on behalf of another—to a younger contemporary, who in the event was to survive him by a number of years. But it is not without some touches of grim hummour, cf. ls.14, 41. On Rhydderch and his family see R.A.Griffiths, *The Principality of Wales in the Later Middle Ages* (1972), 117; D.Hywel, E.Roberts, 'Noddwyr y Beirdd yn Sir Aberteifi', *Ll.C.* X, 83-9.

1. *mi geisiais gêl.* Cf. no.31 (GDG 39), 1, *gwyddwn gêl* 'I know a hiding-place'.

3. *gwn gannoch.* Lit. 'I know a hundred groans'; cf. no.31,31, *gwn ganclwyf.*

5. I take *rhoddiad* 'giver' here as equivalent to *rhodd* 'gift', but it could also be 3 sg. imperf. of *rhoddi*; GMW §132(2).

7. *meingorn.* Lit. 'slenderhorn'. But in this context, Dr Parry suggests 'piercing' is more appropriate.

8. *Na chloch.* On *cloch* 'bell' see introductory n. to no.32 above.
no'r och. Lit. 'than the cry [that] was given'.

11. *syddyn*, an abbreviation for *eisyddyn.* According to T.Richards 'Essyddyn, Ysyddyn is in S. Wales the same as *tyddyn* in N. Wales—a tenement of land.' (Yet in 1.15 Dafydd employs *tyddyn.*)

14. *Ffyddfrawd.* There is no need to deduce from this that Rhydderch and Llywelyn were literally brothers, rather than close friends.
diffoddfrys. Lit. 'sudden his extinction', cf. 1.41.

15-16. *Och Amlyn . . . am Emig.* The popular story of the two faithful friends *Amis* and *Amilun* was translated into Welsh by the second quarter of the 15th century as *Kymdeithas Amlyn ac Amic* (ed. J.G.Evans, Llanbedrog, 1909), for the date of the unique text in the Red Book of Hergest. Since this is too late for Dafydd's life-time, he must have known the tale from some earlier source than the Red Book. Both he and Iolo Goch (IGE² 42, 34-43, 1-2) in alluding to Amlyn and Amic use the Welsh forms of these names, showing that they knew the translation, rather than its English or Anglo-Norman original.

19. *(c)loch y Glyn.* i.e. Glyn Aeron. On *cloch* see n. to no.32 above.

20. *Ail yw.* i.e. Llywelyn's cry was equal to the two previously mentioned.

23. *dierfir*, pres. impers. of vb. *diarfu* 'to disarm'.

47

Little is known of Gruffudd ab Adda apart from the evidence of this poem, which tells us that he was a poet who belonged to Powys Wenwynwyn (ls.17, 36). In the past the tendency has been to deduce too much from the poem concerning Gruffudd's fate. As Dr Parry maintains in his note to 1.47, there can be no doubt but that this is a *marwnad ffug* or 'fictitious elegy', for the statement that Gruffudd was slain in the same manner as that in which one would kill a goose can hardly be intended except as burlesque. Dafydd Jones, Llanfair, claimed in 1567 to have seen the poet's skull at Dolgellau with a dent in it, but this need mean no more than that it testifies to the long survival of a tradition based ultimately on a misinterpretation of this poem. The opening lines imply that Gruffudd was not only a poet but also a skilled musician: this is corroborated by the name of a tune called *Cainc Gruffudd ab Adda* which is referred to in an *englyn*, DGG² p.116. This *englyn*, and two *cywyddau* are the only verses which have come down in Gruffudd's name. His superb *cywydd* to the uprooted birch-tree at Llanidloes (DGG² LXV, OBWV no.54) rivals the best of Dafydd ap Gwilym's verse in its sensitive evocation of the personified tree's ability to feel and to suffer.

1. *Rhagawr* in place of the usual *rhagor* is a false archaism (GDG lxxxix). But Dr Parry points out that the fact that it is essential to the *cynghanedd* shows that it is original to the poet, and not due to a scribal corruption. The involved syntax of the long introductory metaphor has made it necessary to defer the translation of *Rhagawr mawr* to 1.9 below.

8. *Orlais.* See n. to no.10, 1.11 above.

9. *adeilym.* From *adail* 'building' and *llym* 'keen'.

12. *bollt bedryollt*. An arrow (E. 'bolt', EEW 175) with a four-squared head tapering to a point was the kind of arrow shot from a cross-bow.

22. *Beues gweilch*. *Peues* is from Lat. *pagus* 'region'. *Gweilch*, pl. of *gwalch* 'hawk' is used fig. for 'heroes', as in no.45 (GDG 8), l.26; see n.

28. *lle ni cherid*. The bathos of 'where it was not loved', following on the previous eloquent passage, anticipates the further bathos of the conclusion in ls.47-8.

35-6. *Gwenynen . . . Gwenwynwyn dir*. From *circa* 1195 the kingdom of Powys was divided into two halves, named after the princes who ruled them *Powys Wenwynwyn* and *Powys Fadog* (DGG² 217; HW 583-4). Hence Dafydd calls Gruffudd 'bee (*gwenynen*) of poetry', playing on the similarity of the two words.

48. *(g)wladeiddrwydd*. Lit. 'boorishness, ungentlemanliness, discourtesy'. See n. to no.1 (GDG 69), l.44.

50. *Dwred*. *Twred* is from E. 'turret', Fr. *tourette* (here obviously used fig).

48

Madog Benfras ap Gruffudd was a fellow-poet closely contemporary with Dafydd ap Gwilym, and probably also his personal friend, if we are to judge from the mention of him which Dafydd makes in two other poems, besides the present one, GDG nos.25 and 31. Madog came from Marchwiail near Wrexham in Powys, and he is mentioned more than once in the court-records of the bailiwick of Wrexham for the years 1339-40. Dafydd composed this 'elegy' to him, as well as another 'elegy' to the Anglesey poet Gruffudd Gryg (GDG 20): but the fact that these two poets also addressed 'elegies' to Dafydd casts serious doubt on all four poems, as making genuine reference to the occasion of their subject's death. Inspite of the serious pessimism of the opening lines (which recall sentiments expressed in 'The Ruin', no.49 below) I prefer to regard this poem and the three others as gracious compliments paid by living poets to their fellows, according to a literary convention which undoubtedly existed in the 14th century, however difficult it is for us to comprehend it today. His *marwnad* (GDG pp.424-6) and four other *cywyddau* are the only poems which may be ascribed to Madog with any degree of certainty; the group shows no outstanding originality, as do those of certain of his contemporaries, and his poems are strongly under the influence of Dafydd's own verse.

7. *y'm cên*. 3 sg. pres. indic. of a defective verb meaning 'trouble, bother, worry', almost always occurring in this form, as in GDG 148, l.29; but exceptionally in the pl. *pam y'm cenynt*, GDG 30, l.25.

11. *y rhawg* or *rhawg*, adv., lit. 'for a long time'.

12. *Ormail mydr*. *Gormail* 'oppression, tyranny, conquest', hence here 'conqueror'.

16. *fflwch* from E. 'flush' abundant, lavish; here 'generous, liberal'. Cf. no.9, l.8 above.
a phlaid. The meaning of *plaid* here is uncertain, and my rendering is tentative. From its original meaning 'wall' *plaid* came to mean 'party, faction' (GDG 488) hence 'support'.

21. *gwayw*. Dafydd employs *gwayw* with the double meanings of 'spear' and 'pang'; see introductory note to no.9 above.

22. *esgyr*. 3 sg. pres. indic. of *esgor* 'bring forth, give birth to', here used fig., i.e. 'no bardic pupil but will express his feeling of loss'.

24. *Paun* 'peacock'. The peacock being the most aristocratic of birds, is used symbolically to denote the best in any other field; cf. no.2 (GDG 23), l.37 where May is described as a peacock. Madog repays the compliment to Dafydd, describing him as *paun cerdd* (GDG p.424,6), and Gruffudd Gryg describes him as *paun Dyfed* (GDG p.427,8).

25-6. *cad daradr . . . canwyr.* *Cad* here presumably means a poetic contest as in 1.32, rather than a battle; *taradr* is a carpenter's awl for making holes; *canwyr* is his plane. Ifor Williams remarks (DGG² 190) on the poets' fondness for the figurative use of terms of carpentry for their verse, e.g. *naddu gwawd* 'to hew out verse'. Cf. no.5 ls.25-30 above. I translate the sense of *canwyr* rather than its exact meaning, and take it as going with the following line.

27. *Cwplws.* Alternatively 'the coupling of Myrddin's craft of verse'. In *caniatgerdd* I take *cerdd* as retaining its primary meaning of 'art or craft (of poetry)'; see n. to no.43, 1.29 above.

28. *Cwpl* 'principle rafter, support, yoke', etc.; cf. above, and 1.43 below.

29. *tampr* from Fr. *timbre* in an archaic meaning 'bell' (DGG² 215).

30. *Trwmpls* from Fr. *trompel*, and *trimplai* from Fr. *trompille* both have the meaning of 'horn, trumpet'.

32. *A choprs cerdd.* *Coprs* from E. *copperess(e)* 'a worker in copper' (see EEW. 90), meaning that Madog gave a beautiful finish to his work, like copper. Here again the translation gives the sense, rather than the exact word.

a chiprys cad. As in 1.25 *cad* must here mean a poetic contest. *Ciprys* is combined with *copr* also in no.22 (GDG 118), 1.25 (see n.).

33. *digeirdd*, pl. of *digardd* 'faultless, excellent'.

37. *aur mâl.* The 'refined gold' in this instance is the 'gold' of Madog's poetry.

40. *acses* from E. 'access' meaning 'a sudden attack'.

difocsach, Lit. 'without boasting, ostentation, envy'.

43. *capel awen.* Cf. no.23, 1.27 where the Skylark is *cantor o gapel Celi* 'a singer from the Lord's chapel'.

44. *copr pawb wrthaw.* 'each one a copper coin to him'; an example of Dafydd's fondness for coin-imagery; cf. *iawn fwnai* and *ffloringod brig* for the leaves of May in no.2, and the Star as *goldyn* 'a refined coin of yellow gold' no.30 (GDG 67), 1.36.

gwaglaw gwen. Lit. 'empty-handed a girl'; i.e. no girl any longer receives the accustomed tribute of praise-poetry.

45. *gwladaidd.* See n. to no.1, 1.44 above. Cf. no.47, 1.48.

VII. THE POET'S MEDITATIONS (49-56)

49   The Ruin

'You ruined shack with open gable-end,
between the mountain and the pasture,
it would seem grievous to all those
4 who saw you once a hospitable home
and see you now [instead], with ridge-pole broken,
beneath your roof of laths, a dark and shattered house.
Yet once, inside your joyful walls
8 there was a time—a stabbing rebuke—
when there was greater merriment within
than you [have] now, unsightly hovel,
when I saw—I spread your splendid fame abroad—
12 in your corner, there, a lovely girl,
she was kind and gently reared
and shapely, lying intertwined [with me],
and each one's arm (a blessing was the girl's embrace)
16 [was] knotted all about the other,
the girl's arm—[my] desire slaked (?) by one like driven
snow—
beneath the ear of him who foremost [sang her] fame,
and my arm, by a simple trickery,
20 beneath the left ear of the gentle sweet girl:
there was happiness and joy in your greenwood,
but it is not like that today.'

'Mine is the grief (an army(?) under spells)
24 for the course the wild wind took:
a storm from out the bosom of the east
wrought destruction along the stone wall,
the sighing South wind, on its course of wrath
28 [it was which] tore away my roof.'

'Was it the Wind which caused of late this havoc?
Last night it swept right through your roof;
ugly the way in which it tore your spars:
32 A dangerous deception is the world always.
Your corner—mine to interpret with two sighs—
was my bed: it was no lair for pigs.
You were yesterday in happy state
36 [being] a shelter overhead for my sweet love;
today, by Peter—a matter of ease—
no rafter and no cover has been left on you.
So many, so diverse the causes of delusion:
40 can some such deception be this ruined shack?'

'Dafydd, the household's span of work is done,
beneath the cross: it was a decent way of life.'

Yr Adfail (144)

'Tydi, y bwth tinrhwth twn,
Yrhwng gweundir a gwyndwn,
Gwae a'th weles, dygesynt,
4   Yn gyfannedd gyfedd gynt,
Ac a'th wŷl heddiw'n friw frig
Dan do ais, dwndy ysig;
A hefyd ger dy hoywfur
8   Ef a fu ddydd, cerydd cur,
Ynod, ydd oedd ddiddanach
Nog yr wyd, y gronglwyd grach,
Pan welais, pefr gludais glod,
12   Yn dy gongl un deg yngod,
Forwyn, bonheddig fwyn fu,
Hoywdwf yn ymgyhydu,
A braich pob un, gofl fun fudd,
16   Yn gwlm amgylch ei gilydd;
Braich meinir, briwawch manod,
Goris clust goreuwas clod;
A'm braich innau, somau syml,
20   Dan glust asw dyn glwys disyml.
Hawddfyd gan fasw i'th laswydd,
A heddiw nid ydyw'r dydd.'

'Ys mau gŵyn, geirswyn gwersyllt,
24   Am hynt a wnaeth y gwynt gwyllt.
Ystorm o fynwes dwyrain
A wnaeth gur hyd y mur main.
Uchenaid gwynt, gerrynt gawdd,
28   Y deau a'm didoawdd.'

'Ai'r gwynt a wnaeth helynt hwyr?
Da y nithiodd dy do neithiwyr.
Hagr y torres dy esyth;
32   Hudol enbyd yw'r byd byth.
Dy gongl, mau ddeongl ddwyoch,
Gwely ym oedd, nid gwâl moch.
Doe'r oeddud mewn gradd addwyn
36   Yn glyd uwchben fy myd mwyn;
Hawdd o ddadl, heddiw'dd ydwyd,
Myn Pedr, heb na chledr na chlwyd.
Amryw bwnc ymwnc amwyll,
40   Ai hwn yw'r bwth twn bath twyll?'

'Aeth talm o waith y teulu,
Dafydd, â chroes; da foes fu.'

50 The Haycock

Did I gain less of sleeplessness
than profit and reward beside the maiden's home?
It was no easy thing to loiter there
4 with the black rain [falling] so insistently.
Had it so chanced that the door had opened
at night, I would not have ventured within,
lest by a single word the girl forbid me—
8 can it be worse [to be] inside the Haycock?

Your being is a blessing to me, Haycock,
a funny lad with green head, curly, blunt,
it was a good thing that the long-nailed rake
12 gathered you yesterday [upon] the ground.
In a long mantle I have dressed myself in you,
like a green cloak about the lad of song.
I tried to make a bundle out of you
16 [like to] a fragile dove-cot made of grass.
To praise you I will constantly give tongue:
the meadow's fleece, good place to fret at song.

By someone you were shaped faultlessly,
20 in a like manner, broad grey mound,
and of like destiny to [that of] noble lords,
and you are like them too in agony.
By a blue blade you have been boldly slain,
24 the burgess of the hay-field, short and thick.
Tomorrow—joy that is awaiting you—
from your green field, hay, you will be dragged.
Next day, above the tide of stubble
28 you will be hanged, woe's to me, Mary!

I commend your body home
to the hay-loft, and your soul to Heaven.
You will see me like an angel
32 at Judgement Day, above the hay-loft of the house,
coming to knock upon the door [and say]
'Haycock, is the time now ripe?'

51 The Mirror

I never thought—outrageous violence—
that my face was not good and fair
until I took in hand the Mirror
4 and saw my ugliness—it was made obvious—
The Mirror showed to me conclusively
that my aspect is not fair.

Y Mwdwl Gwair (62)

Ai llai fy rhan o anun
No lles a budd ger llys bun?
Nid hawdd godech na llechu
4 A glewed yw y glaw du.
Pei rhôn i'r ddôr egori
Y nos, nis llyfaswn i,
Rhag gwahardd bun ar ungair,
8 Ai gwaeth yn y mwdwl gwair?

    Dawn ym dy fod yn fwdwl,
Digrifwas pengrychlas pŵl.
Da fu'r gribin ewinir
12 Doe a'th gynullodd i dir.
Mi a'th wisgais, maith wasgawd,
Mal cochl gwyrddlas uwch gwas gwawd.
Ceisiais gennyd gael cysellt,
16 Colomendy gwecry gwellt.
Glud y'th folaf â'm tafawd,
Gnu gwaun, da le i gnoi gwawd.

    Erfai o un y'th luniwyd,
20 Un fath, llydan dwynpath llwyd,
Un dramgwydd ag arglwyddi
Teg, ac un artaith wyd di.
Ef a'th las â dur glas glew,
24 Bwrdais y weirglodd byrdew.
Yfory, sydd yty sir,
O'th lasgae, wair, y'th lusgir.
Drennydd, uwch y llanw manwair,
28 Dy grogi, a gwae fi, Fair!

    Cymynnaf dy gorff adref
I'r nen, a'th enaid i'r nef.
Megis angel y'm gwely
32 Ddyddbrawd uwch taflawd y tŷ,
Yn dyfod i gnocio'r drws:
'Y mwdwl gwair, ai madws?'

Y Drych (105)

Ni thybiais, ddewrdrais ddirdra,
Na bai deg f'wyneb a da,
Oni theimlais, waith amlwg,
4 Y drych; a llyna un drwg!
Ym y dywawd o'r diwedd
Y drych nad wyf wych o wedd.

Grown pale for one who is the peer of Enid
8 my cheek is: small its ruddiness.
Like glass my cheek is, after moaning,
and covered with weals of livid hue.
One could almost make a razor
12 of my long nose, is not that a shame?
Is it not luckless that my merry eyes
should be like to blind auger-holes?
my curly head of locks a mockery,
16 each handful falling from the roots.

    Great is the villainy of my fate:
for I am either, it appears to me,
like to [an arrow's] swarthy quiver (?)
20 of evil disposition, or else the Mirror is not true.
If it be on me—I know long passion's nature—
there rests the fault, let me be dead!
if on the Mirror's speckled face
24 the fault was, then woe to its life!

    Like a pale round moon, a mournful orb,
like a load-stone, replete with spells,
pale-coloured, an enchanted jewel,
28 it was magicians who created it:
it is the swiftest kind of dream,
a cold deceiver, brother to the ice,
most evil, most unpleasant lad,
32 perdition to the hateful, thin, and bent-lipped glass!

    Nobody caused my face's wrinkling,
if it be right to credit yonder glass,
except [only] that girl from Gwynedd—
36 it is known there how to spoil [men's] looks.

52 The Poet and his Shadow

    I was yesterday beneath the leaves
waiting for a girl, one who was Elen's peer,
under the green mantle—keeping from the rain—
4 of a birch-tree, like the simpleton I was.
At that I saw a sort of shape,
ugly [he seemed to me], standing alone:
I shied away across [from him]
8 and like a courteous being, I
blessed against the pestilence
my body, with signs of the saints.

    [The Poet]: 'Tell me, and stop your taciturnity,
12 what man is it that is here?'

Melynu am ail Enid
8 Y mae'r grudd, nid mawr y gwrid.
Gwydr yw'r grudd gwedy'r griddfan,
A chlais melynlliw achlân.
Odid na ellid ellyn
12 O'r trwyn hir; pand truan hyn?
Pand diriaid bod llygaid llon
Yn dyllau terydr deillion?
A'r ffluwch bengrech ledechwyrth
16 Bob dyrnaid o'i said a syrth.

Mawr arnaf naid direidi;
Y mae'r naill, yn fy marn i,
Ai 'mod yn gwufr arddufrych,
20 Natur drwg, ai nad da'r drych.
Os arnaf, gwn naws hirnwyf,
Y mae'r bai, poed marw y bwyf!
Os ar y drych brych o bryd
24 Y bu'r bai, wb o'r bywyd!

Lleuad las gron gwmpas graen,
Llawn o hud, llun ehedfaen;
Hadlyd liw, hudol o dlws,
28 Hudolion a'i hadeilws;
Breuddwyd o'r modd ebrwydda',
Bradwr oer a brawd i'r ia.
Ffalstaf, gwir ddifwynaf gwas,
32 Fflam fo'r drych mingam meingas!

Ni'm gwnaeth neb yn wynebgrych,
Os gwiw coeliaw draw i'r drych,
Onid y ferch o Wynedd;
36 Yno y gwŷs ddifwyno gwedd.

Ei Gysgod (141)

Doe'r oeddwn dan oreuddail
Yn aros gwen, Elen ail,
A gochel glaw dan gochl glas
4 Y fedwen, fal ynfydwas.
Nachaf gwelwn ryw eilun
Yn sefyll yn hyll ei hun.
Ysgodigaw draw ar draws
8 Ohonof, fal gŵr hynaws,
A chroesi rhag echrysaint
Y corff mau â swynau saint.

'Dywed, a phaid â'th dewi,
12 Yma wyt ŵr, pwy wyt ti.'

'Give up your questioning, for I
am your own extraordinary Shadow.
For Mary's sake be quiet, and do not hinder me
16   for your own good, from giving you my message.
I have come, [if only] for good manners,
to be beside you here in nakedness,
to show, my fair and noble jewel,
20   what kind of thing you are: enchantment masters you.'

[The Poet]: 'Not so, I am a generous man, you ugly knave,
in seeming like a sprite—I am not so.
With form like to a hunch-backed goat
24   you have indeed a sinister similitude
to some yearning phantom
rather than to a man in decent form.
A herdsman brawling over chequers (?)
28   a witch's-shanks upon black stilts,
shepherd of a dirty load of sprites,
a bogey looking like a tonsured monk,
stud-keeper playing with a hobby-horse,
32   a heron stuffed with eating marshy stalks,
a crane extended to full span
[across] owls' strongholds on the corn-field's edge.
With face like to some foolish pilgrim,
36   a black friar of a man, in tattered rags,
a corpse-like shape, wrapped round in hemp,
where have you been, old farm-yard stick?

'Many a day, let me remind you,
40   I have been with you; woe to you for what I know of you.'

[The Poet]: 'What other harm is there you know
of me, you with a milk-can's neck,
except what every rational person knows
44   throughout the world? You, devil's dung!
I never railed against my native home,
I know I have not slain by stealthy blow,
I never aimed with sling-stone at the hens,
48   nor terrified small children as a sprite,
I do not pervert my natural gifts,
nor did I ever incommode a stranger's wife.'

'By my faith, if I were to make known
52   to those who do not know it, all I know,
in very little time, and needing no persuasion (?)
my faith! you [surely] would be hanged.'

[The Poet]: 'Desist—yours is a sorry snare—
56   from telling henceforth what you know,
as though there were—if it were mine—
stitches upon the corners of the mouth.'

'Myfy wyf, gad d'ymofyn,
Dy gysgod hynod dy hun.
Taw, er Mair, na lestair les,
16   Ym fynegi fy neges.
Dyfod ydd wyf, defod dda,
I'th ymyl yn noeth yma,
I ddangos, em addwyn-gwyn,
20   Rhyw beth wyd; mae rhaib i'th ddwyn.'

'Nage, ŵr hael, anwr hyll,
Nid wyf felly, dwf ellyll.
Godrum gafr o'r un gyfrith,
24   Tebygach wyd, tebyg chwith,
I ddrychiolaeth hiraethlawn
Nog i ddyn mewn agwedd iawn.
Heusor mewn secr yn cecru,
28   Llorpau gwrach ar dudfach du.
Bugail ellyllon bawgoel,
Bwbach ar lun mynach moel.
Grëwr yn chwarae griors,
32   Gryr llawn yn pori cawn cors.
Garan yn bwrw ei gwryd,
Gaerau'r ŵyll, ar gwr yr ŷd.
Wyneb palmer o hurthgen,
36   Brawd du o ŵr mewn brat hen.
Drum corff wedi'i droi mewn carth;
Ble buost, hen bawl buarth?'

'Llawer dydd, yt pes lliwiwn,
40   Gyda thi, gwae di o'th wn.'

'Pa anaf arnaf amgen
A wyddost ti, wddw ystên,
Ond a ŵyr pob synhwyrawl
44   O'r byd oll? Yty baw diawl!
Ni chatgenais fy nghwmwd,
Ni leddais, gwn, leddf ysgŵd,
Ni theflais ieir â thafl fain,
48   Ni fwbechais rai bychain.
Ni wnaf yn erbyn fy nawn,
Ni rwystrais wraig gŵr estrawn.'

'Myn fy nghred, pei managwn
52   I rai na ŵyr hyn a wn,
Dir ennyd cyn torri annog,
'Y nghred y byddud ynghrog.'

'Ymogel, tau y magl tost,
56   Rhag addef rhawg a wyddost,
Mwy no phe bai, tra fai'n fau,
Gowni ar gwr y genau.'

53   Love's Tribulation

My fickle heart has pined,
and love has wrought treachery in my breast.

Once I was—I know a hundred wounds—
4   in the vigour of my youthful prime,
without feebleness or pain,
supporting well the pangs of love,
cajoling song, in complete strength,
8   of a right age, handsome and brave,
making exhilarating minstrelsy,
fulfilled with joy, replete with words,
endowed with health, and in renown,
12   good-looking, active, and agreeable.

But now, affliction quickly comes,
and I am perishing in sorrowful decay.
Gone is the pride which [once] afflicted me,
16   gone the tumultuous (?) passions of my flesh,
the achievements of my voice entirely gone,
grievous [is indeed] my fall.
All desire for a lovely girl has ended,
20   nor is there further word of him who scares off love.

No joyful thought nor passionate desire
arises in me—memory of song—
nor is there merry talk concerning them,
24   nor ever any more of love. Unless a girl should ask?

54   Despondency

A lovely sprightly girl enchanted me:
generous Morfudd, foster-child of May.
She it is that I [now] greet,
4   I am oppressed tonight by love of her.
She sowed within my breast—this shatters it—
love's seed, a wild enchantment.
My punishment: the harvest of my care
8   she will not let me have—this girl of day's bright hue.
Enchantress and lovely goddess,
magic is her speech to me.
She listens readily to any charge
12   against me, so that I obtain no boon.
I may win peace, instruction and reward
today from my erudite love,
tonight an outlaw utterly without redress

Cystudd Cariad (90)

Curiodd anwadal galon,
Cariad a wnaeth brad i'm bron.

Gynt yr oeddwn, gwn ganclwyf,
4 Mewn oed ieuenctid, mau nwyf,
Yn ddilesg, yn ddiddolur,
Yn ddeiliad cariad y cur,
Yn ddenwr gwawd, yn ddinych,
8 Yn dda'r oed, ac yn ddewr wych,
Yn lluniwr berw oferwaith,
Yn llawen iawn, yn llawn iaith,
Yn ddogn o bwynt, yn ddigardd,
12 Yn ddigri, yn heini, yn hardd.

Ac weithian, mae'n fuan fâr,
Edwi 'dd wyf, adwedd afar.
Darfu'r rhyfyg a'm digiawdd,
16 Darfu'r corff, mau darfer cawdd.
Darfu'n llwyr derfyn y llais,
A'r campau, dygn y cwympais.
Darfu'r awen am wenferch,
20 Darfu'r sôn am darfwr serch.

Ni chyfyd ynof, cof cerdd,
Gyngyd llawen nac angerdd,
Na sôn diddan amdanun',
24 Na serch byth, onis eirch bun.

Cystudd y Bardd (102)

Hoywdeg riain a'm hudai,
Hael Forfudd, merch fedydd Mai.
Honno a gaiff ei hannerch,
4 Heinus wyf heno o'i serch.
Heodd i'm bron, hon a hyllt,
Had o gariad, hud gorwyllt.
Heiniar cur, hwn yw'r cerydd,
8 Hon ni ad ym, hoywne dydd.
Hudoles a dwywes deg.
Hud yw ym ei hadameg.
Hawdd y gwrendy gyhudded,
12 Hawdd arnaf, ni chaf ei ched.
Heddwch a gawn, dawn a dysg,
Heddiw gyda'm dyn hyddysg.
Herwr glân heb alanas

16 I am from out her parish and her home.
    Beneath her outlaw's breast she placed
    a man's sharp pang of longing.
    Longer than stays the sea along the shore
20 will last this outlaw's longing for his love.
    I was shackled, and my breast was pierced,
    and it was sorrow's shackle I received.
    It is unlikely that I shall obtain
24 [to live in] peace with my wise gold-haired girl
    —my dire malady has come from this—
    yet more unlikely is it I will get long life.
    From Ynyr she can claim descent—
28 and lacking her I cannot stay alive.

55 A Recantation

    I am Morfudd's poet:
    I sang to her, it was a costly task.
    By Him who rules today
4   my head aches for the fair girl,
    and sickening sorrow wears my brow;
    for my golden girl I die.
    When death comes, agony to the bones,
8   with its sharp arrows,
    life's end will be stupendous,
    man's tongue will become silent.
    Lest there come lamentation with great misery
12 may the Trinity and the Virgin Mary
    forgive me for my great offences,
    Amen, and I shall sing no more.

56 A Prayer

    Anima Christi, sanctifica me.
    Renowned glory of the prophets,
    merciful nature of the Trinity,
    fair soul of blessed Christ crucified,
4   like to a gem, purify me within.

    Corpus Christi, salva me.
    Body of Christ that is most sad because of arrogant
                                            transgression,
    the flesh that is sought in the Communion
    to cause the pure health of the spirit,
8   since You are alive, keep me [too] alive.

16 Heno wyf o'i phlwyf a'i phlas.
   Hyhi a roes, garwloes gŵr,
   Hiraeth dan fron ei herwr.
   Hwy trig no'r môr ar hyd traeth
20 Herwr gwen yn ei hiraeth.
   Hualwyd fi, hoelied f'ais,
   Hual gofal a gefais.
   Hwyr y caf dan ei haur coeth
24 Heddwch gyda'm dyn hoywddoeth,
   Heiniau drwg o hyn a droes,
   Hwyrach ym gaffael hiroes.
   Hon o Ynyr ydd henyw,
28 Hebddi ni byddaf fi byw.

Edifeirwch (106)

Prydydd i Forfudd wyf fi,
Prid o swydd, prydais iddi.
Myn y Gŵr a fedd heddiw
4 Mae gwayw i'm pen am wen wiw,
Ac i'm tâl mae gofalglwyf;
Am aur o ddyn marw ydd wyf.
Pan ddêl, osgel i esgyrn,
8 Angau a'i chwarelau chwyrn,
Dirfawr fydd hoedl ar derfyn,
Darfod a wna tafod dyn.
Y Drindod, rhag cydfod cwyn,
12 A mawr ferw, a Mair Forwyn
A faddeuo 'ngham dramwy,
Amen, ac ni chanaf mwy.

Englynion Yr Offeren (2)

Anima Christi, sanctifica me.
Enwog, trugarog annwyd Tri—ac Un,
   Ogoniant proffwydi,
   Enaid teg croesteg Cristi,
4   Fal glain o fewn glanha fi.

Corpus Christi, salva me.
Corff Crist sy rydrist dros wrhydri—cam,
   Cnawd cymun o'i erchi,
   Iechyd pur ysbryd peri,
8   Can wyd fyw, cadw yn fyw fi.

Sanguis Christi, inebria me.
Blood of Christ, who acts beyond all that is rightfully due,
lest sadly I be exiled and lost,
arise, God's brilliant glory:
12   keep me from the sin of drunkenness.

Aqua lateris Christi, lava me.
Water from the grievous wound of Christ's steadfast side,
sustaining blessedly the Cross,
Sacred Heart, free from perdition,
16   immaculate Circle of Life, cleanse me.

Passio Christi, comforta me.
Passion of Christ of Heaven, Lord of the prophets of the
world,
severe were Your five wounds;
very mighty the true gift of prayer,
20   great Lord, strengthen me.

O bone Iesu, exaudi me.
Gentle, merciful Jesus, come towards me,
expression of the light;
glory of every altar in unending praise,
24   listen without condemning me.

Et ne permittas me separari a te.
And place me—may mine be perfect victory—
by Your side, world's Saviour;
like a bush, serving with perfect strength;
28   with praise unlimited I will praise You.

Ut cum angelis tuis laudem te.
With Your host of angels, almighty Lord,
in the eternal light,
in Heaven it will be made plain
32   how near salvation is; may it be true.

Amen.
May it be true that we are brought to Heaven's fair kingdom
in humble homage,
land of exalted blessing, long nurturing of grace,
36   a feast of glorious perfection.

Sanguis Christi, inebria me.
Gwaed Crist rhag yn drist, dros deithi,—a wna,
 Fy neol a'm colli;
  Cyfod, golau glod Geli,
12 Cadw rhag pechod feddwdod fi.

Aqua lateris Christi, lava me.
Dwfr ystlys dilwfr dolur weli—Crist,
 Croes ddedwydd gynhelwi,
  Dwyfawl gyllawl, heb golli,
16 Diwyd gylch fywyd, golch fi.

Passio Christi, comforta me.
Dioddef Crist nef, naf proffwydi—byd,
 Bu ddygn Dy bym weli,
  Cadarn iawn wiwddawn weddi,
20 Cadarnha, fawr wrda, fi.

O bone Iesu, exaudi me.
Gwâr Iesu trugar, treigl dydi—ataf,
 Ateb y goleuni;
  Gwawr pob allawr fawr foli,
24 Gwrando heb feio fyfi.

Et ne permittas me separari a te.
A gosod, fau fod, fyfi,—gynnydd da,
 Ger dy law, les mwndi;
  Megis perth, wiwnerth weini,
28 Mawl heb dawl, y molaf di.

Ut cum angelis tuis laudem te.
Gyda'th nifer, nêr nerthwir,—engylion,
 Yng ngolau ni chollir,
  Yn y nef y cyhoeddir,
32 Nesed bid gwared, boed gwir.

Amen.
Boed gwir y'n dygir deg frenhiniaeth—nef,
 Yn ufudd wrogaeth,
  Gwlad uchelrad feithrad faeth,
36 Gwledd ddiwagedd ddiwygiaeth.

Notes

49

This poem recalls those earlier laments for ruined and abandoned homesteads which are to be found in the *englynion* cycles associated with Llywarch Hen and Heledd. The theme is a familiar one in the poetry of the Celtic nations, and a number of famous examples have come down in early Irish. *Yr Adfail* 'The Ruin'—and parallels to it—is discussed by R.G.Gruffydd in YB XI (1979), 109-15. I have adopted several of his suggestions in my rendering.

2. *gweundir a gwyndwn.* i.e. between the wild upland country and the pastoral, inhabited lowland.

3. *dygesynt* for *tebygesynt* 'they would have thought, supposed' cf. *debygesynt* no.24 (GDG 122), l.17.

4. *Yn gyfannedd gyfedd.* Lit. 'an abode of carousal'. For *cyfannedd* 'dwelling-place, habitation' etc. see PKM 189.

6. *ais*, pl. of *asen*: usually for 'ribs' etc., but here for laths or fragments of wood used in roofing.

9. *ydd oedd.* Syntactically one would expect *oeddud*, as in l.35 below, to correspond with *Nog yr wyd* in l.10., but there is no MS evidence for this.

10. *(c)rach.* Lit. 'scabby, mean, vile, contemptible'.

17. *briwawch manod. Awch* 'edge, sharpness, vigour, ardour, desire'; *briw* 'broken'; but with *awch*, 'slaked' seems more appropriate. *Manod* lit, 'fine snow' is one of the recurrent traditional formulae for a girl's beauty; cf. *gorlliw eiry mân* no.8 (GDG 42), l.2; *hoen eiry di-frisg* 'like untrodden snow' GDG 33, l.18; *gwynlliw eiry divriw divris(c)* 'of the fair hue of unbroken untrodden snow' GP 11.

18. *goreuwas.* Cf. Gruffudd Gryg's employment of the same epithet for Dafydd, *Yr ywen i oreuwas* DGG[2] LXXXII,I. Since this identical line occurs elsewhere (GDG 53, l.29) in a poem to Morfudd, it seems likely that this is one of the many poems addressed to Morfudd in which she is not actually named.

21. *i'th laswydd.* 'Greenwood' is slightly unexpected here, and can only be metaphorical: the poet had enjoyed as much happiness in the ruined hut as he had at other times in the forest.

22. *nid ydyw'r dydd.* Lit. 'it is not the day'. *Dydd* here refers to *dydd* in l.8 above, the bygone days.

23. The Ruin now speaks. *geirswyn gwersyllt:* the *sangiad* anticipates the following line, and refers to the wind. Dr Gruffydd points out that *gwersyll(t)* can mean 'host, garrison, army' besides the more usual 'camp, watch-tower', etc. He interprets the line to mean that the wind sweeps past the ruin with the force of an attacking army. Alternatively 'a camp, refuge, or look-out'.

30. *da y nithiodd.* Dafydd uses *nithio* 'to winnow' of the Wind again in no. 29 (GDG 117), 13 *cyd nithud ddail* 'though you might winnow leaves'.

33. *mau ddeongl.* GPC cites several instances in which *deongl* is used for the interpretation of a dream or vision: this suggests that it refers here to the *twyll* 'deception, delusion' of l.40 below.

34. *nid gwâl moch*, i.e. it is now a pigsty.

37. *Hawdd o ddadl.* Dr Gruffydd interprets this as referring back to the previous line 'easy was the meeting'. I prefer to take it as referring to the decay which has now transformed the building as Dafydd had known it in the past.

39. *ymwnc* 'frequent, many'; see CL1H 172-3 on *ymwnc, ymwng.*

40. *hwn* 'this' refers back to the previous line; hence 'of that kind,

some such'. I understand the whole as meaning 'is the change which appears to have transformed this building only some kind of delusion?'

41. *y teulu*. Dr Gruffydd suggests that in Dafydd's time *teulu* did not yet mean 'family' in the restricted sense, but rather 'warband, people, household'. He interprets the word here as the equivalent of *toili, teili*, a dialect form of *teulu* known in folk-belief in Ceredigion as denoting ghostly premonitory funerals held by the spirits to give warning of a death. This is conjectural, and so also is his suggestion that *teulu* means the *tylwyth teg* or fairies; in this instance the followers of the magical huntsman Gwyn ap Nudd; cf. *tylwyth Gwyn* no.36 (GDG 68), l.40. His suggestion is that the poet is attributing to them the ruin of the building: I adopt a simpler interpretation of the last two lines.

42. *â chroes*. Cf. DGG² IV, 38, *A gŵr Esyllt dan groesau. Bod dan groes(au)* is explained by Ifor Williams, DGG² 173 as meaning to be lying in a coffin with a cross on one's breast.

da foes fu. Lit. 'it was a good custom'. Dr Gruffydd comments on the remarkable resemblance between this statement and the (amended) line in the poem describing the ruined hall of Rheged, CLIH III, 53, *Coeth gynefod oedd iddi* 'it had a fine custom'; see B.XVI, 276.

50

'Mediaeval English haystacks were small and circular, not much wider than a millstone, *une meule de foin*, as the French say'—C.G. Coulton, *The Mediaeval Village* (Cambridge, 1926), 47 n. In modern terms a haycock, or conical pile of hay. In some such pile as this the frustrated poet claims to have found a shelter, in a poem whose opening is thoroughly in the *fabliau* tradition; cf. nos.39, 40, and particularly no. 41 above. But the Haycock, like the Ruin, is endowed with a personality 'the burgess of the hay-field', l.24 and, like the Ruin, is capable of feeling and suffering. The savage fate which Dafydd foresees for it leads to a sombre metaphor evocative of the potential vicissitudes of contemporary life.

5. *pei rhôn* 'even if it should (be that)', a conjunction frequently employed by Dafydd, e.g. no.37 (GDG 58), ls.33, 47 etc. Cf. GMW 243, n.2.

11. *ewinir*. Ewin 'finger (or toe) nail' + *hir*.

13. *gwasgawd* (-*od*) 'covering, mantle'; cf. *gwasgawd mwythus* no. 17 (GDG 139), l.20; also 'shelter, shade', cf. *gwasgod praff* no.1 (GDG 69), l.13.

14. *gwawd* 'praise-poem'; see n. to no.3, l.43. *Gwas gwawd* means the poet himself.

18. *(c)noi gwawd*. Lit. 'to chew' i.e. 'to compose praise (poetry)'. Dr Parry compares Dafydd Benfras *A ganwyf dy geiniaid ai cny/a genais a genir wedy* 'what I sing your singers will chew, what I have sung will be sung afterwards', MA² 218b, 3-4. It also recalls the traditional method by which the Irish poets, the *filid*, are said to have obtained their inspiration by chewing raw flesh, or in the case of the legendary Finn mac Cumhaill, by chewing his own thumb.

24. *bwrdais*, 'burgess', i.e. an inhabitant of one of the (largely post-Conquest) boroughs established in the principality and in the Marches. But *bwrdais* when used literally does not necessarily imply an Englishman, for some boroughs such as Rhosyr (Newborough) and Oswestry were to a large extent Welsh (see introductory n. to no.40 above).

29-30 *cymynnaf*. In Llywelyn Goch ap Meurig Hen's poem the poet bequeaths Lleucu Llwyd's body to the sanctified earth and her soul to Heaven, DGG² LXXXVIII, 84-8, OBWV 77.

30. *nen* 'roof top' is here apparently parallel to *taflawd tŷ*, l.32 'hay-loft', though elsewhere Dafydd uses it figuratively for 'lord', GDG 15, 30. In *Armes Prydein* l.142 *or nen y safant*, 'nen' apparently means simply 'place': this may corroborate its generalized meaning here, as denoting the place where the hay is stored.

31. *Megis angel.* This recalls the words in which Dafydd portrays himself as visiting his sweetheart in a dream, no.32 (GDG 66), 16.

34. *ai madws!* i.e. 'Is the time ripe for the union of soul and body at the resurrection?'

51

1. *ddewrdrais ddirdra.* Lit. 'bold violence of outrage'.

4. *llyna un drwg.* Lit. 'behold a bad one'.

7. *Enid.* See n. to no.16, l.17 above.

15. *lledechwyrth ffluwch* 'bush or shock of hair, lock of hair'. This is the only recorded instance of the word, and it is interpreted variously in the dictionaries: TW *infrunitus, ynfyd,* etc.; William Llŷn, *Barddoniaeth* 280, *ynfyd;* J.Walters (dictionary, 1770-94) *'extravagant';* T.Richards (dictionary, 1753) *llewyrch* 'foolish, sottish, nonsensical'.

16. *said.* Edge of blade of a weapon, socket; CA 369 (quoting this example.) There is no other instance recorded of the word being used for the roots of the hair.

19. *gwufr arddufrych.* This reading, though corrupt in the MSS, is confirmed as correct by the occurrence of the same *sangiad* in GDG 154,31, where Dafydd applies it to Gruffudd Gryg in the Contention. Davies's dictionary interprets *arddufrych* as *fuscus, infuscus.* PKM 291 explains the word as 'swarthy, dusky', and quotes this example together with IGE[2] 207, 8, where it is applied by the poet to his breast. *cwufr* is from E. 'quiver', used figuratively, as is almost invariably the case when Dafydd employs foreign borrowed words for weapons and accoutrements.

24. *wb* 'alack!' GMW 245.

25-6. Madog Benfras employs two closely similar lines to describe a mirror, *Llygad glas gron gwmpas graen/Llawn hudfawl llun ehedfaen* DGG[2] LXVII, ls.37-8. Here the mirror shows the girl that she is beautiful, and therefore that she has no further need of the poet's praise, and Madog ends the poem with imprecations on the mirror. The lines have just the amount of variation from Dafydd's as might be accounted for by oral dissemination, and imperfect retention by memory by one or the other poet, if not by subsequent oral corruption.

27. *hadlyd.* This is the only mediaeval example of the word recorded, 'withered, languishing, pale, weak, feeble' GPC; later 'corrupt'.

31. *gwas.* Like the inanimate subjects of the two previous poems, the Mirror too is personified.

52

The poet's dialogue with his own Shadow lightly parodies the mediaeval genre of dialogues between the Soul and the Body, such as the poem *Kyvaenad kelvit* in the Black Book of Carmarthen (ed. H.G.Cr. VI), and the further examples edited in B.ii, 127-30; iii, 119-22—all poems which date from the 12th century or earlier. In contrast to the direct accusations made by the Soul to the Body in such poems, the 'loaded' insinuations made by Dafydd's Shadow are the more dramatically effective. Iolo Goch also parodies the genre, IGE[2] XXVI. In his poem the Soul gives a detailed account of a bardic circuit which it claims to have made in its search for its lost Body—all the patrons visited on the way are the poet's living contemporaries. The parodies of both poets are similarly enlivened by the racy colloquial dialogue in which they are framed. Dafydd's vituperation of his Shadow is also one of his richest examples of the use of *dyfalu* in invective.

2. *Elen ail*. The allusion is either to *Elen Fannog*, (Helen of Troy) as in GDG 51, 1.12, or to *Elen Luyddog*, the heroine of The Dream of Maxen; see TYP 341-3.

5. *eilun*. See n. to no. 32 (GDG 66), 15.

7. *Ysgodigaw*, 'to flee, escape, start'; T. Richards 'to be frighted, to winch or kick as a frighted horse'. The word derives from *ysgod* 'shadow', so that there is here a play upon the double meaning.

9. *echryshaint (echrys + haint)* '(contagious) disease, plague'. There is possibly a reference here to the Black Death, which was at its height in Britain 1349-50.

15. *na lestair les*. Lit. 'do not hinder advantage'.

19. The epithets are of course ironic.

20. *rhaib* 'a bewitching'; presumably that of female attraction.

21. *(g)wr hael* refers to Dafydd himself, rather than to his Shadow (Dr Parry's interpretation).

22. *ellyll*. See n. to no. 41,40 above.

27. *secr*, from E. *cheker(e)*, *siecr*, EEW 20. A game played on a squared board like chess or draughts; cf. IGE² IX, 15, *Gwŷr beilch yn chwarae . . . Tawlbwrdd a secr* 'proud men playing draughts and checker'.

23. *godrum*. Cf. no.26, 1.7 above. GPC suggests 'hunch-back(ed), hump-back(ed), burden, shadow', but has no other examples but these two. G compares *godrumyd o dyn bychan* 'a little hunch-back of a man' (?), WM 403, 23-4.

28. *llorpau*. Davies's dictionary gives *llorp = crus, tibia*; T. Richards 'the shank or leg from the knee to the ankle'. This is evidently the meaning here; the word is a variant of *llorf* which has the same meaning. In later usage *llorpau* are the shafts of a cart.

31. *griors*. GPC suggests tentatively 'a prize horse, tall steed, perhaps a game with a wooden hobby-horse (the player imitating the actions of a spirited horse)'. But no other instance is recorded.

33. *yn bwrw ei gwryd*. Lit. 'casting her span', i.e. with wings outstretched.

33-4. There is no connecting link between the two lines, but this seems to be required by the sense, hence I have supplied 'across'.

36. *brawd du*. ie. a Dominican friar. This line too should perhaps be taken with the preceding one.

37. *mewn carth*. ie. wrapped in hemp for burial.

40. *o'th wn*. Lit. 'from (that) I know you'.

45. *Ni chatgenais*. Catganu (from *cad* 'battle' and *canu* 'sing') 'revile, inveigh against'; T. Wiliems, *blasphemo, calumnior*, etc. *fy nghwmwd*. The *cwmwd* or commote was a lesser territorial unit; according to Giraldus it was the fourth part of a *cantref*.

48. *Ni fwbechais*. The verb derives from *bwbach* 'bogey', applied in 1.30 to the Shadow.

50. *(g)wraig gwr estrawn*. The fact that the poet does not here take into account the liaison he claims to have had with the wife of the Aberystwyth merchant *Robin Nordd*, no.15 (GDG 98), ls.13-28—suggests that the preceding lines 45-9 may also conceal allusions to past incidents in the poet's career, which may well have been intelligible to his original audience.

53. *cyn torri annog*. *Annog* 'encouragement, persuasion', etc. Evidently an idiomatic phrase (cf. *torri gair*) for which I suggest a tentative rendering. Dr Parry points out that the *cynghanedd* in the line is defective (initial *D-* being incorrectly answered by *t-*). The line has

probably suffered at the hands of one or more copyists attempting to 'improve' the *cynghanedd*, even at the cost of obscuring the original meaning, which must remain uncertain.

53

8. *yn dda'r oed*. Deliberately ambiguous, since *oed* could mean either 'age (of youth)' or 'love-tryst'.

9. *berw* has here the sense of '(turmoil of) poetic inspiration'. Cf. no. 24, 44 above, and n., and 55, l.12 below.

oferwaith. The *oferfeirdd* were the equivalent of the *clêr* or lower-grade poets; see CD 352. Dafydd describes himself, perhaps slightly disparagingly, as *oferfardd* in no.8 (GDG 42), l.11 (see n.). In the *Trioedd Cerdd* the *ofer gerddor* is contrasted with the more exalted *prydydd* in that his role included satire (GP 136,151). Certain classes of *englyn* were classed as *ofer fesurau*, suitable for satire and ribald songs (CD 352). For discussion of the *Tri Oferfeirdd Ynys Prydein* and some further refs. see TYP 21. On *clêr* see n. to no.43 (GDG 137), l.29.

11. *pwynt* 'plight, condition (of health)', from E. 'point'; EEW 198; DGG² 207. *Pwyntus* is applied to the Nightingale in no.3 (GDG 24), l.26 'in good condition, sleek'.

16. *mau darfer*. In DGG² 219 Ifor Williams suggests *cynnwrf* 'commotion, tumult' *(tarfu)* as the meaning of *tarfer*, which is unrecorded elsewhere. (A doubtful instance in a couplet by Lewis Môn has been subsequently interpreted by this poet's editor, Eurys Rowlands, as *od arfer*, GLM LXXXVIII, 75.)

19. *awen*. Usually 'poetic inspiration', here 'desire, inclination' (GPC *awen*²).

20. *(t)arfwr serch*. Lit. 'the scatterer of love'. The ref. is evidently to *Yr Eiddig* 'the Jealous One'—in this instance probably Morfudd's husband.

54

This poem is a metrical *tour-de-force*, with *cymeriad llythrennol* or initial alliteration maintained throughout (for a poem similarly constructed cf. GDG 95). Lines 15-16 suggest a connection with 'The Wind', no.29 (GDG 117); the allusions to the poet as an 'outlaw' from Morfudd indicate that similar circumstances may have produced both poems.

1. *a'm hudai*; 9. *hudoles*. Cf. no. 12 (GDG 84) where a girl's 'enchantment'—presumably that of Morfudd—is developed through a whole poem.

5. *Heodd i'm bron*. The image of 'sowing' the seeds of love is also elaborated and extended as the subject of no. 6 (GDG 87). Cf. also no. 44 (GDG 7) where Dafydd similarly 'sows' the praise of Ifor Hael.

15. *heb alanas*. *Galanas* was the term given under the native Welsh legal system, *Cyfraith Hywel*, alike to murder and (as here) to the compensation paid for murder by the murderer's kindred to the kindred of the murdered man.

18. *ei herwr* 'her outlaw', i.e. the poet, as in ls.15, 20.

23. *dan ei haur coeth*. Lit. 'under her refined gold'.

27. *Ynyr*. An allusion to the traditional ancestor, in the 13th century of the Vaughans of Nannau, near Dolgellau, Meirionydd; DGG² 177. The Vaughans were patrons of poets throughout many generations. On the basis of the present allusion D. J. Bowen has argued, *Ll.C.* VI (1960), 38 that Morfudd was a member of this family. An 18th century tradition

held that she was buried at Trawsfynydd, loc.cit.107. Genealogies of families descended from Ynyr Nannau are given in P.C. Bartrum's *Welsh Genealogies* 300-1400 (Cardiff, 1974) I, 78-80, but these fail to disclose a 'Morfudd' in the appropriate generation.

55

This semi-penitential poem may be related to the tradition of the *marwysgafn:* the death-bed poems composed by earlier poets such as Meilyr Brydydd (OBWV 20) and Cynddelw Brydydd Mawr (H. Lewis, *Hen Gerddi Crefyddol* XVII) in the 12th century. Poems in the same penitential tradition were composed by contemporaries or near-successors of Dafydd ap Gwilym: Llywelyn Goch ap Meurig Hen (RBP 1301), Siôn Cent (IGE² LXXXIV) and Gruffudd ap Maredudd (RBP 1332-4). Glanmor Williams cites some additional parallels (*The Welsh Church from Conquest to Reformation,* 111), and draws a comparison with the mediaeval English penitential lyric. Such recantations by poets approaching death were indeed a widespread mediaeval genre: one example is the 'retractation' by Geoffrey Chaucer (*circa* 1400) which is affixed to the end of the *Parson's Tale:* the poet prays for divine forgiveness for his 'translacions and enditynges of worldly vanitees' (these include the writing of the other Canterbury Tales). A note by Chaucer's editor, F.N. Robinson, compares with his 'retractation' the recantation poem of Llywelyn Goch.

4. *gwayw* 'spear' is used as frequently by Dafydd in its figurative sense 'pang' as in its literal one; *gwayw yn y pen* 'a headache'. Cf. no.9 (GDG 111) above; and n.

7. *osgel.* 'A cramp in ye bones' according to Lewis Morris, *Llanover* MS,C 4, 147. He gives as his authority 'Dr Thos. Williams (who) says he has heard it in common discourse in some parts of Wales'.

8. *chwarelau.* Pl. of *chwarel,* a borrowing from E. *quarelle* 'bolt from a cross-bow'. EEW 71.

12. *A mawr ferw. Berw* here means 'agitation, turmoil' rather than '(turmoil of) poetic inspiration', as in no.53 (GDG 90), 1.9 above. In the context I understand it as 'distress, misery'.

56

Each *englyn* in this sequence enlarges upon the thought expressed in successive lines of a Latin prayer which was extremely popular in the 14th century throughout western Europe. The authorship of the Latin original is uncertain, but it appears to have been composed before 1340. In Wales no less than three separate translations of this Latin text were made. There is no proof that any one of these is older than the 15th. century, and all are therefore later than the lifetime of Dafydd ap Gwilym. The number of copies in which these translations have come down indicates that the prayer circulated widely both in Latin and in the vernacular. Its popularity may therefore go back over a number of previous years. It belongs to the category of 'private devotions' which accompanied the service of the Mass but did not formally belong to it; these are frequently preserved in Books of Hours of the 14th and 15th centuries. On the whole subject see Brynley Roberts, B.XVI (1956), 268-71; XXV (1973), 145-6. Four religious poems are attributed to Dafydd ap Gwilym, of which two of the others are *cywyddau* and one an *awdl* (GDG nos. 1-4). The extreme compression arising from the intricate metrical rules governing the structure of the *englyn* (see introduction) has necessitated some degree of transposition in the translation of this poem, particularly in the *paladr* or first half of each stanza. Dr Parry points out the absence of *cynghanedd* between ls.25-6, and in l.31.

5. *gwrhydri*. The meanings include 'power, bravado, arrogance', etc. besides 'courage, gallantry, glory'.

7. Alternatively 'spirit that causes pure health'.

9. *dros deithi*. *Teithi* means 'claims, characteristics, endowments' and is cognate with Irish *téchtae* 'legal rightness, that which is in conformity with law'.

14. Alternatively 'the blessedly sustaining Cross'.

15. *Cyllawl* does not occur anywhere else; Dr Parry interprets it as a derivative of *cwll* 'breast, bosom'; hence *dwyfawl gyllawl* 'Sacred Heart'.

23. Among the meanings of *gwawr* 'dawn' is 'brightness, effulgence'; hence 'glory'.

25. Alternatively 'May mine be a good attainment'.

26. *mwndi*. Genitive of Lat. *mundus* 'world'.

27. *Megis perth* 'like a bush'. A reference to the burning bush in which God appeared to Moses on Mount Horeb, *Exodus* ch.3.

30. *ni chollir*. Lit. 'the light which is not extinguished'.

36. *diwagedd*. Lit. 'without emptiness, vanity, unreality'.

diwygiaeth. This is the only instance recorded in GPC. Cf. *diwyg* 'form, aspect, condition', etc.

INDEX OF FIRST LINES

Index of first lines (continued)